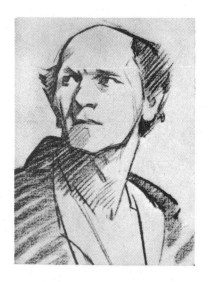
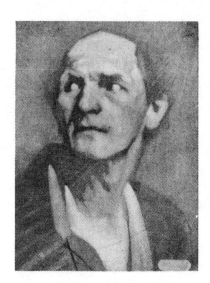
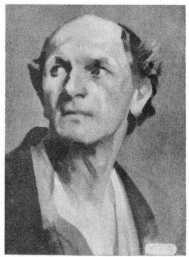
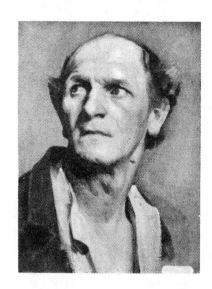

Plate I

FOUR PHOTOGRAPHS OF SAME MONOCHROME PAINTING IN DIFFERENT
STAGES ILLUSTRATING A METHOD OF STUDYING MASS DRAWING
WITH THE BRUSH

THE

PRACTICE & SCIENCE

OF

DRAWING

BY

HAROLD SPEED

Associé de la Société Nationale des Beaux-Arts, Paris; Member of
the Royal Society of Portrait Painters, &c.

With 93 Illustrations & Diagrams

Third Edition

DOVER PUBLICATIONS, INC.
NEW YORK

This Dover edition, first published in 1972, is an unabridged republication of the third edition of the work originally published by Seeley, Service and Co. Ltd., London, in 1917. The Dover edition is published by special arrangement with Seeley, Service and Co., Ltd.

International Standard Book Number
ISBN-13: 978-0-486-22870-9
ISBN-10: 0-486-22870-3

Manufactured in the United States by Courier Corporation
22870315
www.doverpublications.com

PREFACE

PERMIT me in the first place to anticipate the disappointment of any student who opens this book with the idea of finding "wrinkles" on how to draw faces, trees, clouds, or what not, short cuts to excellence in drawing, or any of the tricks so popular with the drawing masters of our grandmothers and still dearly loved by a large number of people. No good can come of such methods, for there are no short cuts to excellence. But help of a very practical kind it is the aim of the following pages to give; although it may be necessary to make a greater call upon the intelligence of the student than these Victorian methods attempted.

It was not until some time after having passed through the course of training in two of our chief schools of art, that the author got any idea of what drawing really meant. What was taught was the faithful copying of a series of objects, beginning with the simplest forms, such as cubes, cones, cylinders, &c. (an excellent system to begin with at present in danger of some neglect), after which more complicated objects in plaster of Paris were attempted, and finally copies of the human head and figure posed in suspended animation and supported by blocks, &c. In so far as this was accurately done, all this mechanical training of eye and hand was excellent; but it was not enough. And when with an eye trained to the closest mechanical

PREFACE

accuracy the author visited the galleries of the Continent and studied the drawings of the old masters, it soon became apparent that either his or their ideas of drawing were all wrong. Very few drawings could be found sufficiently "like the model" to obtain the prize at either of the great schools he had attended. Luckily there was just enough modesty left for him to realise that possibly they were in some mysterious way right and his own training in some way lacking. And so he set to work to try and climb the long uphill road that separates mechanically accurate drawing from artistically accurate drawing.

Now this journey should have been commenced much earlier, and perhaps it was due to his own stupidity that it was not; but it was with a vague idea of saving some students from such wrong-headedness, and possibly straightening out some of the path, that he accepted the invitation to write this book.

In writing upon any matter of experience, such as art, the possibilities of misunderstanding are enormous, and one shudders to think of the things that may be put down to one's credit, owing to such misunderstandings. It is like writing about the taste of sugar, you are only likely to be understood by those who have already experienced the flavour; by those who have not, the wildest interpretation will be put upon your words. The written word is necessarily confined to the things of the understanding because only the understanding has written language; whereas art deals with ideas of a different mental texture, which words can only vaguely suggest. However, there are a large number of people who, although they cannot

PREFACE

be said to have experienced in a full sense any works of art, have undoubtedly the impelling desire which a little direction may lead on to a fuller appreciation. And it is to such that books on art are useful. So that although this book is primarily addressed to working students, it is hoped that it may be of interest to that increasing number of people who, tired with the rush and struggle of modern existence, seek refreshment in artistic things. To many such in this country modern art is still a closed book; its point of view is so different from that of the art they have been brought up with, that they refuse to have anything to do with it. Whereas, if they only took the trouble to find out something of the point of view of the modern artist, they would discover new beauties they little suspected.

If anybody looks at a picture by Claude Monet from the point of view of a Raphael, he will see nothing but a meaningless jargon of wild paint-strokes. And if anybody looks at a Raphael from the point of view of a Claude Monet, he will, no doubt, only see hard, tinny figures in a setting devoid of any of the lovely atmosphere that always envelops form seen in nature. So wide apart are some of the points of view in painting. In the treatment of form these differences in point of view make for enormous variety in the work. So that no apology need be made for the large amount of space occupied in the following pages by what is usually dismissed as mere theory; but what is in reality the first essential of any good practice in drawing. To have a clear idea of what it is you wish to do, is the first necessity of any successful performance. But our exhibitions are full of works that show how seldom this is the case in art. Works showing much ingenuity and ability, but no artistic brains; pictures that are little more than school studies, exercises in the representation of carefully or carelessly arranged objects, but cold to any artistic intention.

At this time particularly some principles, and a clear intellectual understanding of what it is you are trying to do, are needed. We have no set traditions to guide us. The times when the student accepted the style and traditions of his master and blindly followed them until he found himself, are gone. Such conditions belonged to an age when intercommunication was difficult, and when the artistic horizon was restricted to a single town or province. Science has altered all that, and we may regret the loss of local colour and singleness of aim this growth of art in separate compartments produced; but it is unlikely that such conditions will occur again. Quick means of transit and cheap methods of reproduction have brought the art of the whole world to our doors. Where formerly the artistic food at the disposal of the student was restricted to the few pictures in his vicinity and some prints of others, now there is scarcely a picture of note in the world that is not known to the average student, either from personal inspection at our museums and loan exhibitions, or from excellent photographic reproductions. Not only European art, but the art of the East, China and Japan, is part of the formative influence by which he is surrounded; not to mention the modern science of light and colour that has had such an influence on technique. It is no wonder that a period of artistic indigestion is upon us. Hence the student has need of sound principles and a clear understanding of the science of his art, if he would select from this mass of material those things which answer to his own inner need for artistic expression.

The position of art to-day is like that of a river where many tributaries meeting at one point, suddenly turn the steady flow to turbulence, the many streams jostling each other and the different currents pulling hither and thither. After a time these newly-met forces will adjust themselves to the altered condition, and a larger, finer stream be the result. Something analogous to this would seem to be happening in art at the present time, when all nations and all schools are acting and reacting upon each other, and art is losing its national characteristics. The hope of the future is that a larger and deeper art, answering to the altered conditions of humanity, will result.

There are those who would leave this scene of struggling influences and away up on some bare primitive mountain-top start a new stream, begin all over again. But however necessary it may be to give the primitive mountain waters that were the start of all the streams a more prominent place in the new flow onwards, it is unlikely that much can come of any attempt to leave the turbulent waters, go backwards, and start again; they can only flow onwards. To speak more plainly, the complexity of modern art influences may make it necessary to call attention to the primitive principles of expression that should never be lost sight of in any work, but hardly justifies the attitude of those anarchists in art who would flout the heritage of culture we possess and attempt a new start. Such attempts however when sincere are interesting and may be productive of some new vitality, adding to the weight of the main stream. But it must be along the main stream, along lines in harmony with tradition that the chief advance must be looked for.

Although it has been felt necessary to devote much space to an attempt to find principles that may be said to be at the basis of the art of all nations, the executive side of the question has not been neglected. And it is hoped that the logical method for the study of drawing from the two opposite points of view of line and mass here advocated may be useful, and help students to avoid some of the confusion that results from attempting simultaneously the study of these different qualities of form expression.

CONTENTS

LIST OF PLATES

LIST OF PLATES

LIST OF PLATES

LIST OF DIAGRAMS

LIST OF DIAGRAMS

THE PRACTICE AND SCIENCE OF DRAWING

I

INTRODUCTION

THE best things in an artist's work are so much a matter of intuition, that there is much to be said for the point of view that would altogether discourage intellectual inquiry into artistic phenomena on the part of the artist. Intuitions are shy things and apt to disappear if looked into too closely. And there is undoubtedly a danger that too much knowledge and training may supplant the natural intuitive feeling of a student, leaving only a cold knowledge of the means of expression in its place. For the artist, if he has the right stuff in him, has a consciousness, in doing his best work, of something, as Ruskin has said, "not in him but through him." He has been, as it were, but the agent through which it has found expression.

Talent can be described as "that which we have," and Genius as "that which has us." Now, although we may have little control over this power that "has us," and although it may be as well to abandon oneself unreservedly to its influence, there can be little doubt as to its being the business of the artist to see to it that his talent be so developed, that he may prove a fit instrument for the expression of whatever it may be given him to express; while it must be left to his individual temperament to decide how far it is advisable to pursue any intellectual analysis of the elusive things that are the true matter of art.

Provided the student realises this, and that art training can only deal with the perfecting of a means of expression and that the real matter of art lies above this and is beyond the scope of teaching, he cannot have too much of it. For although he must ever be a child before the influences that move him, if it is not with the knowledge of the grown man that he takes off his coat and approaches the craft of painting or drawing, he will be poorly equipped to make them a means of conveying to others in adequate form the things he may wish to express. Great things are only done in art when the creative instinct of the artist has a well-organised executive faculty at its disposal.

Of the two divisions into which the technical study of painting can be divided, namely Form and Colour, we are concerned in this book with Form alone. But before proceeding to our immediate subject, something should be said as to the nature of art generally, not with the ambition of arriving at any final result in a short chapter, but merely in order to give an idea of the point of view from which the following pages are written, so that misunderstandings may be avoided.

The variety of definitions that exist justifies some inquiry. The following are a few that come to mind:

" Art is nature expressed through a personality."

INTRODUCTION

But what of architecture? Or music? Then there is Morris's

"Art is the expression of pleasure in work."

But this does not apply to music and poetry. Andrew Lang's

"Everything which we distinguish from nature"

seems too broad to catch hold of, while Tolstoy's

"An action by means of which one man, having experienced a feeling, intentionally transmits it to others"

is nearer the truth, and covers all the arts, but seems, from its omitting any mention of rhythm, very inadequate.

Now the facts of life are conveyed by our senses to the consciousness within us, and stimulate the world of thought and feeling that constitutes our real life. Thought and feeling are very intimately connected, few of our mental perceptions, particularly when they first dawn upon us, being unaccompanied by some feeling. But there is this general division to be made, on one extreme of which is what we call pure intellect, and on the other pure feeling or emotion. The arts, I take it, are a means of giving expression to the emotional side of this mental activity, intimately related as it often is to the more purely intellectual side. The more sensual side of this feeling is perhaps its lowest, while the feelings associated with the intelligence, the little sensitivenesses of perception that escape pure intellect, are possibly its noblest experiences.

Pure intellect seeks to construct from the facts brought to our consciousness by the senses, an accurately measured world of phenomena, uncoloured by the human equation in each of us. It seeks to create a point of view outside the human standpoint, one more stable and accurate, unaffected by the ever-changing current of human life. It therefore invents mechanical instruments to do the measuring of our sense perceptions, as their records are more accurate than human observation unaided.

But while in science observation is made much more effective by the use of mechanical instruments in registering facts, the facts with which art deals, being those of feeling, can only be recorded by the feeling instrument—man, and are entirely missed by any mechanically devised substitutes.

The artistic intelligence is not interested in things from this standpoint of mechanical accuracy, but in the effect of observation on the living consciousness—the sentient individual in each of us. The same fact accurately portrayed by a number of artistic intelligences should be different in each case, whereas the same fact accurately expressed by a number of scientific intelligences should be the same.

But besides the feelings connected with a wide range of experience, each art has certain emotions belonging to the particular sense perceptions connected with it. That is to say, there are some that only music can convey : those connected with sound ; others that only painting, sculpture, or architecture can convey : those connected with the form and colour that they severally deal with.

In abstract form and colour—that is, form and colour unconnected with natural appearances—there is an emotional power, such as there is in music, the sounds of which have no direct connection with anything in nature, but only with that mysterious sense we have, the sense of Harmony, Beauty, or Rhythm (all three but different aspects of the same thing).

This inner sense is a very remarkable fact, and will be found to some extent in all, certainly all civilised, races. And when the art of a remote people like the Chinese and Japanese is understood, our senses of harmony are found to be wonderfully in agreement. Despite the fact that their art has developed on lines widely different from our own, none the less, when the surprise at its newness has worn off and we begin to understand it, we find it conforms to very much the same sense of harmony.

But apart from the feelings connected directly with the means of expression, there appears to be much in common between all the arts in their most profound expression ; there seems to be a common centre in our inner life that they all appeal to. Possibly at this centre are the great primitive emotions common to all men. The religious group, the deep awe and reverence men feel when contemplating the great mystery of the Universe and their own littleness in the face of its vastness —the desire to correspond and develop relationship with the something outside themselves that is felt to be behind and through all things. Then there are those connected with the joy of life, the throbbing of the great life spirit, the gladness of being, the desire of the sexes; and also those connected with the sadness and mystery of death and decay, &c.

The technical side of an art is, however, not concerned with these deeper motives but with the things of sense through which they find expression; in the case of painting, the visible universe.

The artist is capable of being stimulated to artistic expression by all things seen, no matter what; to him nothing comes amiss. Great pictures have been made of beautiful people in beautiful clothes and of squalid people in ugly clothes, of beautiful architectural buildings and the ugly hovels of the poor. And the same painter who painted the Alps painted the Great Western Railway.

The visible world is to the artist, as it were, a wonderful garment, at times revealing to him the Beyond, the Inner Truth there is in all things. He has a consciousness of some correspondence with something the other side of visible things and dimly felt through them, a "still, small voice" which he is impelled to interpret to man. It is the expression of this all-pervading inner significance that I think we recognise as beauty, and that prompted Keats to say:

"Beauty is truth, truth beauty."

And hence it is that the love of truth and the love of beauty can exist together in the work of the artist. The search for this inner truth is the search for beauty. People whose vision does not penetrate beyond the narrow limits of the commonplace, and to whom a cabbage is but a vulgar vegetable, are surprised if they see a beautiful picture painted of one, and say that the artist has idealised it, meaning that he has consciously altered its appearance on some idealistic formula; whereas he has probably only honestly given expression to a truer, deeper vision than they had been aware of. The commonplace is not the true, but only the shallow, view of things.

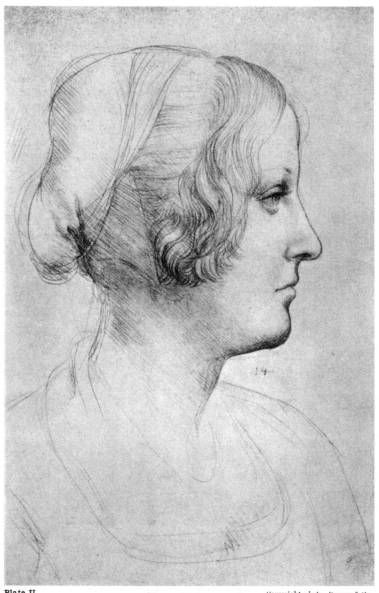

DRAWING BY LEONARDO DA VINCI FROM THE
ROYAL COLLECTION AT WINDSOR

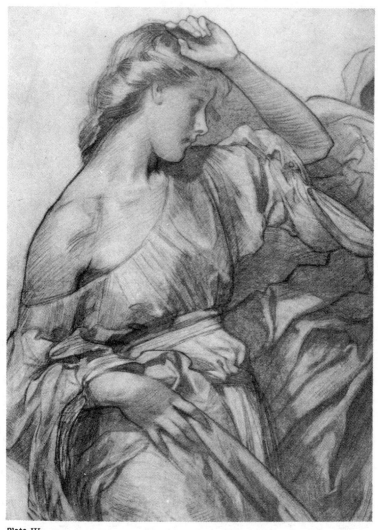

Plate III

STUDY FOR "APRIL"

In red chalk on toned paper.

INTRODUCTION

Fromentin's

" Art is the expression of the invisible by means of the visible "

expresses the same idea, and it is this that gives to art its high place among the works of man.

Beautiful things seem to put us in correspondence with a world the harmonies of which are more perfect, and bring a deeper peace than this imperfect life seems capable of yielding of itself. Our moments of peace are, I think, always associated with some form of beauty, of this spark of harmony within corresponding with some infinite source without. Like a mariner's compass, we are restless until we find repose in this one direction. In moments of beauty (for beauty is, strictly speaking, a state of mind rather than an attribute of certain objects, although certain things have the power of inducing it more than others) we seem to get a glimpse of this deeper truth behind the things of sense. And who can say but that this sense, dull enough in most of us, is not an echo of a greater harmony existing somewhere the other side of things, that we dimly feel through them, evasive though it is.

But we must tread lightly in these rarefied regions and get on to more practical concerns. By finding and emphasising in his work those elements in visual appearances that express these profounder things, the painter is enabled to stimulate the perception of them in others.

In the representation of a fine mountain, for instance, there are, besides all its rhythmic beauty of form and colour, associations touching deeper chords in our natures—associations connected with its size, age, and permanence, &c.; at any rate we have more feelings than form and colour of themselves are capable of arousing. And these things must be felt by the painter, and his picture painted under the influence of these feelings, if he is instinctively to select those elements of form and colour that convey them. Such deeper feelings are far too intimately associated even with the finer beauties of mere form and colour for the painter to be able to neglect them; no amount of technical knowledge will take the place of feeling, or direct the painter so surely in his selection of what is fine.

There are those who would say, "This is all very well, but the painter's concern is with form and colour and paint, and nothing else. If he paints the mountain faithfully from that point of view, it will suggest all these other associations to those who want them." And others who would say that the form and colour of appearances are only to be used as a language to give expression to the feelings common to all men. "Art for art's sake" and "Art for subject's sake." There are these two extreme positions to consider, and it will depend on the individual on which side his work lies. His interest will be more on the æsthetic side, in the feelings directly concerned with form and colour; or on the side of the mental associations connected with appearances, according to his temperament. But neither position can neglect the other without fatal loss. The picture of form and colour will never be able to escape the associations connected with visual things, neither will the picture all for subject be able to get away from its form and colour. And it is wrong to say "If he paints the mountain faithfully from the form and colour point of view it will suggest all those other associations to those who want them," unless, as is possible with a simple-minded painter, he be unconsciously moved by deeper feelings, and impelled to select the significant things while only conscious of his paint. But the chances are that his picture will convey the things he was thinking about, and, in consequence, instead of impressing us with the grandeur of the mountain, will say something very like "See what a clever painter I am!" Unless the artist has painted his picture under the influence of the deeper feelings the scene was capable of producing, it is not likely anybody will be so impressed when they look at his work.

And the painter deeply moved with high ideals as to subject matter, who neglects the form and colour through which he is expressing them, will find that his work has failed to be convincing. The immaterial can only be expressed through the material in art, and the painted symbols of the picture must be very perfect if subtle and elusive meanings are to be conveyed. If he cannot paint the commonplace aspect of our mountain, how can he expect to paint any expression of the deeper things in it? The fact is, both positions are incomplete. In all good art the matter expressed and the manner of its expression are so intimate as to have become one. The deeper associations connected with the mountain are only matters for art in so far as they affect its appearance and take shape as form and colour in the mind of the artist, informing the whole process of the painting, even to the brush strokes. As in a good poem, it is impossible to consider the poetic idea apart from the words that express it: they are fired together at its creation.

Now an expression by means of one of our different sense perceptions does not constitute art, or the boy shouting at the top of his voice, giving expression to his delight in life but making a horrible noise, would be an artist. If his expression is to be adequate to convey his feeling to others, there must be some arrangement. The expression must be ordered, rhythmic, or whatever word most fitly conveys the idea of those powers, conscious or unconscious, that select and arrange the sensuous material of art, so as to make the most telling impression, by bringing it into relation with our innate sense of harmony. If we can find a rough definition that will include all the arts, it will help us to see in what direction lie those things in painting that make it an art. The not uncommon idea, that painting is "the production by means of colours of more or less perfect representations of natural objects" will not do. And it is devoutly to be hoped that science will perfect a method of colour photography finally to dispel this illusion.

What, then, will serve as a working definition? There must be something about feeling, the expression of that individuality the secret of which everyone carries in himself; the expression of that ego that perceives and is moved by the phenomena of life around us. And, on the other hand, something about the ordering of its expression.

But who knows of words that can convey a just idea of such subtle matter? If one says "Art is the rhythmic expression of Life, or emotional consciousness, or feeling," all are inadequate. Perhaps the "rhythmic expression of life" would be the more perfect definition. But the word "life" is so much more associated with eating and drinking in the popular mind, than with the spirit or force or whatever you care to call it, that exists behind consciousness and is the animating factor of our whole being, that it will hardly serve a useful purpose. So that, perhaps, for a rough, practical definition that will at least point away from the mechanical performances that so often pass for art, "the **Rhythmic expression of Feeling**" will do: for by Rhythm is meant that ordering of the materials of art (form and colour, in the case of painting) so as to bring them into relationship with our innate sense of harmony which gives them their expressive power. Without this relationship we have no direct means of making the sensuous material of art awaken an answering echo in others. The boy shouting at the top of his voice, making a horrible noise, was not an artist because his expression was inadequate—was not related to the underlying sense of harmony that would have given it expressive power.

Let us test this definition with some simple cases. Here is a savage, shouting and flinging his arms and legs about in wild delight; he is not an artist, although he may be moved by life and feeling. But let this shouting be done on some ordered plan, to a rhythm expressive of joy and delight, and his leg and arm movements governed by it also, and he has become an artist, and singing and dancing (possibly the oldest of the arts) will result.

Or take the case of one who has been deeply moved by something he has seen, say a man killed by a wild beast, which he wishes to tell his friends. If he just explains the facts as he saw them, making no effort to order his words so as to make the most telling impression upon his hearers and convey to them something of the feelings that are stirring in him, if he merely does this, he is not an artist, although the recital of such a terrible incident may be

27

moving. But the moment he arranges his words so as to convey in a telling manner not only the plain facts, but the horrible feelings he experienced at the sight, he has become an artist. And if he further orders his words to a rhythmic beat, a beat in sympathy with his subject, he has become still more artistic, and a primitive form of poetry will result.

Or in building a hut, so long as a man is interested solely in the utilitarian side of the matter, as are so many builders to-day, and just puts up walls as he needs protection from wild beasts, and a roof to keep out the rain, he is not yet an artist. But the moment he begins to consider his work with some feeling, and arranges the relative sizes of his walls and roof so that they answer to some sense he has for beautiful proportion, he has become an artist, and his hut has some architectural pretensions. Now if his hut is of wood, and he paints it to protect it from the elements, nothing necessarily artistic has been done. But if he selects colours that give him pleasure in their arrangement, and if the forms his colour masses assume are designed with some personal feeling, he has invented a primitive form of decoration.

And likewise the savage who, wishing to illustrate his description of a strange animal he has seen, takes a piece of burnt wood and draws on the wall his idea of what it looked like, a sort of catalogue of its appearance, he is not necessarily an artist. It is only when he draws under the influence of some feeling, of some pleasure he felt in the appearance of the animal, that he becomes an artist.

Of course in each case it is assumed that the men have the power to be moved by these things, and whether they are good or poor artists will

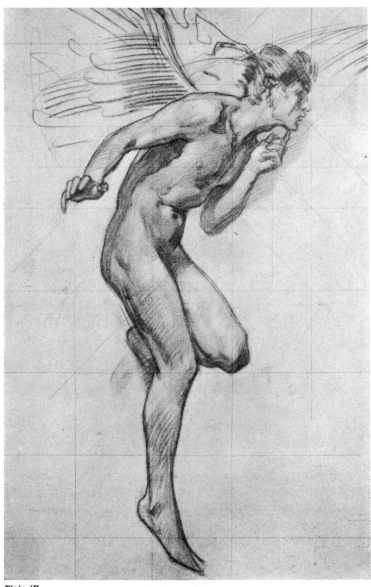

STUDY ON TISSUE-PAPER IN RED CHALK FOR FIGURE OF BOREAS

depend on the quality of their feeling and the fitness of its expression.

The purest form of this "rhythmic expression of feeling" is music. And as Walter Pater shows us in his essay on "The School of Giorgione," "music is the type of art." The others are more artistic as they approach its conditions. Poetry, the most musical form of literature, is its most artistic form. And in the greatest pictures form, colour, and idea are united to thrill us with harmonies analogous to music.

The painter expresses his feelings through the representation of the visible world of Nature, and through the representation of those combinations of form and colour inspired in his imagination, that were all originally derived from visible nature. If he fails from lack of skill to make his representation convincing to reasonable people, no matter how sublime has been his artistic intention, he will probably have landed in the ridiculous. And yet, so great is the power of direction exercised by the emotions on the artist that it is seldom his work fails to convey something, when genuine feeling has been the motive. On the other hand, the painter with no artistic impulse who makes a laboriously commonplace picture of some ordinary or pretentious subject, has equally failed as an artist, however much the skilfulness of his representations may gain him reputation with the unthinking.

The study, therefore, of the representation of visible nature and of the powers of expression possessed by form and colour is the object of the painter's training.

And a command over this power of representation and expression is absolutely necessary if he is to be capable of doing anything worthy of his art.

INTRODUCTION

This is all in art that one can attempt to teach. The emotional side is beyond the scope of teaching. You cannot teach people how to feel. All you can do is to surround them with the conditions calculated to stimulate any natural feeling they may possess. And this is done by familiarising students with the best works of art and nature.

It is surprising how few art students have any idea of what it is that constitutes art. They are impelled, it is to be assumed, by a natural desire to express themselves by painting, and, if their intuitive ability is strong enough, it perhaps matters little whether they know or not. But to the larger number who are not so violently impelled, it is highly essential that they have some better idea of art than that it consists in setting down your canvas before nature and copying it.

Inadequate as this imperfect treatment of a profoundly interesting subject is, it may serve to give some idea of the point of view from which the following pages are written, and if it also serves to disturb the "copying theory" in the minds of any students and encourages them to make further inquiry, it will have served a useful purpose.

II

DRAWING

By drawing is here meant **the expression of form upon a plane surface.**

Art probably owes more to form for its range of expression than to colour. Many of the noblest things it is capable of conveying are expressed by form more directly than by anything else. And it is interesting to notice how some of the world's greatest artists have been very restricted in their use of colour, preferring to depend on form for their chief appeal. It is reported that Apelles only used three colours, black, red, and yellow, and Rembrandt used little else. Drawing, although the first, is also the last, thing the painter usually studies. There is more in it that can be taught and that repays constant application and effort. Colour would seem to depend much more on a natural sense and to be less amenable to teaching. A well-trained eye for the appreciation of form is what every student should set himself to acquire with all the might of which he is capable.

It is not enough in artistic drawing to portray accurately and in cold blood the appearance of objects. To express form one must first be moved by it. There is in the appearance of all objects, animate and inanimate, what has been called an **emotional significance,** a hidden rhythm that is not

31

DRAWING

caught by the accurate, painstaking, but cold artist.
The form significance of which we speak is never
found in a mechanical reproduction like a photograph. You are never moved to say when looking
at one, " What fine form."

It is difficult to say in what this quality consists.
The emphasis and selection that is unconsciously
given in a drawing done directly under the guidance
of strong feeling, are too subtle to be tabulated ; they
escape analysis. But it is this selection of the significant and suppression of the non-essential that
often gives to a few lines drawn quickly, and having
a somewhat remote relation to the complex appearance of the real object, more vitality and truth than
are to be found in a highly-wrought and painstaking
drawing, during the process of which the essential
and vital things have been lost sight of in the
labour of the work; and the non-essential, which is
usually more obvious, has been allowed to creep in
and obscure the original impression. Of course, had
the finished drawing been done with the mind centred
upon the particular form significance aimed at, and
every touch and detail added in tune to this idea,
the comparison might have been different. But it
is rarely that good drawings are done this way.
Fine things seem only to be seen in flashes, and the
nature that can carry over the impression of one of
these moments during the labour of a highly-wrought
drawing is very rare, and belongs to the few great
ones of the craft alone.

It is difficult to know why one should be moved
by the expression of form; but it appears to have
some physical influence over us. In looking at a
fine drawing, say of a strong man, we seem to identify
ourselves with it and feel a thrill of its strength in

DRAWING

our own bodies, prompting us to set our teeth, stiffen our frame, and exclaim "That's fine." Or, when looking at the drawing of a beautiful woman, we are softened by its charm and feel in ourselves something of its sweetness as we exclaim, "How beautiful." The measure of the feeling in either case will be the extent to which the artist has identified himself with the subject when making the drawing, and has been impelled to select the expressive elements in the forms.

Art thus enables us to experience life at second hand. The small man may enjoy somewhat of the wider experience of the bigger man, and be educated to appreciate in time a wider experience for himself. This is the true justification for public picture galleries. Not so much for the moral influence they exert, of which we have heard so much, but that people may be led through the vision of the artist to enlarge their experience of life. This enlarging of the experience is true education, and a very different thing from the memorising of facts that so often passes as such. In a way this may be said to be a moral influence, as a larger mind is less likely to harbour small meannesses. But this is not the kind of moral influence usually looked for by the many, who rather demand a moral story told by the picture; a thing not always suitable to artistic expression.

One is always profoundly impressed by the expression of a sense of bulk, vastness, or mass in form. There is a feeling of being lifted out of one's puny self to something bigger and more stable. It is this splendid feeling of bigness in Michael Angelo's figures that is so satisfying. One cannot come away from the contemplation of that wonderful ceiling of

33

his in the Vatican without the sense of having experienced something of a larger life than one had known before. Never has the dignity of man reached so high an expression in paint, a height that has been the despair of all who have since tried to follow that lonely master. In landscape also this expression of largeness is fine: one likes to feel the weight and mass of the ground, the vastness of the sky and sea, the bulk of a mountain.

On the other hand one is charmed also by the expression of lightness. This may be noted in much of the work of Botticelli and the Italians of the fifteenth century. Botticelli's figures seldom have any weight; they drift about as if walking on air, giving a delightful feeling of otherworldliness. The hands of the Madonna that hold the Child might be holding flowers for any sense of support they express. It is, I think, on this sense of lightness that a great deal of the exquisite charm of Botticelli's drawing depends.

The feathery lightness of clouds and of draperies blown by the wind is always pleasing, and Botticelli nearly always has a light wind passing through his draperies to give them this sense.

As will be explained later, in connection with academic drawing, it is eminently necessary for the student to train his eye accurately to observe the forms of things by the most painstaking of drawings. In these school studies feeling need not be considered, but only a cold accuracy. In the same way a singer trains himself to sing scales, giving every note exactly the same weight and preserving a most mechanical time throughout, so that every note of his voice may be accurately under his control and be equal to the subtlest variations he may afterwards

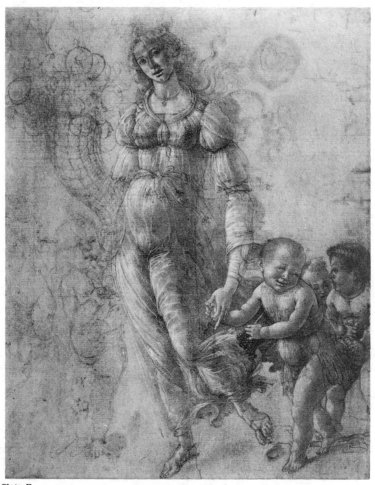

Plate V

FROM A STUDY BY BOTTICELLI

In the Print Room at the British Museum.

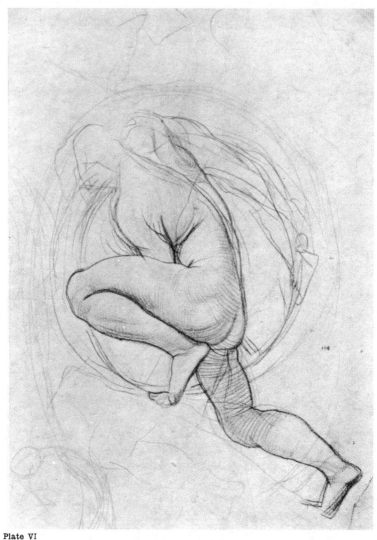

Plate VI

STUDY IN NATURAL RED CHALK BY ALFRED STEPHENS
From the collection of Charles Ricketts and Charles Shannon

want to infuse into it at the dictates of feeling. For how can the draughtsman who does not know how to draw accurately the cold, commonplace view of an object, hope to give expression to the subtle differences presented by the same thing seen under the excitement of strong feeling?

These academic drawings, too, should be as highly finished as hard application can make them, so that the habit of minute visual expression may be acquired. It will be needed later, when drawing of a finer kind is attempted, and when in the heat of an emotional stimulus the artist has no time to consider the smaller subtleties of drawing, which by then should have become almost instinctive with him, leaving his mind free to dwell on the bigger qualities.

Drawing, then, to be worthy of the name, must be more than what is called accurate. It must present the form of things in a more vivid manner than we ordinarily see them in nature. Every new draughtsman in the history of art has discovered a new significance in the form of common things, and given the world a new experience. He has represented these qualities under the stimulus of the feeling they inspired in him, hot and underlined, as it were, adding to the great book of sight the world possesses in its art, a book by no means completed yet.

So that to say of a drawing, as is so often said, that it is not true because it does not present the commonplace appearance of an object accurately, may be foolish. Its accuracy depends on the completeness with which it conveys the particular emotional significance that is the object of the drawing. What this significance is will vary

DRAWING

enormously with the individual artist, but it is only by this standard that the accuracy of the drawing can be judged.

It is this difference between scientific accuracy and artistic accuracy that puzzles so many people. Science demands that phenomena be observed with the unemotional accuracy of a weighing machine, while artistic accuracy demands that things be observed by a sentient individual recording the sensations produced in him by the phenomena of life. And people with the scientific habit that is now so common among us, seeing a picture or drawing in which what are called facts have been expressed emotionally, are puzzled, if they are modest, or laugh at what they consider a glaring mistake in drawing if they are not, when all the time it may be their mistaken point of view that is at fault.

But while there is no absolute artistic standard by which accuracy of drawing can be judged, as such standard must necessarily vary with the artistic intention of each individual artist, this fact must not be taken as an excuse for any obviously faulty drawing that incompetence may produce, as is often done by students, who when corrected, say that they "saw it so." For there undoubtedly exists a rough physical standard of rightness in drawing, any violent deviations from which, even at the dictates of emotional expression, is productive of the gro-tesque. This physical standard of accuracy in his work it is the business of the student to acquire in his academic training; and every aid that science can give by such studies as Perspective, Anatomy, and, in the case of Landscape, even Geology and Botany, should be used to increase the accuracy of

36

his representations. For the strength of appeal in artistic work will depend much on the power the artist possesses of expressing himself through representations that arrest everyone by their truth and naturalness. And although, when truth and naturalness exist without any artistic expression, the result is of little account as art, on the other hand, when truly artistic expression is clothed in representations that offend our ideas of physical truth, it is only the few who can forgive the offence for the sake of the genuine feeling they perceive behind it.

How far the necessities of expression may be allowed to override the dictates of truth to physical structure in the appearance of objects, will always be a much debated point. In the best drawing the departures from mechanical accuracy are so subtle that I have no doubt many will deny the existence of such a thing altogether. Good artists of strong natural inspiration, but simple minds, are often quite unconscious of doing anything but being as mechanically accurate as possible, when painting.

Yet however much it may be advisable to let yourself go in artistic work, during your academic training let your aim be a searching accuracy.

III

VISION

It is necessary to say something about Vision in the first place, if we are to have any grasp of the idea of form.

An act of vision is not so simple a matter as the student who asked her master if she should "paint nature as she saw nature" would seem to have thought. And his answer, "Yes, madam, provided you don't see nature as you paint nature," expressed the first difficulty the student of painting has to face: the difficulty of learning to see.

Let us roughly examine what we know of vision. Science tells us that all objects are made visible to us by means of light; and that white light, by which we see things in what may be called their normal aspect, is composed of all the colours of the solar spectrum, as may be seen in a rainbow; a phenomenon caused, as everybody knows, by the sun's rays being split up into their component parts.

This light travels in straight lines and, striking objects before us, is reflected in all directions. Some of these rays passing through a point situated behind the lenses of the eye, strike the retina. The multiplication of these rays on the retina produces a picture of whatever is before the eye, such as can be seen on the ground glass at the back of a photographer's camera, or on the table of a camera obscura, both of which instruments are constructed roughly on the same principle as the human eye.

These rays of light when reflected from an object, and again when passing through the atmosphere, undergo certain modifications. Should the object be a red one, the yellow, green, and blue rays, all, in fact, except the red rays, are absorbed by the object, while the red is allowed to escape. These red rays striking the retina produce certain effects which convey to our consciousness the sensation of red, and we say "That is a red object." But there may be particles of moisture or dust in the air that will modify the red rays so that by the time they reach the eye they may be somewhat different. This modification is naturally most effective when a large amount of atmosphere has to be passed through, and in things very distant the colour of the natural object is often entirely lost, to be replaced by atmospheric colours, as we see in distant mountains when the air is not perfectly clear. But we must not stray into the fascinating province of colour.

What chiefly concerns us here is the fact that the pictures on our retinas are flat, of two dimensions, the same as the canvas on which we paint. If you examine these visual pictures without any prejudice, as one may with a camera obscura, you will see that they are composed of masses of colour in infinite variety and complexity, of different shapes and gradations, and with many varieties of edges; giving to the eye the illusion of nature with actual depths and distances, although one knows all the time that it is a flat table on which one is looking.

Seeing then that our eyes have only flat pictures containing two - dimension information about the objective world, from whence is this knowledge of distance and the solidity of things? How do we *see* the third dimension, the depth and thickness, by means of flat pictures of two dimensions?

The power to judge distance is due principally to our possessing two eyes situated in slightly different positions, from which we get two views of objects, and also to the power possessed by the eyes of focussing at different distances, others being out of focus for the time being. In a picture the eyes can only focus at one distance (the distance the eye is from the plane of the picture when you are looking at it), and this is one of the chief causes of the perennial difficulty in painting backgrounds. In nature they are out of focus when one is looking at an object, but in a painting the background is necessarily on the same focal plane as the object. Numerous are the devices resorted to by painters to overcome this difficulty, but they do not concern us here.

The fact that we have two flat pictures on our two retinas to help us, and that we can focus at different planes, would not suffice to account for our knowledge of the solidity and shape of the objective world, were these senses not associated with another sense all important in ideas of form, the sense of touch.

This sense is very highly developed in us, and the earlier period of our existence is largely given over to feeling for the objective world outside ourselves. Who has not watched the little baby hands feeling for everything within reach, and without its reach, for the matter of that; for the infant has no knowledge yet of what is and what is not within its reach. Who has not offered some bright object to a young child and watched its clumsy attempts to feel for it, almost as clumsy at first as if it were blind as it has not yet learned to focus distances. And when he has at last got hold of it, how eagerly he feels it all over, looking intently at it all the time; thus learning early to associate the "feel of an object" with its appearance. In this way by degrees he acquires those ideas of roughness and smoothness, hardness and softness, solidity, &c., which later on he will be able to distinguish by vision alone, and without touching the object.

Our survival depends so much on this sense of touch, that it is of the first importance to us. We must know whether the ground is hard enough for us to walk on, or whether there is a hole in front of us; and masses of colour rays striking the retina, which is what vision amounts to, will not of themselves tell us. But associated with the knowledge accumulated in our early years, by connecting touch with sight, we do know when certain combinations of colour rays strike the eye that there is a road for us to walk on, and that when certain other combinations occur there is a hole in front of us, or the edge of a precipice.

And likewise with hardness and softness, the child who strikes his head against the bed-post is forcibly reminded by nature that such things are to be avoided, and feeling that it is hard and that hardness has a certain look, it avoids that kind of thing in the future. And when it strikes its head against the pillow, it learns the nature of softness, and associating this sensation with the appearance of the pillow, knows in future that when softness is observed it need not be avoided as hardness must be.

VISION

Sight is therefore not a matter of the eye alone. A whole train of associations connected with the objective world is set going in the mind when rays of light strike the retina refracted from objects. And these associations vary enormously in quantity and value with different individuals; but the one we are here chiefly concerned with is this universal one of touch. Everybody "sees" the shape of an object, and "sees" whether it "looks" hard or soft, &c. Sees, in other words, the "feel" of it.

If you are asked to think of an object, say a cone, it will not, I think, be the visual aspect that will occur to most people. They will think of a circular base from which a continuous side slopes up to a point situated above its centre, as one would feel it. The fact that in almost every visual aspect the base line is that of an ellipse, not a circle, comes as a surprise to people unaccustomed to drawing.

But above these cruder instances, what a wealth of associations crowd in upon the mind, when a sight that moves one is observed. Put two men before a scene, one an ordinary person and the other a great poet, and ask them to describe what they see. Assuming them both to be possessed of a reasonable power honestly to express themselves, what a difference would there be in the value of their descriptions. Or take two painters both equally gifted in the power of expressing their visual perceptions, and put them before the scene to paint it. And assuming one to be a commonplace man and the other a great artist, what a difference will there be in their work. The commonplace painter will paint a commonplace picture, while the form and colour will be the means of stirring deep associ-

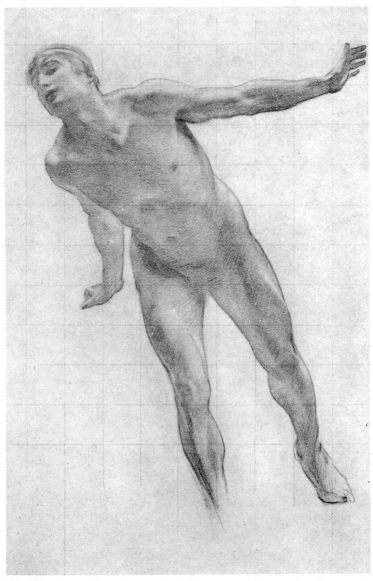

Plate VII

STUDY FOR THE FIGURE OF APOLLO IN THE PICTURE
"APOLLO AND DAPHNE"

In natural red chalk rubbed with finger; the high lights are picked out with rubber.

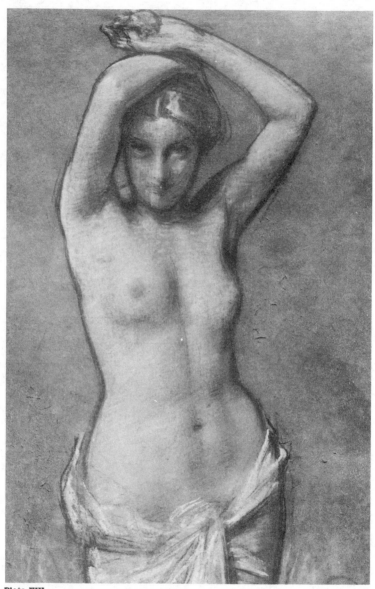

Plate VIII

STUDY FOR A PICTURE

In red conté chalk and white pastel rubbed on toned paper.

ations and feelings in the mind of the other, and will move him to paint the scene so that the same splendour of associations may be conveyed to the beholder.

But to return to our infant mind. While the development of the perception of things has been going on, the purely visual side of the question, the observation of the picture on the retina for what it is as form and colour, has been neglected— neglected to such an extent that when the child comes to attempt drawing, **sight is not the sense he consults.** The mental idea of the objective world that has grown up in his mind is now associated more directly with touch than with sight, with the felt shape rather than the visual appearance. So that if he is asked to draw a head, he thinks of it first as an object having a continuous boundary in space. This his mind instinctively conceives as a line. Then, hair he expresses by a row of little lines coming out from the boundary, all round the top. He thinks of eyes as two points or circles, or as points in circles, and the nose either as a triangle or an L-shaped line. If you feel the nose you will see the reason of this. Down the front you have the L line, and if you feel round it you will find the two sides meeting at the top and a base joining them, suggesting the triangle. The mouth similarly is an opening with a row of teeth, which are gener- ally shown although so seldom seen, but always apparent if the mouth is felt (see diagram A). This is, I think, a fair type of the first drawing the ordi- nary child makes—and judging by some ancient scribbling of the same order I remember noticing scratched on a wall at Pompeii, and by savage draw- ing generally, it appears to be a fairly universal type. It is a very remarkable thing which, as far as I know, has not yet been pointed out, that in these first attempts at drawing the vision should not be consulted. A blind man would not draw differently, could he but see to draw. Were vision the first sense consulted, and were the simplest visual

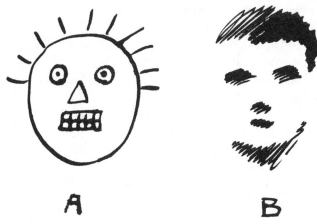

A   B

Diagram I

A, Type of First Drawing made by Children, showing how Vision has not been consulted

B, Type of what might have been expected if crudest expression of Visual Appearance had been attempted

appearance sought after, one might expect something like diagram B, the shadows under eyes, nose, mouth, and chin, with the darker mass of the hair being the simplest thing the visual appearance can be reduced to. But despite this being quite as easy to do, it does not appeal to the ordinary child as the other type does, because it does not satisfy the sense of touch that forms so large a part of the idea of an object in the mind. All architectural elevations and geometrical projections generally appeal to this mental idea of form. They consist of views of a building or object that could never possibly be seen by anybody, assuming as they do that the eye of the spectator is exactly in front of every part of the building at the same time, a physical impossibility. And yet so removed from the actual visual appearance is our mental idea of objects that such drawings do convey a very accurate idea of a building or object. And of course they have great advantage as working drawings in that they can be scaled.

If so early the sense of vision is neglected and relegated to be the handmaiden of other senses, it is no wonder that in the average adult it is in such a shocking state of neglect. I feel convinced that with the great majority of people vision is seldom if ever consulted for itself, but only to minister to some other sense. They look at the sky to see if it is going to be fine; at the fields to see if they are dry enough to walk on, or whether there will be a good crop of hay; at the stream not to observe the beauty of the reflections from the blue sky or green fields dancing upon its surface or the rich colouring of its shadowed depths, but to calculate how deep it is or how much power it would supply to work a mill, how many fish it contains, or some other association alien to its visual aspect. If one looks up at a fine mass of cumulus clouds above a London street, the ordinary passer-by who follows one's gaze expects to see a balloon or a flying-machine at least, and when he sees it is only clouds he is apt to wonder what one is gazing at. The beautiful form and colour of the cloud seem to be unobserved. Clouds mean nothing to him but an accumulation of water dust that may bring rain. This accounts in some way for the number of good paintings that are incomprehensible to the majority of people. It is only those pictures that pursue the visual aspect of objects to a sufficient completion to contain the suggestion of these other associations, that they understand at all. Other pictures, they say, are not finished enough. And it is so seldom that a picture can have this petty realisation and at the same time be an expression of those larger emotional qualities that constitute good painting.

The early paintings of the Pre-Raphaelite Brotherhood appear to be a striking exception to this. But in their work the excessive realisation of all details was part of the expression and gave emphasis to the poetic idea at the basis of their pictures, and was therefore part of the artistic intention. In these paintings the fiery intensity with which every little detail was painted made their picture a ready medium for the expression of poetic thought, a sort of "painted poetry," every detail being selected on account of some symbolic meaning it had, bearing on the poetic idea that was the object of the picture.

But to those painters who do not attempt "painted poetry," but seek in painting a poetry of its own, a visual poetry, this excessive finish (as it is called) is irksome, as it mars the expression of those qualities in vision they wish to express. Finish in art has no connection with the amount of detail in a picture, but has reference only to the completeness with which the emotional idea the painter set out to express has been realised.

VISION

The visual blindness of the majority of people is greatly to be deplored, as nature is ever offering them on their retina, even in the meanest slum, a music of colour and form that is a constant source of pleasure to those who can see it. But so many are content to use this wonderful faculty of vision for utilitarian purposes only. It is the privilege of the artist to show how wonderful and beautiful is all this music of colour and form, so that people, having been moved by it in his work, may be encouraged to see the same beauty in the things around them. This is the best argument in favour of making art a subject of general education : that it should teach people to see. Everybody does not need to draw and paint, but if everybody could get the faculty of appreciating the form and colour on their retinas as form and colour, what a wealth would always be at their disposal for enjoyment ! The Japanese habit of looking at a landscape upside down between their legs is a way of seeing without the deadening influence of touch associations. Thus looking, one is surprised into seeing for once the colour and form of things with the association of touch for the moment forgotten, and is puzzled at the beauty. The odd thing is that although thus we see things upside down, the pictures on our retinas are for once the right way up ; for ordinarily the visual picture is inverted on the retina, like that on the ground glass at the back of a photographic camera.

To sum up this somewhat rambling chapter, I have endeavoured to show that there are two aspects from which the objective world can be apprehended. There is the purely mental perception founded chiefly on knowledge derived from our sense of touch associated with vision, whose primitive instinct is to put an outline round objects as representing their boundaries in space. And secondly, there is the visual perception, which is concerned with the visual aspects of objects as they appear on the retina; an arrangement of colour shapes, a sort of mosaic of colour. And these two aspects give us two different points of view from which the representation of visible things can be approached.

When the representation from either point of view is carried far enough, the result is very similar. Work built up on outline drawing to which has been added light and shade, colour, aerial perspective, &c., may eventually approximate to the perfect visual appearance. And inversely, representations approached from the point of view of pure vision, the mosaic of colour on the retina, if pushed far enough, may satisfy the mental perception of form with its touch associations. And of course the two points of view are intimately connected. You cannot put an accurate outline round an object without observing the shape it occupies in the field of vision. And it is difficult to consider the "mosaic of colour forms" without being very conscious of the objective significance of the colour masses portrayed. But they present two entirely different and opposite points of view from which the representation of objects can be approached. In considering the subject of drawing I think it necessary to make this division of the subject, and both methods of form expression should be studied by the student. Let us call the first method Line Drawing and the second Mass Drawing. Most modern drawing is a mixture of both these points of view, but they should be studied separately if confusion is to be avoided. If the student neglects line drawing, his work will lack the expressive significance of form that only a feeling for lines seems to have the secret of conveying; while, if he neglects mass drawing, he will be poorly equipped when he comes to express form with a brush full of paint to work with.

IV

LINE DRAWING

Most of the earliest forms of drawing known to us in history, like those of the child we were discussing in the last chapter, are largely in the nature of outline drawings. This is a remarkable fact considering the somewhat remote relation lines have to the complete phenomena of vision. Outlines can only be said to exist in appearances as the boundaries of masses. But even here a line seems a poor thing from the visual point of view; as the boundaries are not always clearly defined, but are continually merging into the surrounding mass and losing themselves to be caught up again later on and defined once more. Its relationship with visual appearances is not sufficient to justify the instinct for line drawing. It comes, I think, as has already been said, from the sense of touch. When an object is felt there is no merging in the surrounding mass, but a firm definition of its boundary, which the mind instinctively conceives as a line.

There is a more direct appeal to the imagination in line drawing than in possibly anything else in pictorial art. The emotional stimulus given by fine design is due largely to line work. The power a line possesses of instinctively directing the eye along its course is of the utmost value also, enabling the artist to concentrate the attention of the beholder where he wishes. Then there is a harmonic sense in lines and their relationships, a music of line that is found at the basis of all good art. But this subject will be treated later on when talking of line rhythm.

Most artists whose work makes a large appeal to the imagination are strong on the value of line. Blake, whose visual knowledge was such a negligible quantity, but whose mental perceptions were so magnificent, was always insisting on its value. And his designs are splendid examples of its powerful appeal to the imagination.

On this basis of line drawing the development of art proceeded. The early Egyptian wall paintings were outlines tinted, and the earliest wall sculpture was an incised outline. After these incised lines some man of genius thought of cutting away the surface of the wall between the outlines and modelling it in low relief. The appearance of this may have suggested to the man painting his outline on the wall the idea of shading between his outlines.

At any rate the next development was the introduction of a little shading to relieve the flatness of the line-work and suggest modelling. And this was as far as things had gone in the direction of the representation of form, until well on in the Italian Renaissance. Botticelli used nothing else than an outline lightly shaded to indicate form. Light and shade were not seriously perceived until Leonardo da Vinci. And a wonderful discovery it was thought to be, and was, indeed, although it seems difficult to understand where men's eyes had been for so long with the phenomena of light and shade before them all the time. But this is only another proof of what cannot be too often insisted on, namely that the eye only sees what it is on the look-out for, and it may even be there are things just as wonderful yet to be discovered in vision.

But it was still the touch association of an object that was the dominant one; it was within the outline demanded by this sense that the light and shade were to be introduced as something as it were put on the object. It was the "solids in space" idea that art was still appealing to.

"The first object of a painter is to make a simple flat surface appear like a relievo, and some of its parts detached from the ground; he who excels all others in that part of the art deserves the greatest praise,"[1] wrote Leonardo da Vinci, and the insistence on this "standing out" quality, with its appeal to the touch sense as something great in art, sounds very strange in these days. But it must be remembered that the means of creating this illusion were new to all and greatly wondered at.

And again, in paragraph 176 of his treatise, Leonardo writes: "The knowledge of the outline is of most consequence, and yet may be acquired to great certainty by dint of study; as the outlines of the human figure, particularly those which do not bend, are invariably the same. But the knowledge of the situation, quality and quantity of shadows, being infinite, requires the most extensive study."

The outlines of the human figure are "invariably the same"? What does this mean? From the visual point of view we know that the space occupied by figures in the field of our vision is by no means "invariably the same," but of great variety. So it cannot be the visual appearance he is speaking about.

[1] Leonardo da Vinci, *Treatise on Painting*, paragraph 178.

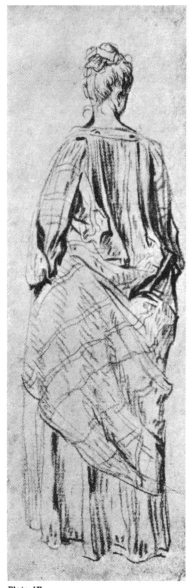

Plate IX

STUDY BY WATTEAU

From an original drawing in the collection of Charles Ricketts and Charles Shannon.

LINE DRAWING

It can only refer to the mental idea of the shape of the members of the human figure. The remark "particularly those that do not bend" shows this also, for when the body is bent up even the mental idea of its form must be altered. There is no hint yet of vision being exploited for itself, but only in so far as it yielded material to stimulate this mental idea of the exterior world.

All through the work of the men who used this light and shade (or chiaroscuro, as it was called) the outline basis remained. Leonardo, Raphael, Michael Angelo, Titian, and the Venetians were all faithful to it as the means of holding their pictures together; although the Venetians, by fusing the edges of their outline masses, got very near the visual method to be introduced later by Velazquez.

In this way, little by little, starting from a basis of simple outline forms, art grew up, each new detail of visual appearance discovered adding, as it were, another instrument to the orchestra at the disposal of the artist, enabling him to add to the somewhat crude directness and simplicity of the early work the graces and refinements of the more complex work, making the problem of composition more difficult but increasing the range of its expression.

But these additions to the visual formula used by artists was not all gain; the simplicity of the means at the disposal of a Botticelli gives an innocence and imaginative appeal to his work that it is difficult to think of preserving with the more complete visual realisation of later schools. When the realisation of actual appearance is most complete, the mind is liable to be led away by side issues connected with the things represented, instead of seeing the emotional intentions of the artist expressed through them. The mind is apt to leave the picture and looking, as it were, not at it but through it, to pursue a train of thought associated with the objects represented as real objects, but alien to the artistic intention of the picture. There is nothing in these early formulæ to disturb the contemplation of the emotional appeal of pure form and colour. To those who approach a picture with the idea that the representation of nature, the " making it look like the real thing," is the sole object of painting, how strange must be the appearance of such pictures as Botticelli's.

The accumulation of the details of visual observation in art is liable eventually to obscure the main idea and disturb the large sense of design on which so much of the imaginative appeal of a work of art depends. The large amount of new visual knowledge that the naturalistic movements of the nineteenth century brought to light is particularly liable at this time to obscure the simpler and more primitive qualities on which all good art is built. At the height of that movement line drawing went out of fashion, and charcoal, and an awful thing called a stump, took the place of the point in the schools. Charcoal is a beautiful medium in a dexterous hand, but is more adaptable to mass than to line drawing. The less said about the stump the better, although I believe it still lingers on in some schools.

Line drawing is happily reviving, and nothing is so calculated to put new life and strength into the vagaries of naturalistic painting and get back into art a fine sense of design.

This obscuring of the direct appeal of art by the accumulation of too much naturalistic detail, and the loss of power it entails, is the cause of artists having occasionally gone back to a more primitive convention. There was the Archaistic movement in Greece, and men like Rossetti and Burne-Jones found a better means of expressing the things that moved them in the technique of the fourteenth century. And it was no doubt a feeling of the weakening influence on art, as an expressive force, of the elaborate realisations of the modern school, that prompted Puvis de Chavannes to invent for himself his large primitive manner. It will be noticed that in these instances it is chiefly the insistence upon outline that distinguishes these artists from their contemporaries.

Art, like life, is apt to languish if it gets too far away from primitive conditions. But, like life also, it is a poor thing and a very uncouth affair if it has nothing but primitive conditions to recommend it. Because there is a decadent art about, one need not make a hero of the pavement artist. But without going to the extreme of flouting the centuries of culture that art inherits, as it is now fashionable in many places to do, students will do well to study at first the early rather than the late work of the different schools, so as to get in touch with the simple conditions of design on which good work is built. It is easier to study these essential qualities when they are not overlaid by so much knowledge of visual realisation. The skeleton of the picture is more apparent in the earlier than the later work of any school.

The finest example of the union of the primitive with the most refined and cultured art the world has ever seen is probably the Parthenon at Athens, a building that has been the wonder of the artistic world for over two thousand years. Not only are the fragments of its sculptures in the British Museum amazing, but the beauty and proportions of its architecture are of a refinement that is, I think, never even attempted in these days. What architect now thinks of correcting the poorness of hard, straight lines by very slightly curving them? Or of slightly sloping inwards the columns of his façade to add to the strength of its appearance? The amount of these variations is of the very slightest and bears witness to the pitch of refinement attempted. And yet, with it all, how simple! There is something of the primitive strength of Stonehenge in that solemn row of columns rising firmly from the steps without any base. With all its magnificence, it still retains the simplicity of the hut from which it was evolved.

Something of the same combination of primitive grandeur and strength with exquisite refinement of visualisation is seen in the art of Michael Angelo. His followers adopted the big, muscular type of their master, but lost the primitive strength he expressed; and when this primitive force was lost sight of, what a decadence set in!

This is the point at which art reaches its highest mark: when to the primitive strength and simplicity of early art are added the infinite refinements and graces of culture without destroying or weakening the sublimity of the expression.

In painting, the refinement and graces of culture take the form of an increasing truth to natural appearances, added bit by bit to the primitive baldness of early work; until the point is reached, as it was in the nineteenth century, when apparently the whole facts of visual nature are incorporated. From this wealth of visual material, to which must be added the knowledge we now have of the arts of the East, of China, Japan, and India, the modern artist has to select those things that appeal to him ; has to select those elements that answer to his inmost need of expressing himself as an artist. No wonder a period of artistic dyspepsia is upon us, no wonder our exhibitions, particularly those on the Continent, are full of strange, weird things. The problem before the artist was never so complex, but also never so interesting. New forms, new combinations, new simplifications are to be found. But the steadying influence and discipline of line work were never more necessary to the student.

The primitive force we are in danger of losing depends much on line, and no work that aims at a sublime impression can dispense with the basis of a carefully wrought and simple line scheme.

The study, therefore, of pure line drawing is of great importance to the painter, and the numerous drawings that exist by the great masters in this method show how much they understood its value.

And the revival of line drawing, and the desire there is to find a simpler convention founded on this basis, are among the most hopeful signs in the art of the moment.

V

MASS DRAWING

IN the preceding chapter it has, I hope, been shown that outline drawing is an instinct with Western artists and has been so from the earliest times; that this instinct is due to the fact that the first mental idea of an object is the sense of its form as a felt thing, not a thing seen; and that an outline drawing satisfies and appeals directly to this mental idea of objects.

But there is another basis of expression directly related to visual appearances that in the fulness of time was evolved, and has had a very great influence on modern art. This form of drawing is based on the consideration of the flat appearances on the retina, with the knowledge of the felt shapes of objects for the time being forgotten. In opposition to line drawing, we may call this Mass Drawing.

The scientific truth of this point of view is obvious. If only the accurate copying of the appearances of nature were the sole object of art (an idea to be met with among students) the problem of painting would be simpler than it is, and would be likely ere long to be solved by the photographic camera.

This form of drawing is the natural means of expression when a brush full of paint is in your hands. The reducing of a complicated appearance

58

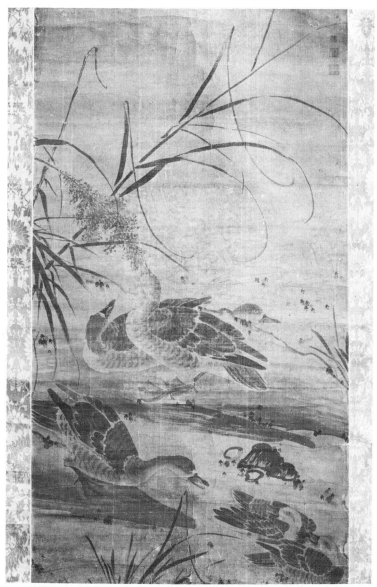

Plate X

EXAMPLE OF FIFTEENTH-CENTURY CHINESE WORK
BY LUI LIANG (BRITISH MUSEUM)

Showing how early Chinese masters had developed the mass-drawing point of view.

to a few simple masses is the first necessity of the painter. But this will be fully explained in a later chapter treating more practically of the practice of mass drawing.

The art of China and Japan appears to have been more influenced by this view of natural appearances than that of the West has been, until quite lately. The Eastern mind does not seem to be so obsessed by the objectivity of things as is the Western mind. With us the practical sense of touch is all powerful. "I know that is so, because I felt it with my hands" would be a characteristic expression with us. Whereas I do not think it would be an expression the Eastern mind would use. With them the spiritual essence of the thing seen appears to be the more real, judging from their art. And who is to say they may not be right? This is certainly the impression one gets from their beautiful painting, with its lightness of texture and avoidance of solidity. It is founded on nature regarded as a flat vision, instead of a collection of solids in space. Their use of line is also much more restrained than with us, and it is seldom used to accentuate the solidity of things, but chiefly to support the boundaries of masses and suggest detail. Light and shade, which suggest solidity, are never used, a wide light where there is no shadow pervades everything, their drawing being done with the brush in masses.

When, as in the time of Titian, the art of the West had discovered light and shade, linear perspective, aerial perspective, &c., and had begun by fusing the edges of the masses to suspect the necessity of painting to a widely diffused focus, they had got very near considering appearances as a visual whole. But it was not until Velazquez that a picture was painted that was founded entirely on visual appearances, in which a basis of objective outlines was discarded and replaced by a structure of tone masses.

When he took his own painting room with the little Infanta and her maids as a subject, Velazquez seems to have considered it entirely as one flat visual impression. The focal attention is centred on the Infanta, with the figures on either side more or less out of focus, those on the extreme right being quite blurred. The reproduction here given unfortunately does not show these subtleties, and flattens the general appearance very much. The focus is nowhere sharp, as this would disturb the contemplation of the large visual impression. And there, I think, for the first time, the whole gamut of natural vision, tone, colour, form, light and shade, atmosphere, focus, &c., considered as one impression, were put on canvas.

All sense of design is lost. The picture has no surface; it is all atmosphere between the four edges of the frame, and the objects are within. Placed as it is in the Prado, with the light coming from the right as in the picture, there is no break between the real people before it and the figures within, except the slight yellow veil due to age.

But wonderful as this picture is, as a "tour de force," like his Venus of the same period in the National Gallery, it is a painter's picture, and makes but a cold impression on those not interested in the technique of painting. With the cutting away of the primitive support of fine outline design and the absence of those accents conveying a fine form

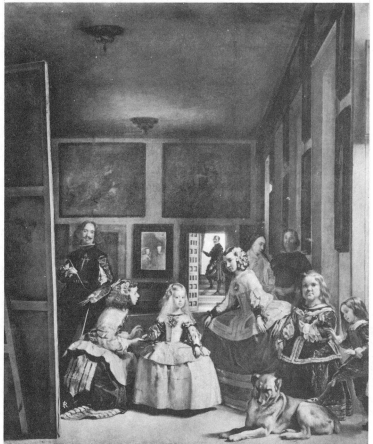

Plate XI   *Photo Anderson*

LAS MENIÑAS. BY VELAZQUEZ (PRADO)

Probably the first picture ever painted entirely from the visual or impressionist standpoint.

stimulus to the mind, art has lost much of its emotional significance.

But art has gained a new point of view. With this subjective way of considering appearances—this "impressionist vision," as it has been called— The Impression-many things that were too ugly, either from shape or association, to yield material for the ist Point of View. painter, were yet found, when viewed as part of a scheme of colour sensations on the retina which the artist considers emotionally and rhythmically, to lend themselves to new and beautiful harmonies and "ensembles" undreamt of by the earlier formulæ. And further, many effects of light that were too hopelessly complicated for painting, considered on the old light and shade principles (for instance, sunlight through trees in a wood), were found to be quite paintable, considered as an impression of various colour masses. The early formula could never free itself from the object as a solid thing, and had consequently to confine its attention to beautiful ones. But from the new point of view, form consists of the shape and qualities of masses of colour on the retina; and what objects happen to be the outside cause of these shapes matters little to the impressionist. Nothing is ugly when seen in a beautiful aspect of light, and aspect is with them everything.

This consideration of the visual appearance in the first place necessitated an increased dependence on the model. As he does not now draw from his mental perceptions the artist has nothing to select the material of his picture from until it has existed as a seen thing before him: until he has a visual impression of it in his mind. With the older point of view (the representation by a pictorial description, as it were, based on the mental idea of an object), the model was not so necessary. In the case of the Impressionist the mental perception is arrived at from the visual impression, and in the older point of view the visual impression is the result of the mental perception. Thus it happens that the Impressionist movement has produced chiefly pictures inspired by the actual world of visual phenomena around us, the older point of view producing most of the pictures deriving their inspiration from the glories of the imagination, the mental world in the mind of the artist. And although interesting attempts are being made to produce imaginative works founded on the impressionist point of view of light and air, the loss of imaginative appeal consequent upon the destruction of contours by scintillation, atmosphere, &c., and the loss of line rhythm it entails, have so far prevented the production of any very satisfactory results. But undoubtedly there is much new material brought to light by this movement waiting to be used imaginatively; and it offers a new field for the selection of expressive qualities.

This point of view, although continuing to some extent in the Spanish school, did not come into general recognition until the last century in France. The most extreme exponents of it are the body of artists who grouped themselves round Claude Monet. This impressionist movement, as the critics have labelled it, was the result of a fierce determination to consider nature solely from the visual point of view, making no concessions to any other associations connected with sight. The result was an entirely new vision of nature, startling and repulsive to eyes unaccustomed to observation from a purely visual point of view and used only to seeing the "feel of things," as it were. And the first results were naturally rather crude. But a great amount of new visual facts were brought to light, particularly those connected with the painting of sunlight and half light effects. Indeed the whole painting of strong light has been permanently affected by the work of this group of painters. Emancipated from the objective world, they no longer dissected the object to see what was inside it, but studied rather the anatomy of the light refracted from it to their eyes. Finding this to be composed of all the colours of the rainbow as seen in the solar spectrum, and that all the effects nature produced are done with different proportions of these colours, they took them, or the nearest pigments they could get to them, for their palette, eliminating the earth colours and black. And further, finding that nature's colours (the rays of coloured light) when mixed produced different results than their corresponding pigments mixed together, they determined to use their paints as pure as possible, placing them one against the other to be mixed as they came to the eye, the mixture being one of pure colour rays, not pigments, by this means.

But we are here only concerned with the movement as it affected form, and must avoid the fascinating province of colour.

Those who had been brought up in the old school of outline form said there was no drawing in these impressionist pictures, and from the point of view of the mental idea of form discussed in the last chapter, there was indeed little, although, had the impression been realised to a sufficiently definite focus, the sense of touch and solidity would probably have been satisfied. But the particular field of this new point of view, the beauty of tone and colour relations considered as an impression apart from objectivity, did not tempt them to carry their work so far as this, or the insistence on these particular qualities would have been lost.

But interesting and alluring as is the new world of visual music opened up by this point of view, it is beginning to be realised that it has failed somehow to satisfy. In the first place, the implied assumption that one sees with the eye alone is wrong:

" In every object there is inexhaustible meaning; the eye sees in it what the eye brings means of seeing,"[1]

and it is the mind behind the eye that supplies this means of perception: **one sees with the mind.** The ultimate effect of any picture, be it impressionist, post, anti, or otherwise—is its power to stimulate these mental perceptions within the mind.

But even from the point of view of the *true* visual perception (if there is such a thing) that modern art has heard so much talk of, the copying of the retina picture is not so great a success. The impression carried away from a scene that has moved us is not its complete visual aspect. Only those things that are significant to the felt impression have been retained by the mind; and if the picture is to be a true representation of this, the significant facts must be sorted out from the mass of irrelevant matter and presented in a lively manner. The impressionist's habit of painting before nature entirely is not calculated to do this. Going time after time to the same place, even if similar weather conditions are waited for, although well enough for studies, is against the production of a fine picture. Every

[1] Goethe, quoted in Carlyle's *French Revolution*, chap. i.

time the artist goes to the selected spot he receives a different impression, so that he must either paint all over his picture each time, in which case his work must be confined to a small scale and will be hurried in execution, or he must paint a bit of to-day's impression alongside of yesterday's, in which case his work will be dull and lacking in oneness of conception.

And further, in decomposing the colour rays that come to the eye and painting in pure colour, while great addition was made to the power of expressing light, yet by destroying the definitions and enveloping everything in a scintillating atmos-phere, the power to design in a large manner was lost with the wealth of significance that the music of line can convey.

But impressionism has opened up a view from which much interesting matter for art is to be gleaned. And everywhere painters are selecting from this, and grafting it on to some of the more traditional schools of design.

Our concern here is with the influence this point of view has had upon draughtsmanship. The influ-ence has been considerable, particularly with those draughtsmen whose work deals with the rendering of modern life. It consists in drawing from the ob-servation of the silhouette occupied by objects in the field of vision, observing the flat appearance of things as they are on the retina. This is, of course, the only accurate way in which to observe visual shapes. The difference between this and the older point of view is its insistence on the observation of the flat visual impression to the exclusion of the tactile or touch sense that by the association of ideas we have come to expect in things seen. An increased truth to the character of appearances has been the result, with a corresponding loss of plastic form expression.

On pages 66 and 67 a reproduction of a drawing in the British Museum, attributed to Michael Angelo, is contrasted with one in the Louvre by Degas. The one is drawn from the line point of view and the other from the mass. They both contain lines, but in the one case the lines are the contours of felt forms and in the other the boundaries of visual masses. In the Michael Angelo the silhouette is only the result of the overlapping of rich forms considered in the round. Every muscle and bone has been mentally realised as a concrete thing and the drawing made as an expression of this idea. Note the line rhythm also; the sense of energy and movement conveyed by the swinging curves; and compare with what is said later (page 162) about the rhythmic significance of swinging curves.

Then compare it with the Degas and observe the totally different attitude of mind in which this drawing has been approached. Instead of the outlines being the result of forms felt as concrete things, the silhouette is everywhere considered first, the plastic sense (nowhere so great as in the other) being arrived at from the accurate consideration of the mass shapes.

Notice also the increased attention to individual character in the Degas, observe the pathos of those underfed little arms, and the hand holding the tired ankle—how individual it all is. What a different tale this little figure tells from that given before the footlights! See with what sympathy the contours have been searched for those accents expressive of all this.

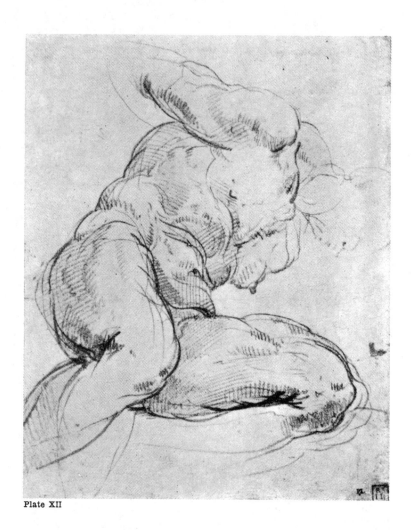

Plate XII

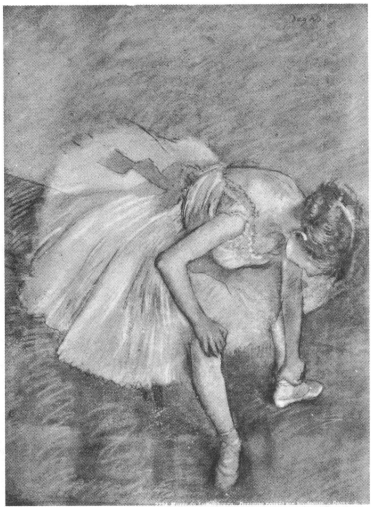

Plate XIII *Photo Levy*

Study by Degas (Luxembourg)

In contrast with Michael Angelo's drawing, note the preoccupation with the silhouette, the spaces occupied by the different masses in the field of vision; how the appearance of solid forms is the result of accurately portraying this visual appearance.

MASS DRAWING

How remote from individual character is the Michael Angelo in contrast with this! Instead of an individual he gives us the expression of a glowing mental conception of man as a type of physical strength and power.

The rhythm is different also, in the one case being a line rhythm, and in the other a consideration of the flat pattern of shapes or masses with a play of lost-and-foundness on the edges (see later, pages 192 *et seq.*, variety of edges). It is this feeling for rhythm in Degas's drawing and the sympathetic searching for and emphasis of those points expressive of character, that keep it from being the mechanical performance which so much concern with scientific visual accuracy might well have made it, and which has made mechanical many of the drawings of Degas's followers who unintelligently copy his method.

VI

THE ACADEMIC AND CONVENTIONAL

THE terms Academic and Conventional are much used in criticism and greatly feared by the criticised, often without either party appearing to have much idea of what is meant. New so-called schools of painting seem to arrive annually with the spring fashions, and sooner or later the one of last year gets called out of date, if not conventional and academic. And as students, for fear of having their work called by one or other of these dread terms, are inclined to rush into any new extravagance that comes along, some inquiry as to their meaning will not be out of place before we pass on to the chapters dealing with academic study.

It has been the cry for some time that Schools of Art turned out only academic students. And one certainly associates a dead level of respectable mediocrity with much school work. We can call to mind a lot of dull, lifeless, highly-finished work, **imperfectly perfect**, that has won the prize in many a school competition. Flaubert says "a form deadens," and it does seem as if the necessary formality of a school course had some deadening influence on students; and that there was some important part of the artist's development which it has failed to recognise and encourage.

The freer system of the French schools has been

in many cases more successful. But each school was presided over by an artist of distinction, and this put the students in touch with real work and thus introduced vitality. In England, until quite lately, artists were seldom employed in teaching, which was left to men set aside for the purpose, without any time to carry on original work of their own. The Royal Academy Schools are an exception to this. There the students have the advantage of teaching from some distinguished member or associate who has charge of the upper school for a month at a time. But as the visitor is constantly changed, the less experienced students are puzzled by the different methods advocated, and flounder hopelessly for want of a definite system to work on; although for a student already in possession of a good grounding there is much to be said for the system, as contact with the different masters widens their outlook.

But perhaps the chief mistake in Art Schools has been that they have too largely confined themselves to training students mechanically to observe and portray the thing set before them to copy, an antique figure, a still-life group, a living model sitting as still and lifeless as he can. Now this is all very well as far as it goes, but the real matter of art is not necessarily in all this. And if the real matter of art is neglected too long the student may find it difficult to get in touch with it again.

These accurate, painstaking school studies are very necessary indeed as a training for the eye in observing accurately, and the hand in reproducing the appearances of things, because it is through the reproduction of natural appearances and the knowledge of form and colour derived from such study that the student will afterwards find the means of giving expression to his feelings. But when valuable prizes and scholarships are given for them, and *not* for really artistic work, they do tend to become the end instead of the means.

It is of course improbable that even school studies done with the sole idea of accuracy by a young artist will in all cases be devoid of artistic feeling; it will creep in, if he has the artistic instinct. But it is not enough **encouraged,** and the prize is generally given to the drawing that is most complete and like the model in a commonplace way. If a student, moved by a strong feeling for form, lets himself go and does a fine thing, probably only remotely like the model to the average eye, the authorities are puzzled and don't usually know what to make of it.

There are schools where the most artistic qualities are encouraged, but they generally neglect the academic side; and the student leaves them poorly equipped for fine work. Surely it would be possible to make a distinction, giving prizes for academic drawings which should be as thoroughly accurate in a mechanical way as industry and application can make them, and also for artistic drawings, in which the student should be encouraged to follow his bent, striving for the expression of any qualities that delight him, and troubling less about mechanical accuracy. The use of drawing as an expression of something felt is so often left until after the school training is done that many students fail to achieve it altogether. And rows of lifeless pictures, made up of models copied in different attitudes, with studio properties around them, are the result, and pass for art in many quarters. Such pictures often display considerable ability, for as Burne-Jones says in one of his letters, " It is very difficult to paint even a bad picture." But had the ability been differently directed, the pictures might have been good.

It is difficult to explain what is wrong with an academic drawing, and what is the difference between it and a fine drawing. But perhaps this difference can be brought home a little more clearly if you will pardon a rather fanciful simile. I am told that if you construct a perfectly fitted engine —the piston fitting the cylinder with absolute accuracy and the axles their sockets with no space between, &c.—it will not work, but be a lifeless mass of iron. There must be enough play between the vital parts to allow of some movement ; " dither " is, I believe, the Scotch word for it. The piston must be allowed some play in the opening of the cylinder through which it passes, or it will not be able to move and show any life. And the axles of the wheels in their sockets, and, in fact, all parts of the machine where life and movement are to occur, must have this play, this " dither." It has always seemed to me that the accurately fitting engine was like a good academic drawing, in a way a perfect piece of workmanship, but lifeless. Imperfectly perfect, because there was no room left for the play of life. And to carry the simile further, if you allow too great a play between the parts, so that they fit one over the other too loosely, the engine will lose power and become a poor rickety thing. There must be the smallest amount of play that will allow of its working. And the more perfectly made the engine, the less will the amount of this " dither " be.

The word " dither " will be a useful name to give

that elusive quality, that play on mechanical accuracy, existing in all vital art. **It is this vital quality that has not yet received much attention in art training.**

It is here that the photograph fails, it can only at best give mechanical accuracy, whereas art gives the impression of a live, individual consciousness. Where the recording instrument is a live individual, there is no mechanical standard of accuracy possible, as every recording instrument is a different personality. And it is the subtle differences in the individual renderings of nature that are the life-blood of art. The photograph, on account of its being chained to mechanical accuracy, has none of this play of life to give it charm. It only approaches artistic conditions when it is blurred, vague, and indefinite, as in so-called artistic photography, for then only can some amount of this vitalising play, this "dither" be imagined to exist.

It is this perfect accuracy, this lack of play, of variety, that makes the machine-made article so lifeless. Wherever there is life there is variety, and the substitution of the machine-made for the hand-made article has impoverished the world to a greater extent than we are probably yet aware of. Whereas formerly, before the advent of machinery, the commonest article you could pick up had a life and warmth which gave it individual interest, now everything is turned out to such a perfection of deadness that one is driven to pick up and collect, in sheer desperation, the commonest rubbish still surviving from earlier periods.

But to return to our drawings. If the variations from strict accuracy made under the influence

72

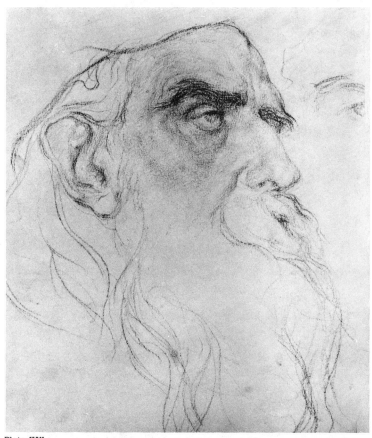

Plate XIV

DRAWING IN RED CHALK BY ERNEST COLE

Example of unacademic drawing made in the author's class at the Goldsmiths' College
School of Art.

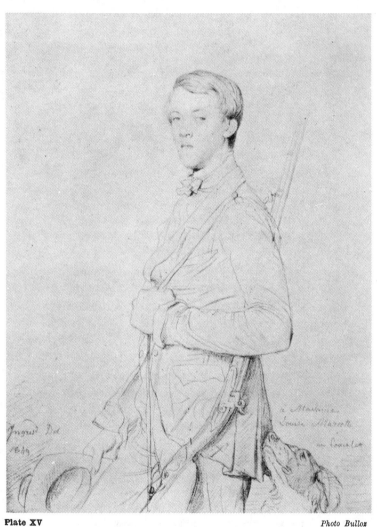

Plate XV   *Photo Bulloz*

FROM A PENCIL DRAWING BY INGRES

of feeling are too great, the result will be a caricature. The variations in a beautiful drawing are so subtle as often to defy detection. The studies of Ingres are an instance of what I mean. How true and instinct with life are his lines, and how easily one might assume that they were merely accurate. But no merely accurate work would have the impelling quality these drawings possess. If the writer may venture an opinion on so great an artist, the subtle difference we are talking about was sometimes missed by even Ingres himself, when he transferred his drawings to the canvas; and the pictures have in some cases become academic and lifeless. Without the stimulus of nature before him it was difficult to preserve the "dither" in the drawing, and the life has escaped. This is the great difficulty of working from studies; it is so easy to lose those little points in your drawing that make for vitality of expression, in the process of copying in cold blood.

The fact is: it is only the academic that can be taught. And it is no small thing if this is well done in a school. The qualities that give vitality and distinction to drawing must be appreciated by the student himself, and may often assert themselves in his drawing without his being aware that he is doing aught but honestly copying. And if he has trained himself thoroughly he will not find much difficulty when he is moved to vital expression. All the master can do is to stand by and encourage whenever he sees evidence of the real thing. But there is undoubtedly this danger of the school studies becoming the end instead of the means.

A drawing is not necessarily academic because it is thorough, but only because it is dead. Neither

THE ACADEMIC AND CONVENTIONAL

is a drawing necessarily academic because it is done in what is called a conventional style, any more than it is good because it is done in an unconventional style. The test is whether it has life and conveys genuine feeling.

There is much foolish talk about conventional art, as if art could ever get away from conventions, if it would. The convention will be more natural or more abstract according to the nature of the thing to be conveyed and the medium employed to express it. But naturalism is just as much a convention as any of the other isms that art has lately been so assailed with. For a really unconventional art there is Madame Tussaud's Waxworks. There, even the convention of a frame and flat surface are done away with, besides the painted symbols to represent things. They have **real** natural chairs, tables, and floors, real clothes, and even real hair. Realism everywhere, but no life. And we all know the result. There is more expression of life in a few lines scribbled on paper by a good artist than in all the reality of the popular show.

It would seem that, after a certain point, the nearer your picture approaches the actual illusion of natural appearance, the further you are from the expression of life. One can never hope to surpass the illusionary appearance of a **tableau vivant**. There you have real, living people. But what an awful deathlike stillness is felt when the curtain is drawn aside. The nearer you approach the actual in all its completeness, the more evident is the lack of that **movement** which always accompanies life. You cannot express life by copying laboriously

74

natural appearances. Those things in the appearance that convey vital expression and are capable of being translated into the medium he is working with, have to be sought by the artist, and the painted symbols of his picture made accordingly. This lack of the movement of life is never noticed in a good picture, on the other hand the figures are often felt to move.

Pictures are blamed for being conventional when it is lack of vitality that is the trouble. If the convention adopted has not been vitalised by the emotion that is the reason of the painting, it will, of course, be a lifeless affair. But however abstract and unnaturalistic the manner adopted, if it has been truly felt by the artist as the right means of expressing his emotional idea, it will have life and should not be called conventional in the commonly accepted offensive use of the term.

It is only when a painter consciously chooses a manner not his own, which he does not comprehend and is incapable of firing with his own personality, that his picture is ridiculous and conventional in the dead sense.

But every age differs in its temperament, and the artistic conventions of one age seldom fit another. The artist has to discover a convention for himself, one that fits his particular individuality. But this is done simply and naturally—not by starting out with the intention of flouting all traditional conventions on principle; nor, on the other hand, by accepting them all on principle, but by simply following his own bent and selecting what appeals to him in anything and everything that comes within the range of his vision. The result is likely to be something very different from the violent exploits in peculiarity that have been masquerading as originality lately. **Originality is more concerned with sincerity than with peculiarity.**

The struggling and fretting after originality that one sees in modern art is certainly an evidence of vitality, but one is inclined to doubt whether anything really original was ever done in so forced a way. The older masters, it seems, were content sincerely to try and do the best they were capable of doing. And this continual striving to do better led them almost unconsciously to new and original results. Originality is a quality over which an artist has as little influence as over the shape and distinction of his features. All he can do is to be sincere and try and find out the things that really move him and that he really likes. If he has a strong and original character, he will have no difficulty in this, and his work will be original in the true sense. And if he has not, it is a matter of opinion whether he is not better employed in working along the lines of some well-tried manner that will at any rate keep him from doing anything really bad, than in struggling to cloak his own commonplaceness under violent essays in peculiarity and the avoidance of the obvious at all costs.

But while speaking against fretting after eccentricity, don't let it be assumed that any discouragement is being given to genuine new points of view. In art, when a thing has once been well done and has found embodiment in some complete work of art, it has been done once for all. The circumstances that produced it are never likely to occur again. That is why those painters who continue to reproduce a picture of theirs (we do not mean literally) that had been a success in the first instance, never

76

afterwards obtain the success of the original performance. Every beautiful work of art is a new creation, the result of particular circumstances in the life of the artist and the time of its production, that have never existed before and will never recur again. Were any of the great masters of the past alive now, they would do very different work from what they did then, the circumstances being so entirely different. So that should anybody seek to paint like Titian now, by trying to paint like Titian did in his time, he could not attempt anything more unlike the spirit of that master; which in its day, like the spirit of all masters, was most advanced. But it is only by a scrupulously sincere and truthful attitude of mind that the new and original circumstances in which we find ourselves can be taken advantage of for the production of original work. And self-conscious seeking after peculiarity only stops the natural evolution and produces abortions.

But do not be frightened by conventions, the different materials in which the artist works impose their conventions. And as it is through these materials that he has to find expression, what expressive qualities they possess must be studied, and those facts in nature selected that are in harmony with them. The treatment of hair by sculptors is an extreme instance of this. What are those qualities of hair that are amenable to expression in stone? Obviously they are few, and confined chiefly to the mass forms in which the hair arranges itself. The finest sculptors have never attempted more than this, have never lost sight of the fact that it was stone they were working with, and never made any attempt to create an illusion of real hair. And in the same way, when working in bronze, the fine artist never loses sight of the fact that it is bronze with which he is working. How sadly the distinguished painter to whom a misguided administration entrusted the work of modelling the British emblem overlooked this, may be seen any day in Trafalgar Square, the lions there possessing none of the splendour of bronze but looking as if they were modelled in dough, and possessing in consequence none of the vital qualities of the lion. It is interesting to compare them with the little lion Alfred Stevens modelled for the railing of the British Museum, and to speculate on what a thrill we might have received every time we passed Trafalgar Square, had he been entrusted with the work, as he might have been.

And in painting, the great painters never lose sight of the fact that it is paint with which they are expressing themselves. And although paint is capable of approaching much nearer the actual appearance of nature than stone or bronze, they never push this to the point where you forget that it is paint. This has been left for some of the smaller men.

And when it comes to drawing, the great artists have always confined themselves to the qualities in nature that the tool they were drawing with was capable of expressing, and no others. Whether working with pen, pencil, chalk, or charcoal, they always created a convention within which unlimited expression has been possible.

To sum up, academic drawing is all that can be really taught, and is as necessary to the painter as the practising of exercises is to the musician, that his powers of observation and execution may be trained. But the vital matter of art is not in all this necessary training. And this fact the student should always keep in mind, and be ever ready to give rein to those natural enthusiasms which, if he is an artist, he will find welling up within him. The danger is that the absorbing interest in his academic studies may take up his whole attention, to the neglect of the instinctive qualities that he should possess the possession of which alone will entitle him to be an artist.

VII

THE STUDY OF DRAWING

WE have seen that there are two extreme points of view from which the representation of form can be approached, that of outline directly related to the mental idea of form with its touch association on the one hand, and that of mass connected directly with the visual picture on the retina on the other.

Now, between these two extreme points of view there are an infinite variety of styles combining them both and leaning more to the one side or the other, as the case may be. But it is advisable for the student to study both separately, for there are different things to be learnt and different expressive qualities in nature to be studied in both.

From the study of outline drawing the eye is trained to accurate observation and learns the expressive value of a line. And the hand is also trained to definite statement, the student being led on by degrees from simple outlines to approach the full realisation of form in all the complexity of light and shade.

But at the same time he should study mass drawing with paint from the purely visual point of view, in order to be introduced to the important study of tone values and the expression of form by means of planes. And so by degrees he will learn accurately to observe and portray the tone masses (their shapes and values) to which all visual appearances can be reduced; and he will gradually arrive at the full realisation of form—a realisation that will bring him to a point somewhat similar to that arrived at from the opposite point of view of an outline to which has been added light and shade, &c.

But unless both points of view are studied, the student's work will be incomplete. If form be studied only from the outline point of view, and what have been called sculptor's drawings alone attempted, the student will lack knowledge of the tone and atmosphere that always envelop form in nature. And also he will be poorly equipped when he comes to exchange the pencil for a brush and endeavours to express himself in paint.

And if his studies be only from the mass point of view, the training of his eye to the accurate observation of all the subtleties of contours and the construction of form will be neglected. And he will not understand the mental form stimulus that the direction and swing of a brush stroke can give. These and many things connected with expression can best be studied in line work.

Let the student therefore begin on the principles adopted in most schools, with outline studies of simple casts or models, and gradually add light and shade. When he has acquired more proficiency he may approach drawing from the life. This is sufficiently well done in the numerous schools of art that now exist all over the country. But, at the same time (and this, as far as I know, is not done anywhere), the student should begin some simple form of mass drawing in paint, simple exer-

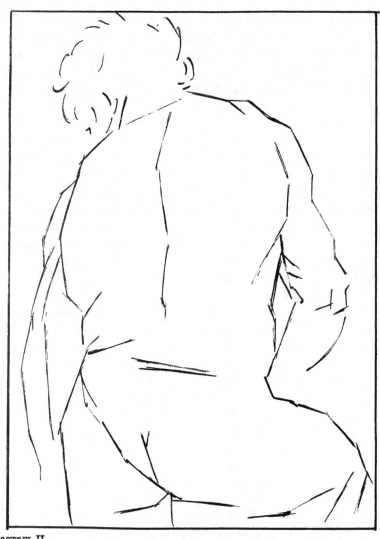

Diagram II

SHOWING WHERE SQUARENESSES MAY BE LOOKED FOR
IN THE DRAWING ON THE OPPOSITE PAGE

82

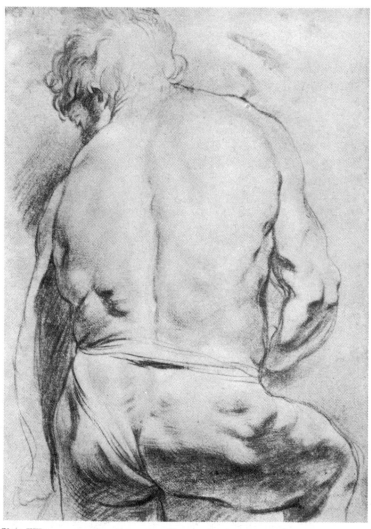

Plate XVI

STUDY BY RUBENS FROM THE COLLECTION OF CHARLES RICKETTS
AND CHARLES SHANNON

A splendid example of Rubens' love of rich, full forms. Compare with the diagram opposite,
and note the flatnesses that give strength to the forms.

cises, as is explained later in the chapter on Mass Drawing, Practical, being at first attempted and criticised solely from the point of view of tone values.

From lack of this elementary tone study, the student, when he approaches painting for the first time, with only his outline and light and shade knowledge, is entirely at sea. With brushes and paint he is presented with a problem of form expressions entirely new. And he usually begins to flounder about, using his paint as much like chalk on paper as possible. And timid of losing his outlines, he fears to put down a mass, as he has no knowledge of reducing appearances to a structure of tone masses or planes.

I would suggest, therefore, that the student should study simultaneously from these two points of view, beginning with their most extreme positions, that is, bare outline on the one side and on the other side tone masses criticised for their accuracy of values only in the first instance. As he advances, the one study will help the other. The line work will help the accuracy with which he observes the shapes of masses, and when he comes to light and shade his knowledge of tone values will help him here. United at last, when complete light and shade has been added to his outline drawings and to his mass drawing an intimate knowledge of form, the results will approximate and the two paths will meet. But if the qualities appertaining to either point of view are not studied separately, the result is confusion and the "muddling through" method so common in our schools of art.

VIII

LINE DRAWING: PRACTICAL

SEEING that the first condition of your drawing
is that it has to be made on a flat surface, no
matter whether it is to be in line or mass you
intend to draw, it is obvious that appearances must
be reduced to terms of a flat surface before they
can be expressed on paper. And this is the first
difficulty that confronts the student in attempting
to draw a solid object. He has so acquired the
habit of perceiving the solidity of things, as was
explained in an earlier chapter, that no little
difficulty will be experienced in accurately seeing
them as a flat picture.

As it is only from one point of view that things
Observing can be drawn, and as we have two eyes,
Solids as a therefore two points of view, the closing of
Flat Copy. one eye will be helpful at first.

The simplest and most mechanical way of observing things as a flat subject is to have a piece
of cardboard with a rectangular hole cut out of the
middle, and also pieces of cotton threaded through
it in such a manner that they make a pattern of
squares across the opening, as in the accompanying
sketch. To make such a frame, get a piece of stiff
cardboard, about 12 inches by 9 inches, and cut a
rectangular hole in the centre, 7 inches by 5 inches,
as in Diagram III. Now mark off the inches on

all sides of the opening, and taking some black thread, pass it through the point A with a needle (fixing the end at this point with sealing-wax),

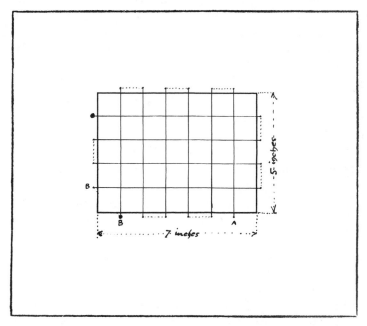

Diagram III

A DEVICE FOR ENABLING STUDENTS TO OBSERVE
APPEARANCES AS A FLAT SUBJECT

and across the opening to the corresponding point on the opposite side. Take it along to the next point, as shown by the dotted line, and pass it through and across the opening again, and so on, until B is reached, when the thread should be held by some sealing-wax quite taut everywhere. Do the same for the other side. This frame should be held between the eye and the object to be drawn (one eye being closed) in a perfectly vertical position, and with the rectangular sides of the opening vertical and horizontal. The object can then be observed as a flat copy. The trellis of cotton will greatly help the student in seeing the subject to be drawn in two dimensions, and this is the first technical difficulty the young draughtsman has to overcome. It is useful also in training the eye to see the proportions of different parts one to another, the squares of equal size giving one a unit of measurement by which all parts can be scaled.

Vertical and horizontal lines are also of the utmost importance in that first consideration for setting out a drawing, namely the fixing of salient points, and getting their relative positions. Fig. Z, on page 87, will illustrate what is meant. Let A B C D E be assumed to be points of some importance in an object you wish to draw. Unaided, the placing of these points would be a matter of considerable difficulty. But if you assume a vertical line drawn from A, the positions of B, C, D, and E can be observed in relation to it by noting the height and length of horizontal lines drawn from them to this vertical line. This vertical can be drawn by holding a plumb line at arm's length (closing one eye, of course) and bringing it to a position where it will cover the point A on your subject. The position of the other points on either side of this vertical line can then be observed. Or a knitting-needle can be held vertically before you at arm's length, giving you a line passing through point A. The advantage of the needle is that comparative measurements can be taken with it.

Fixing Positions of Salient Points.

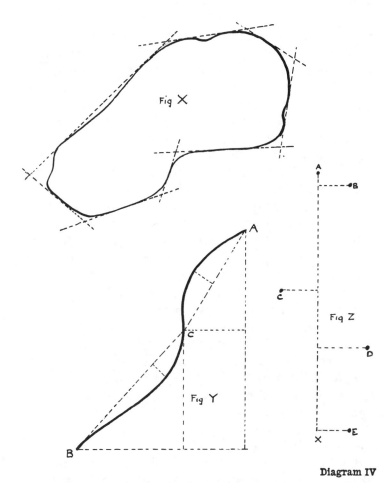

Diagram IV

SHOWING THREE PRINCIPLES OF CONSTRUCTION USED
IN OBSERVING FIG. X, MASSES; FIG. Y, CURVES;
FIG. Z, POSITION OF POINTS

LINE DRAWING: PRACTICAL

In measuring comparative distances the needle should always be held at arm's length and the eye kept in one position during the operation; and, whether held vertically or horizontally, always kept in a vertical plane, that is, either straight up and down, or across at right angles to the line of your vision. If these things are not carefully observed, your comparisons will not be true. The method employed is to run the thumb-nail up the needle until the distance from the point so reached to the top exactly corresponds with the distance on the object you wish to measure. Having this carefully noted on your needle, without moving the position of your eye, you can move your outstretched arm and compare it with other distances on the object. It is never advisable to compare other than vertical and horizontal measurements. In our diagram the points were drawn at random and do not come in any obvious mathematical relationship, and this is the usual circumstance in nature. But point C will be found to be a little above the half, and point D a little less than a third of the way up the vertical line. How much above the half and less than the third will have to be observed by eye and a corresponding amount allowed in setting out your drawing. In the horizontal distances, E will be found to be one-fourth the distance from X to the height of C on the right of our vertical line, and C a little more than this distance to the left, while the distance on the right of D is a little less than one-fifth of the whole height. The height of B is so near the top as to be best judged by eye, and its distance to the right is the same as E. These measurements are never to be taken as absolutely accurate, but are a great help to beginners in train-

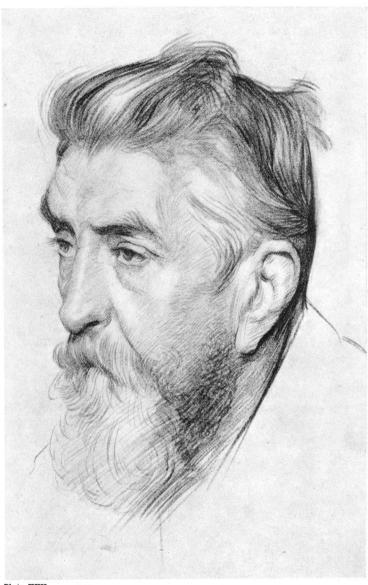

Plate XVII

DEMONSTRATION DRAWING MADE BEFORE THE STUDENTS OF THE
GOLDSMITHS COLLEGE SCHOOL OF ART

Illustrating how different directions of lines can help expression of form.

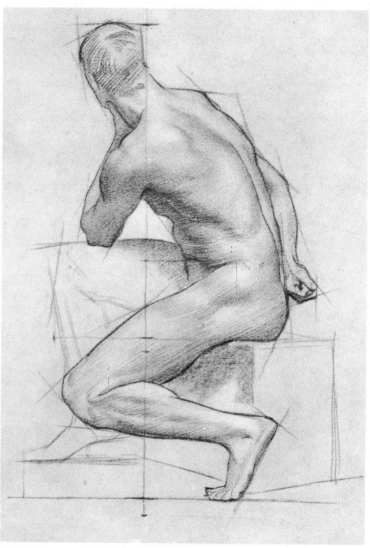

Plate XVIII

Study illustrating Method of Drawing

Note the different stages. 1st. Centre line and transverse lines for settling position of salient points. 2nd. Blocking in, as shown in further leg. 3rd. Drawing in the forms and shading, as shown in front leg. 4th. Rubbing with fingers (giving a faint middle tone over the whole), and picking out high lights with bread, as shown on back and arms.

LINE DRAWING: PRACTICAL

ing the eye, and are at times useful in every artist's work.

It is useful if one can establish a unit of measurement, some conspicuous distance that does not vary in the object (if a living model a great many distances will be constantly varying), and with which all distances can be compared.

In setting out a drawing, this fixing of certain salient points is the first thing for the student to do. The drawing reproduced on page 89 has been made to illustrate the method of procedure it is advisable to adopt in training the eye to accurate observation. It was felt that a vertical line drawn through the pit of the arm would be the most useful for taking measurements on, and this was first drawn and its length decided upon. Train yourself to draw between limits decided upon at the start. This power will be of great use to you when you wish to place a figure in an exact position in a picture. The next thing to do is to get the relative heights of different points marked upon this line. The fold at the pit of the stomach was found to be exactly in the centre. This was a useful start, and it is generally advisable to note where the half comes first, and very useful if it comes in some obvious place. Other measurements were taken in the same way as our points A B C D E in the diagram on page 87, and horizontal lines drawn across, and the transverse distances measured in relation to the heights. I have left these lines on the drawing, and also different parts of it unfinished, so as to show the different stages of the work. These guide lines are done mentally later on, when the student is more advanced, and with more accuracy than the clumsy knitting-needle.

LINE DRAWING: PRACTICAL

But before the habit of having constantly in mind a vertical and horizontal line with which to compare positions is acquired, they should be put in with as much accuracy as measuring can give.

The next thing to do is to block out the spaces corresponding to those occupied by the model **Blocking** in the field of your vision. The method **in your** employed to do this is somewhat similar **Drawing.** to that adopted by a surveyor in drawing the plan of a field. Assuming he had an irregular shaped one, such as is drawn in Fig. X, page 87, he would proceed to invest it with straight lines, taking advantage of any straightness in the boundary, noting the length and the angles at which these straight lines cut each other, and then reproducing them to scale on his plan. Once having got this scaffolding accurately placed, he can draw the irregularities of the shape in relation to these lines with some certainty of getting them right.

You should proceed in very much the same way to block out the spaces that the forms of your drawing are to occupy. I have produced these blocking-out lines beyond what was necessary in the accompanying drawing (page 87), in order to show them more clearly.

There is yet another method of construction useful in noting accurately the shape of a curved **How to ob-** line, which is illustrated in Fig. Y, page 87. **serve the** First of all, fix the positions of the ex- **Shape of** tremities of the line by means of the vertical **Curves.** and horizontal. And also, as this is a double curve, the point at which the curvature changes from one direction to the other: point C. By drawing lines CA, CB and noting the distances your curves travel from these straight lines, and particularly the relative position of the farthest points reached, their curvature can be accurately observed and copied. In noting the varying curvature of forms, this construction should always be in your mind to enable you to observe them accurately. First note the points at which the curvature begins and ends, and then the distances it travels from a line joining these two points, holding up a pencil or knitting-needle against the model if need be.

A drawing being blocked out in such a state as the further leg and foot of our demonstration drawing (page 89), it is time to begin the drawing proper. So far you have only been pegging out the ground it is going to occupy. This initial scaffolding, so necessary to train the eye, should be done as accurately as possible, but don't let it interfere with your freedom in expressing the forms afterwards. The work up to this point has been mechanical, but it is time to consider the subject with some feeling for form. Here knowledge of the structure of bones and muscles that underlie the skin will help you to seize on those things that are significant and express the form of the figure. And the student cannot do better than study the excellent book by Sir Alfred D. Fripp on this subject, entitled **Human Anatomy for Art Students**. Notice particularly the swing of the action, such things as the pull occasioned by the arm resting on the farther thigh, and the prominence given to the forms by the straining of the skin at the shoulder. Also the firm lines of the bent back and the crumpled forms of the front of the body. Notice the overlapping of the con-

The Drawing proper.

tours, and where they are accentuated and where more lost, &c., drawing with as much feeling and conviction as you are capable of. You will have for some time to work tentatively, feeling for the true shapes that you do not yet rightly see, but as soon as you feel any confidence, remember it should be your aim to express yourself freely and swiftly.

There is a tendency in some quarters to discourage this blocking in of the forms in straight lines, and certainly it has been harmful to the freedom of expression in the work of some students. They not only begin the drawing with this mechanical blocking in, but continue it in the same mechanical fashion, cutting up almost all their curves into flatnesses, and never once breaking free from this scaffolding to indulge in the enjoyment of free line expression. This, of course, is bad, and yet the character of a curved line is hardly to be accurately studied in any other way than by observing its relation to straight lines. The inclination and length of straight lines can be observed with certainty. But a curve has not this definiteness, and is a very unstable thing to set about copying unaided. Who but the highly skilled draughtsman could attempt to copy our random shape at Fig. X, page 87, without any guiding straight lines? And even the highly skilled draughtsman would draw such straight lines mentally. So that some blocking out of the curved forms, either done practically or in imagination, must be adopted to rightly observe any shapes. But do not forget that this is only a scaffolding, and should always be regarded as such and kicked away as soon as real form expression with any feeling begins.

LINE DRAWING: PRACTICAL

But it will be some years before the beginner has got his eye trained to such accuracy of observation that he can dispense with it.

In the case of foreshortenings, the eye, unaided by this blocking out, is always apt to be led astray. And here the observation of the shape of the background against the object will be of great assistance. The appearance of the foreshortened object is so unlike what you know it to be as a solid thing, that it is as well to concentrate the attention on the background rather than on the form in this blocking-out process. And in fact, in blocking out any object, whether foreshortened or not, the shape of the background should be observed as carefully as any other shape. But in making the drawing proper, the forms must be observed in their inner relations. That is to say, the lines bounding one side of a form must be observed in relation to the lines bounding the other side; as the true expression of form, which is the object of drawing, depends on the true relationship of these boundaries. The drawing of the two sides should be carried on simultaneously, so that one may constantly compare them. *In Blocking-in observe Shape of the Background as much as the Object.*

The boundaries of forms with any complexity, such as the human figure, are not continuous lines. One form overlaps another, like the lines of a range of hills. And this overlapping should be sought for and carefully expressed, the outlines being made up of a series of overlappings. *Boundaries a series of Overlappings.*

In Line Drawing shading should only be used to aid the expression of form. It is not advisable to aim at representing the true tone values. *Shading.*

LINE DRAWING: PRACTICAL

In direct light it will be observed that a solid object has some portion of its surface in light, while other portions, those turned away from the light, are in shadow. Shadows are also cast on the ground and surrounding objects, called cast shadows. The parts of an object reflecting the most direct light are called the high lights. If the object have a shiny surface these lights are clear and distinct; if a dull surface, soft and diffused. In the case of a very shiny surface, such as a glazed pot, the light may be reflected so completely that a picture of the source of light, usually a window, will be seen.

In the diagram on page 95, let A represent the plan of a cone, B C the opening of a window, and D the eye of the spectator, and E F G the wall of a room. Light travels in straight lines from the window, strikes the surface of the cone, and is reflected to the eye, making the angle of incidence equal to the angle of reflection, the angle of incidence being that made by the light striking an object, and the angle of reflection that made by the light in leaving the surface.

It will be seen that the lines B 1 D, C 2 D are the limits of the direct rays of light that come to the eye from the cone, and that therefore between points 1 and 2 will be seen the highest light. If the cone have a perfect reflecting surface, such as a looking-glass has, this would be all the direct light that would be reflected from the cone to the eye. But assuming it to have what is called a dull surface, light would be reflected from other parts also, although not in so great a quantity. If what is called a dull surface is looked at under a microscope it will be found to be quite rough,

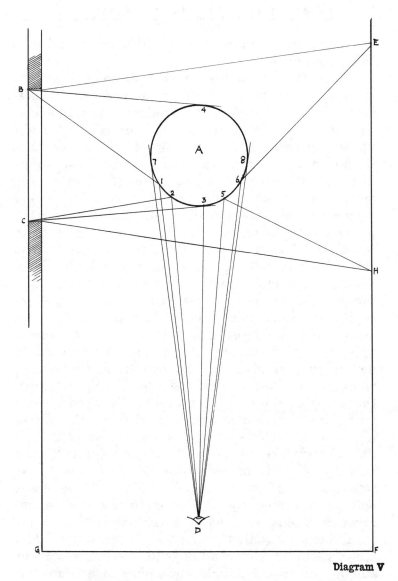

Diagram **V**

PLAN OF CONE A, LIT BY WINDOW BC; POSITION OF
    EYE D. ILLUSTRATING PRINCIPLES OF LIGHT AND
    SHADE

95

i.e. made up of many facets which catch light at different angles.

Lines B4, C3 represent the extreme limits of light that can be received by the cone, and therefore at points 3 and 4 the shadow will commence. The fact that light is reflected to the eye right up to the point 3 does not upset the theory that it can only be reflected from points where the angle of incidence can equal the angle of reflection, as it would seem to do, because the surface being rough presents facets at different angles, from some of which it can be reflected to the eye right up to point 3. The number of these facets that can so reflect is naturally greatest near the high lights, and gets gradually less as the surface turns more away; until the point is reached where the shadows begin, at which point the surface positively turns away from the light and the reflection of direct light ceases altogether. After point 3 there would be no light coming to the eye from the object, were it not that it receives reflected light. Now, the greatest amount of reflected light will come from the direction opposite to that of the direct light, as all objects in this direction are strongly lit. The surface of the wall between points E and H, being directly opposite the light, will give most reflection. And between points 5 and 6 this light will be reflected by the cone to the eye in its greatest intensity, since at these points the angles of incidence equal the angles of reflection. The other parts of the shadow will receive a certain amount of reflected light, lessening in amount on either side of these points. We have now rays of light coming to the eye from the cone between the extreme points 7 and 8. From 7 to 3 we have the light, including the half tones. Between 1 and 2 the high light. Between 3 and 8 the shadows with the greatest amount of reflected light between 5 and 6.

I should not have troubled the reader with this tedious diagram were it not that certain facts about light and shade can be learned from it. The first is that the high lights come much more within the edge of the object than you would have expected With the light directly opposite point 7, one might have thought the highest light would have come there, and that is where many students put it, until the loss of roundness in the appearance of their work makes them look more carefully for its position. So remember always to look out for high lights within the contours of forms, not on the edges.

The next thing to notice is that **the darkest part of the shadow will come nearest the lights between points 3 and 5.** This is the part turned most away from the direction of the greatest amount of reflected light, and therefore receiving least. The lightest part of the shadow will be in the middle, rather towards the side away from the light, generally speaking. The shadow cast on the ground will be dark, like the darkest part of the shadow on the cone, as its surface is also turned away from the chief source of reflected light.

Although the artist will very seldom be called upon to draw a cone, the same principles of light and shade that are so clearly seen in such a simple figure obtain throughout the whole of nature. This is why the much abused drawing and shading from whitened blocks and pots is so useful. Nothing so clearly impresses the general laws of light and shade as this so-called dull study.

LINE DRAWING: PRACTICAL

This lightening of shadows in the middle by reflected light and darkening towards their edges is a very important thing to remember, the heavy, smoky look students' early work is so prone to, being almost entirely due to their neglect through ignorance of this principle. Nothing is more awful than shadows darker in the middle and gradually lighter towards their edges. Of course, where there is a deep hollow in the shadow parts, as at the armpit and the fold at the navel in the drawing on page 89, you will get a darker tone. But this does not contradict the principle that generally shadows are lighter in the middle and darker towards the edges. Note the luminous quality the observation of this principle gives the shadow on the body of our demonstration drawing.

This is a crude statement of the general principles of light and shade on a simple round object. In one with complex surfaces the varieties of light and shade are infinite. But the same principles hold good. The surfaces turned more to the source of light receive the greatest amount, and are the lightest. And from these parts the amount of light lessens through what are called the half tones as the surface turns more away, until a point is reached where no more direct light is received, and the shadows begin. And in the shadows the same law applies: those surfaces turned most towards the source of reflected light will receive the most, and the amount received will gradually lessen as the surface turns away, until at the point immediately before where the half tones begin the amount of reflected light will be very little, and in consequence the darkest part of the shadows may be looked for. There may, of course, be other sources of direct

light on the shadow side that will entirely alter
and complicate the effect. Or one may draw in a
wide, diffused light, such as is found in the open
air on a grey day; in which case there will be little
or no shadow, the modelling depending entirely on
degrees of light and half tone.

In studying the principles of simple light and
shade it is advisable to draw from objects of one
local colour, such as white casts. In parti-coloured
objects the problem is complicated by the different
tones of the local colour. In line drawing it is as
well to take as little notice as possible of these
variations which disturb the contemplation of pure
form and do not belong to the particular province of
form expression with which we are here concerned.

Although one has selected a strong half light
and half shade effect to illustrate the general principles of light and shade, it is not advisable in
making line drawings to select such a position. A
point of view with a fairly wide light at your back
is the best. In this position little shadow will be
seen, most of the forms being expressed by the play
of light and half tone. The contours, as they are
turned away from the light, will naturally be darker,
and against a light background your subject has an
appearance with dark edges that is easily expressed
by a line drawing. Strong light and shade effects
should be left for mass drawing. You seldom see
any shadows in Holbein's drawings; he seems to
have put his sitters near a wide window, close
against which he worked. Select also a background
as near the tone of the highest light on the object to
be drawn as possible. This will show up clearly the
contour. In the case of a portrait drawing, a newspaper hung behind the head answers very well and

is always easily obtained. The tone of it can be varied by the distance at which it is placed from the head, and by the angle at which it is turned away from or towards the light.

Don't burden a line drawing with heavy half tones and shadows; keep them light. The beauty that is the particular province of line drawing is the beauty of contours, and this is marred by heavy light and shade. Great draughtsmen use only just enough to express the form, but never to attempt the expression of tone. Think of the half tones as part of the lights and not as part of the shadows.

There are many different methods of drawing in line, and a student of any originality will find one that suits his temperament. But I will try and illustrate one that is at any rate logical, and that may serve as a fair type of line drawing generally.

The appearance of an object is first considered as a series of contours, some forming the boundaries of the form against the background, and others the boundaries of the subordinate forms within these bounding lines. The light and shade and differences of local colour (like the lips, eyebrows, and eyes in a head) are considered together as tones of varying degrees of lightness and darkness, and suggested by means of lines drawn parallel across the drawing from left to right, and from below upwards, or vice versa, darker and closer together when depth is wanted, and fainter and farther apart where delicacy is demanded, and varying in thickness when gradation is needed. This rule of parallel shading is broken only when strongly marked forms, such as the swinging lines of hair, a prominent bone or straining muscles, &c., demand it. This parallel shading gives a great beauty of

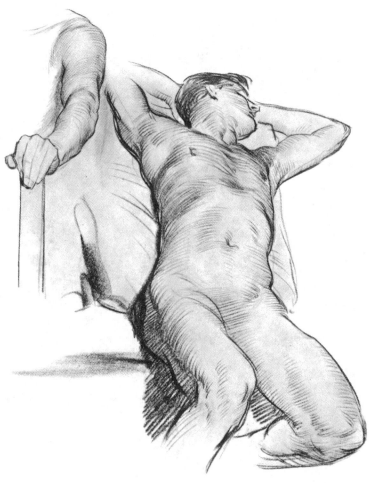

Plate XIX

ILLUSTRATING CURVED LINES SUGGESTING FULLNESS
AND FORESHORTENING

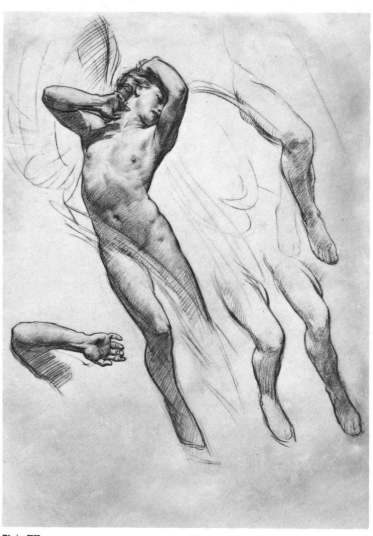

Plate **XX**

STUDY FOR THE FIGURE OF LOVE IN THE PICTURE "LOVE LEAVING
PSYCHE" ILLUSTRATING A METHOD OF DRAWING

The lines of shading following a convenient parallel direction unless prominent
forms demand otherwise.

LINE DRAWING: PRACTICAL

surface and fleshiness to a drawing. The lines
following, as it were, the direction of the light
across the object rather than the form, give a
unity that has a great charm. It is more suited
to drawings where extreme delicacy of form is desired, and is usually used in silver point work, a
medium capable of the utmost refinement.

In this method the lines of shading not being
much varied in direction or curved at all, a minimum
amount of that "form stimulus" is conveyed. The
curving of the lines in shading adds considerably to
the force of the relief, and suggests much stronger
modelling. In the case of foreshortened effects,
where the forms are seen at their fullest, arching
one over the other, some curvature in the lines of
shading is of considerable advantage in adding to
the foreshortened look. (See illustration, page 100.)

Lines drawn down the forms give an appearance of great strength and toughness, a tense look.
And this quality is very useful in suggesting such
things as joints and sinews, rocks, hard ground, or
gnarled tree-trunks, &c. In figure drawing it is an
interesting quality to use sparingly, with the shading done on the across-the-form principle; and to
suggest a difference of texture or a straining of the
form. Lines of shading drawn in every direction,
crossing each other and resolving themselves into
tone effects, suggest atmosphere and the absence
of surface form. This is more often used in the
backgrounds of pen and ink work and is seldom
necessary in pencil or chalk drawing, as they are
more concerned with form than atmosphere. Pen
and ink is more often used for elaborate pictorial
effects in illustration work, owing to the ease with
which it can be reproduced and printed; and it is

here that one often finds this muddled quality of line spots being used to fill up interstices and make the tone even.

Speaking generally, lines of shading drawn across the forms suggest softness, lines drawn in curves fulness of form, lines drawn down the forms hardness, and lines crossing in all directions so that only a mystery of tone results, atmosphere. And if these four qualities of line be used judiciously, a great deal of expressive power is added to your shading. And, as will be explained in the next chapter, somewhat the same principle applies to the direction of the swing of the brush in painting.

Shading lines should never be drawn backwards and forwards from left to right (scribbled), except possibly where a mystery of shadow is wanted and the lines are being crossed in every direction; but never when lines are being used to express form. They are not sufficiently under control, and also the little extra thickness that occurs at the turn is a nuisance.

The crossing of lines in shading gives a more opaque look. This is useful to suggest the opaque appearance of the darker passage that occurs in that part of a shadow nearest the lights; and it is sometimes used in the half tones also.

Draughtsmen vary very much in their treatment of hair, and different qualities of hair require different treatment. The particular beauty of it that belongs to point drawing is the swing and flow of its lines. These are especially apparent in the lights. In the shadows the flow of line often stops, to be replaced by a mystery of shadow. So that a play of swinging lines alternating with shadow passages, drawn like all the other shadows

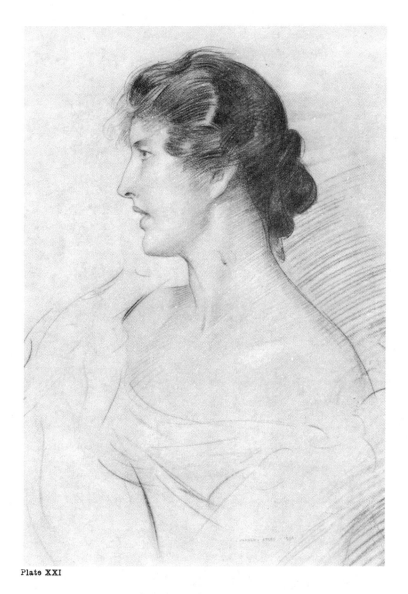

Plate XXI

STUDY IN RED CHALK

Illustrating a treatment of hair in line-work.

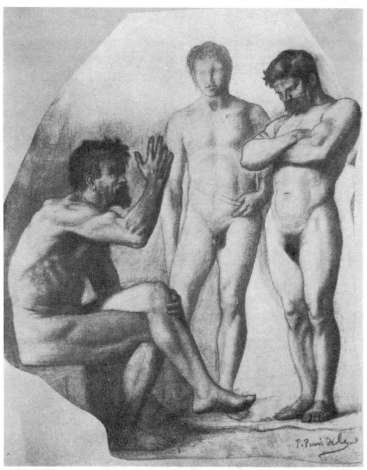

Plate XXII

STUDY FOR DECORATION AT AMIENS "REPOSE"
BY PUVIS DE CHAVANNES

Note how the contours are searched for expressive forms, the power given to the seated
figure by the right angle of the raised arm, and the contrast between the upright vigour
of the right-hand figure with the softer lines of the middle one

with parallel lines not following the form, is often effective, and suggests the quality of hair in nature. The swinging lines should vary in thickness along their course, getting darker as they pass certain parts, and gradating into lighter lines at other parts according to the effect desired. (See illustration, page 102.)

To sum up, in the method of line drawing we are trying to explain (the method employed for most of the drawings by the author in this book) the lines of shading are made parallel in a direction that comes easy to the hand, unless some quality in the form suggests their following other directions. So that when you are in doubt as to what direction they should follow, draw them on the parallel principle. This preserves a unity in your work, and allows the lines drawn in other directions for special reasons to tell expressively.

As has already been explained, it is not sufficient in drawing to concentrate the attention on copying accurately the visual appearance of anything, important as the faculty of accurate observation is. Form to be expressed must first be appreciated. And here the science of teaching fails. "You can take a horse to the fountain, but you cannot make him drink," and in art you can take the student to the point of view from which things are to be appreciated, but you cannot make him see. How, then, is this appreciation of form to be developed? Simply by feeding. Familiarise yourself with all the best examples of drawing you can find, trying to see in nature the same qualities. Study the splendid drawing by Puvis de Chavannes reproduced on page 103. Note the way the contours have been searched for expressive qualities. Look how the expressive line of the back of the seated figure has been "felt," the powerful expression of the upraised arm with its right angle (see later page 155, chapter on line rhythm). And then observe the different types of the two standing figures; the practical vigour of the one and the soft grace of the other, and how their contours have been studied to express this feeling, &c. There is a mine of knowledge to be unearthed in this drawing.

There never was an age when such an amount of artistic food was at the disposal of students. Cheap means of reproduction have brought the treasures of the world's galleries and collections to our very doors in convenient forms for a few pence. The danger is not from starvation, but indigestion. Students are so surfeited with good things that they often fail to digest any of them; but rush on from one example to another, taking but snapshot views of what is offered, until their natural powers of appreciation are in a perfect whirlwind of confused ideas. What then is to be done? You cannot avoid the good things that are hurled at you in these days, but when you come across anything that strikes you as being a particularly fine thing, feed deeply on it. Hang it up where you will see it constantly; in your bedroom, for instance, where it will entertain your sleepless hours, if you are unfortunate enough to have any. You will probably like very indifferent drawings at first, the pretty, the picturesque and the tricky will possibly attract before the sublimity of finer things. But be quite honest and feed on the best that you genuinely like, and when you have thoroughly digested and comprehended that, you will weary of it and long for something better, and so, gradually, be led on to appreciate the best you are capable of appreciating.

Before closing this chapter there are one or two points connected with the drawing of a head that might be mentioned, as students are not always sufficiently on the look out for them.

In our diagram on page 107, let Fig. 1 represent a normal eye. At Fig. 2 we have removed the skin and muscles and exposed the two main structural features in the form of the eye, namely the bony ring of the socket and the globe containing the lenses and retina. Examining this opening, we find from A to B that it runs smoothly into the bony prominence at the top of the nose, and that the rest of the edge is sharp, and from point C to E quite free. It is at point A, starting from a little hole, that the sharp edge begins; and near this point the corner of the eye is situated: A, Figs. 1, 2, 3. From points A to F the bony edge of the opening is very near the surface and should be looked for.

The next thing to note is the fact that the eyebrow at first follows the upper edge of the bony opening from B to C, but that from point C it crosses the free arch between C and D and soon ends. So that considering the under side of the eyebrow, whereas from point C towards B there is usually a cavernous hollow, from C towards D there is a prominence. The character of eyes varies greatly, and this effect is often modified by the fleshy fulness that fills in the space between the eyelid and the brow, but some indication of a change is almost always to be observed at a point somewhere about C, and should be looked out for. Any bony prominence from this point towards D should be carefully constructed. Look out for the bone, therefore, between the points C D and A F.

Never forget when painting an eye that what we call the white of the eye is part of a sphere and will therefore have the light and shade of a sphere. It will seldom be the same tone all over; if the light is coming from the right, it will be in shade towards the left and vice versa. Also the eyelids are bands of flesh placed on this spherical surface. They will therefore partake of the modelling of the sphere and not be the same tone all across. Note particularly the sudden change of plane usually marked by a fold, where the under eyelid meets the surface coming from the cheek bone. The neglect to construct these planes of the under eyelid is a very common fault in poorly painted eyes. Note also where the upper eyelid comes against the flesh under the eyebrow (usually a strongly marked fold) and the differences of planes that occur at this juncture. In some eyes, when there is little loose flesh above the eyelid, there is a deep hollow here, the eyelid running up under the bony prominence, C D. This is an important structural line, marking as it does the limit of the spherical surface of the eyeball, on which surface the eyelids are placed.

Fig. 4 is a rough diagram of the direction it is usual for the hairs forming the eyebrow to take. From A a few scant hairs start radiating above the nose and quite suddenly reach their thickest and strongest growth between B and E. They continue, still following a slightly radiating course until D. These hairs are now met by another lot, starting from above downwards, and growing from B to C. An eyebrow is considered by the draughts-

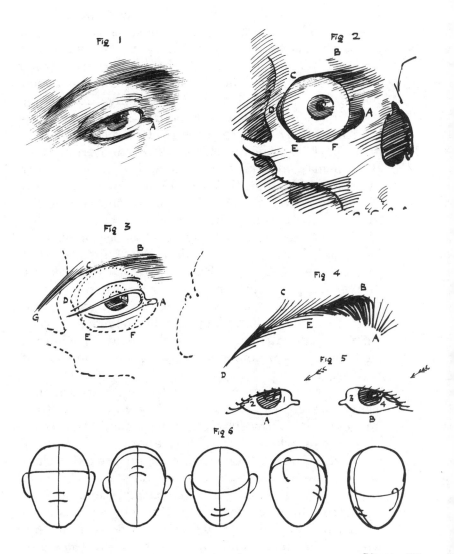

Diagram **VI**

ILLUSTRATING SOME POINTS CONNECTED WITH THE EYES
NOT ALWAYS OBSERVED IN DRAWING A HEAD

man as a tone of a certain shape and qualities of edge. And what interests us here is to note the effect of this order of growth upon its appearance as tone. The meeting of the strong growth of hair upwards with the downward growth between points B and E creates what is usually the darkest part of the eyebrow at this point. And the coming together of the hairs towards D often makes another dark part in this direction. The edge from C to B is nearly always a soft one, the tone melting into the flesh, and this should be looked out for, giving as it does a pretty variety to the run of the line. Another thing that tends to make this edge soft is the fact that a bony prominence is situated here and has usually a high light upon it that crosses the eyebrow. From C to D you usually find a sharper edge, the hairs running parallel to the line of the eyebrow, while from D to E and A to B a softer boundary can be looked for. The chief accent will generally be found at B, where a dark mass often comes sharply against the tone of the forehead.

The eyelashes do not count for much in drawing a head, except in so far as they affect the tone impression. In the first place they shade the white of the eye when the light is above, as is usually the case. They are much thicker on the outer than on the inner side of the eyelids, and have a tendency to grow in an outward direction, so that when the light comes from the left, as is shown by arrow, Fig. 5, the white of the eye at A 1 will not be much shaded, and the light tone will run nearly up to the top. But at B 4, which should be the light side of this eye, the thick crop of eyelashes will shade it somewhat and the light will not run far up in consequence, while B 3, A 2 will be in the shade from the turning away from the direction of the light of the spherical surface of the whites of the eyes.

These may seem small points to mention, but the observance of such small points makes a great difference to the construction of a head.

Fig. 6 gives a series of blocks all exactly alike in outline, with lines showing how the different actions of the head affect the guide lines on which the features hang; and how these actions can be suggested even when the contours are not varied. These archings over should be carefully looked out for when the head is in any but a simple full face position.

IX

MASS DRAWING: PRACTICAL

THIS is the form of drawing with which painting in the oil medium is properly concerned. The distinction between drawing and painting that is sometimes made is a wrong one in so far as it conveys any idea of painting being distinct from drawing. Painting is drawing (*i.e.* the expression of form) with the added complication of colour and tone. And with a brush full of paint as your tool, some form of mass drawing must be adopted. So that at the same time that the student is progressing with line drawing, he should begin to accustom himself to this other method of seeing, by attempting very simple exercises in drawing with the brush.

Most objects can be reduced broadly into three tone masses, the lights (including the high lights), the half tones, and the shadows. And the habit of reducing things into a simple equation of three tones as a foundation on which to build complex appearances should early be sought for.

Here is a simple exercise in mass drawing with the brush that is, as far as I know, never offered to the young student. Select a simple object: some of those casts of fruit hanging up that are common in art schools will do. Place it in a strong light and shade, preferably by artificial light, as it is not so subtle, and therefore easier; the

Exercise in Mass Drawing.

110

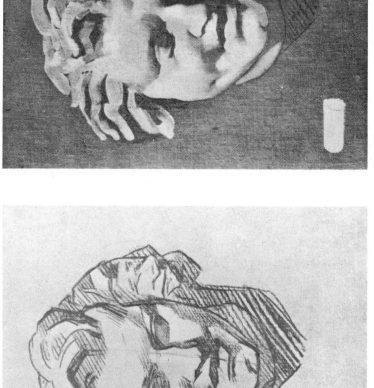

Plate XXIII

SET OF FOUR PHOTOGRAPHS OF THE SAME PAINTING FROM A CAST IN DIFFERENT STAGES

No. 1. Blocking out the shape of spaces to be occupied by masses.

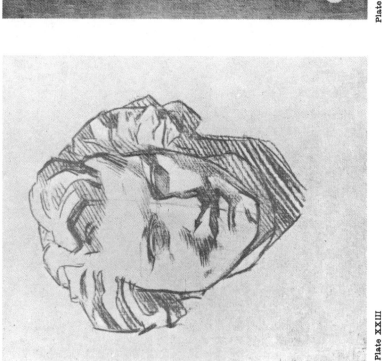

Plate XXIIIa

No. 2. A middle tone having been scrumbled over the whole, the lights are now painted; their shapes and the play of lost-foundedness on their edges being observed. Gradations are got by thinner paint, which is mixed with the wet middle tone of the ground, and is darkened.

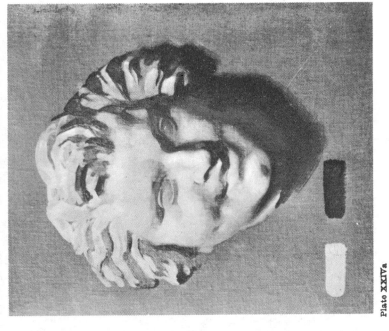

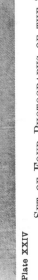

light coming from either the right or left hand, but not from in front. Try and arrange it so that the tone of the ground of your cast comes about equal to the half tones in the relief.

First draw in the outlines of the **masses** strongly in charcoal, noting the shapes of the shadows carefully, taking great care that you get their shapes blocked out in square lines in true proportion relative to each other, and troubling about little else. Let this be a setting out of the ground upon which you will afterwards express the form, rather than a drawing—the same scaffolding, in fact, that you were advised to do in the case of a line drawing, only, in that case, the drawing proper was to be done with a point, and in this case the drawing proper is to be done with a brush full of paint. Fix the charcoal **well** with a spray diffuser and the usual solution of white shellac in spirits of wine.

Taking raw umber and white (oil paint), mix up a tone that you think equal to the half tones of the cast before you. Extreme care should be taken in matching this tone. Now scumble this with a big brush equally over the whole canvas (or whatever you are making your study on). Don't use much medium, but if it is too stiff to go on thinly enough, put a little oil with it, but no turpentine. By scumbling is meant rubbing the colour into the canvas, working the brush from side to side rapidly, and laying just the **thinnest solid tone** that will cover the surface. If this is properly done, and your drawing was well fixed, you will just be able to see it through the paint. Now mix up a tone equal to the highest lights on the cast, and map out simply the shapes of the light masses on your study, leaving the

111

scumbled tone for the half tones. Note carefully where the light masses come sharply against the half tones and where they merge softly into them.

You will find that the scumbled tone of your ground will mix with the tone of the lights with which you are painting, and darken it somewhat. This will enable you to get the amount of variety you want in the tone of the lights. The thicker you paint the lighter will be the tone, while the thinner paint will be more affected by the original half tone, and will consequently be darker. When this is done, mix up a tone equal to the darkest shadow, and proceed to map out the shadows in the same way as you did the lights; noting carefully where they come sharply against the half tone and where they are lost. In the case of the shadows the thicker you paint the darker will be the tone; and the thinner, the lighter.

When the lights and shadows have been mapped out, if this has been done with any accuracy, your work should be well advanced. And it now remains to correct and refine it here and there, as you feel it wants it. Place your work alongside the cast, and walk back to correct it. Faults that are not apparent when close, are easily seen at a little distance.

I don't suggest that this is the right or only way of painting, but I do suggest that exercises of this description will teach the student many of the rudimentary essentials of painting, such elementary things as how to lay a tone, how to manage a brush, how to resolve appearances into a simple structure of tones, and how to manipulate your paint so as to express the desired shape. This elementary paint drawing is, as far as I know, never given as an exercise, the study of drawing at present being confined to paper and charcoal or chalk mediums. Drawing in charcoal is the nearest thing to this "paint drawing," it being a sort of mixed method, half line and half mass drawing. But although allied to painting, it is a very different thing from expressing form with paint, and no substitute for some elementary exercise with the brush. The use of charcoal to the neglect of line drawing often gets the student into a sloppy manner of work, and is not so good a training to the eye and hand in clear, definite statement. Its popularity is no doubt due to the fact that you can get much effect with little knowledge. Although this painting into a middle tone is not by any means the only method of painting, I do feel that it is the best method for studying form expression with the brush.

But, when you come to colour, the fact of the opaque middle tone (or half tone) being first painted over the whole will spoil the clearness and transparency of your shadows, and may also interfere with the brilliancy of the colour in the lights. When colour comes to be considered it may be necessary to adopt many expedients that it is as well not to trouble too much about until a further stage is reached. But there is no necessity for the half tone to be painted over the shadows. In working in colour the half tone or middle tone of the lights can be made, and a middle tone of the shadows, and these two first painted separately, the edges where they come together being carefully studied and finished. Afterwards the variety of tone in the lights and the shadows can be added. By this means the difference in the quality of the colour between lights and shadows is preserved. This is an important consideration, as there is generally a strong contrast between them, the shadows usually being warm if the lights are cool and vice versa; and such contrasts greatly affect the vitality of colouring.

Try always to do as much as possible with one stroke of the brush; paint has a vitality when the touches are deft, that much handling and continual touching kills. Look carefully at the shape and variety of the tone you wish to express, and try and manipulate the swing of your brush in such a way as to get in one touch as near the quality of shape and gradation you want. Remember that the lightest part of your touch will be where the brush first touches the canvas when you are painting lights into a middle tone; and that as the amount of paint in the brush gets less, so the tone will be more affected by what you are painting into, and get darker. And in painting the shadows, the darkest part of your stroke will be where the brush first touches the canvas; and it will gradually lighten as the paint in your brush gets less and therefore more affected by the tone you are painting into. If your brush is very full it will not be influenced nearly so much. And if one wants a touch that shall be distinct, as would be the case in painting the shiny light on a glazed pot, a very full brush would be used. But generally speaking, get your effects with as little paint as possible. Thinner paint is easier to refine and manipulate. There will be no fear of its not being solid if you are painting into a solidly scumbled middle tone.

Many charming things are to be done with a mixture of solid and transparent paint, but it is well at first not to complicate the problem too much, and therefore to leave this until later on, when you are competent to attack problems of colour. Keep your early work both in monochrome and colour quite solid, but as thin as you can, reserving thicker paint for those occasions when you wish to put a touch that shall not be influenced by what you are painting into.

It will perhaps be as well to illustrate a few of the different brush strokes, and say something about the different qualities of each. These are only given as typical examples of the innumerable ways a brush may be used as an aid to very elementary students; every artist will, of course, develop ways of his own.

The touch will of necessity depend in the first instance upon the shape of the brush, and these shapes are innumerable. But there are two classes into which they can roughly be divided, flat and round. The round brushes usually sold, which we will call Class A, have rather a sharp point, and this, although helpful in certain circumstances, is against their general usefulness. But a round brush with a round point is also made, and this is much more convenient for mass drawing. Where there is a sharp point the central hairs are much longer, and consequently when the brush is drawn along and pressed so that all the hairs are touching the canvas, the pressure in the centre, where the long hairs are situated, is different from that at the sides. This has the effect of giving a touch that is not equal in quality all across, and the variety thus given is difficult to manipulate. I should therefore advise the student to try the blunt-ended round brushes first, as they give a much more even touch, and one much more suited to painting in planes of tone.

The most extreme flat brushes (Class B) are thin and rather short, with sharp square ends, and have been very popular with students. They can be relied upon to give a perfectly flat, even tone, but with a rather hard sharp edge at the sides, and also at the commencement of the touch. In fact, they make touches like little square bricks. But as the variety that can be got out of them is limited, and the amount of paint they can carry so small that only short strokes can be made, they are not the best brush for general use. They are at times, when great refinement and delicacy are wanted, very useful, but are, on the whole, poor tools for the draughtsman in paint. Some variety can be got by using one or other of their sharp corners, by which means the smallest possible touch can be made to begin with, which can be increased in size as more pressure is brought to bear, until the whole surface of the brush is brought into play. They are also often used to paint across the form, a manner illustrated in the second touch, columns 1 and 2 of the illustration on page 117.

A more useful brush (Class C) partakes of the qualities of both flat and round. It is made with much more hair than the last, is longer, and has a square top with rounded corners. This brush carries plenty of paint, will lay an even tone, and, from the fact that the corners are rounded and the pressure consequently lessened at the sides, does not leave so hard an edge on either side of your stroke.

Another brush that has recently come into fashion is called a filbert shape (Class D) by the makers. It is a fine brush to draw with, as being

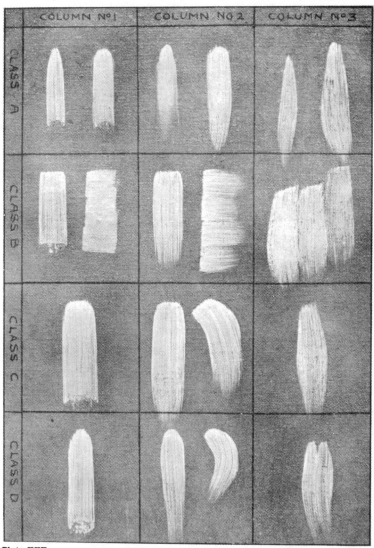

Plate XXV

ILLUSTRATING SOME TYPICAL BRUSH STROKES MADE WITH
FOUR CLASSES OF BRUSH

Class A, round; Class B, flat; Class C, full flat brush with rounded corners;
Class D, filbert shape.

flat it paints in planes, and having a rounded top is capable of getting in and out of a variety of contours. They vary in shape, some being more pointed than others. The blunt-ended form is the best for general use. Either this class of brush or Class C are perhaps the best for the exercises in mass drawing we have been describing. But Class A should also be tried, and even Class B, to find out which suits the particular individuality of the student.

On opposite page a variety of touches have been made in turn by these different shaped brushes.

In all the strokes illustrated it is assumed that the brush is moderately full of paint of a consistency a little thinner than that usually put up by colour-men. To thin it, mix a little turpentine and linseed oil in equal parts with it; and get it into easy working consistency before beginning your work, so as not to need any medium.

In the first column (No. 1), a touch firmly painted with an equal pressure all along its course is given. This gives you a plane of tone with firm edges the width of your brush, getting gradually darker or lighter as your brush empties, according to the length of the stroke and to whether you are painting into a lighter or darker ground.

In column No. 2 a drag touch is illustrated. This is a very useful one. The brush is placed firmly on the canvas and then dragged from the point lightly away, leaving a gradated tone. A great deal of the modelling in round objects is to be expressed by this variety of handling. The danger is that its use is apt to lead to a too dexterous manner of painting; a dexterity more concerned with the clever manner in which a thing is painted than with the truth expressed.

117

MASS DRAWING: PRACTICAL

Column No. 3. This is a stroke lightly and quickly painted, where the brush just grazes the surface of the canvas. The paint is put on in a manner that is very brilliant, and at the same time of a soft quality. If the brush is only moderately full, such touches will not have any hard edges, but be of a light, feathery nature. It is a most useful manner of putting on paint when freshness of colour is wanted, as it prevents one tone being churned up with another and losing its purity. And in the painting of hair, where the tones need to be kept very separate, and at the same time not hard, it is very useful. But in monochrome painting from the cast it is of very little service.

Another method of using a brush is hatching, the drawing of rows of parallel lines in either equal or varying thicknesses. This method will lighten or darken a tone in varying degree, according to whether the lines are thick, thin, or gradated—somewhat in the same way that lines of shading are drawn in line work. In cases where the correction of intricate modelling is desired and where it would be very difficult to alter a part accurately by a deft stroke of the brush, this method is useful to employ. A dry brush can be drawn across the lines to unite them with the rest of the work afterwards. This method of painting has lately been much used by those artists who have attempted painting in separate, pure colours, after the so-called manner of Claude Monet, although so mechanical a method is seldom used by that master.

As your power of drawing increases (from the line drawing you have been doing), casts of hands and heads should be attempted in the same manner as has been described. Illustrations are given of

118

MASS DRAWING: PRACTICAL

exercises of this description on pages 110 and 122. Unfortunately the photographs, which were taken from the same study at different stages during the painting, are not all alike, the first painting of the lights being too darkly printed in some cases. But they show how much can be expressed with the one tone, when variety is got by using the middle tone to paint into. The two tones used are noted in the right-hand lower corner.

Try to train yourself to do these studies at one sitting. But if you find you cannot manage this, use slower drying colours, say bone brown and zinc white, which will keep wet until the next day.

When you begin studying from the life, proceed in the same way with monochrome studies painted into a middle tone.

And what are you to do if you find, when you have finished, that it is all wrong? I should advise you to let it dry, and then scumble a middle tone right over the whole thing, as you did at first, which will show the old work through, and you can then correct your drawing and proceed to paint the lights and shadows as before. And if only a part of it is wrong, when it is quite dry rub a little poppy oil thinned with turpentine over the work, as little as will serve to cover the surface. If it is found difficult to get it to cover, breathe on the canvas, the slightest moisture will help it to bite. When this is done, wipe it off with the palm of your hand or an old piece of clean linen. Now paint a middle tone right over the part you wish to retouch, being careful about joining it up to the surrounding work, and proceed as before, drawing in the light and shadow masses.

This form of drawing you will probably find more difficult at first. For the reason already explained

119

it seems natural to observe objects as made up of outlines, not masses. The frame with cottons across it should be used to flatten the appearance, as in making outline drawings. And besides this a black glass should be used. This can easily be made by getting a small piece of glass—a photographic negative will do—and sticking some black paper on the back; turning it over the front to keep the raw edges of the glass from cutting the fingers. Or the glass can be painted on the back with black paint. Standing with your back to the object and your painting, hold this glass close in front of one of your eyes (the other being closed), so that you can see both your painting and the object. Seeing the tones thus reduced and simplified, you will be enabled more easily to correct your work.

I should like to emphasise the importance of the setting-out work necessary for brush-drawing. While it is not necessary to put expressive work into this preparatory work, the utmost care should be taken to ensure its accuracy as far as it goes. It is a great nuisance if, after you have put up some of your fair structure, you find the foundations are in the wrong place and the whole thing has to be torn down and shifted. It is of the utmost necessity to have the proportions and the main masses settled at this early stage, and every device of blocking out with square lines and measuring with your knitting-needle, &c., should be adopted to ensure the accuracy of these large proportions. The variations and emphases that feeling may dictate can be done in the painting stage. This initial stage is not really a drawing at all, but a species of mapping out, and as such it should be regarded. The only excuse for making the elaborate preparatory drawings on canvas students sometimes do, is that it enables them to learn the subject, so that when they come to paint it, they already know something about it. But the danger of making these preparatory drawings interesting is that the student fears to cover them up and lose an outline so carefully and lovingly wrought; and this always results in a poor painting. When you take up a brush to express yourself, it must be with no fear of hurting a careful drawing. Your drawing is going to be done with the brush, and only the general setting out of the masses will be of any use to you in the work of this initial stage. Never paint with the poor spirit of the student who fears to lose his drawing, or you will never do any fine things in painting. Drawing (expressing form) is the thing you should be doing all the time. And in art, "he that would save his work must often lose it," if you will excuse the paraphrase of a profound saying which, like most profound sayings, is applicable to many things in life besides what it originally referred to. It is often necessary when a painting is nearly right to destroy the whole thing in order to accomplish the apparently little that still divides it from what you conceive it should be. It is like a man rushing a hill that is just beyond the power of his motor-car to climb, he must take a long run at it. And if the first attempt lands him nearly up at the top but not quite, he has to go back and take the long run all over again, to give him the impetus that shall carry him right through.

Another method of judging tone drawing is our old method of half closing the eyes. This, by lowering the tone and widening the focus, enables you to correct the work more easily.

In tone drawing there is not only the shape of

the masses to be considered, but their **values**—that is, their position in an imagined scale from dark to light. The relation of the different tones in this way—the values, as it is called—is an extremely important matter in painting. But it more properly belongs to the other department of the subject, namely Colour, and this needs a volume to itself. But something more will be said on this subject when treating of Rhythm.

We saw, in speaking of line drawing, how the character of a line was found by observing its flatnesses and its relation to straight lines. In the same way **the character of modelling is found by observing its planes.** So that in building up a complicated piece of form, like a head or figure, the planes (or flat tones) should be sought for everywhere. As a carver in stone blocks out his work in square surfaces, the modelling of a figure or any complex surface that is being studied should be set out in planes of tone, painting in the first instance the larger ones, and then, to these, adding the smaller; when it will be seen that the roundnesses have, with a little fusing of edges here and there, been arrived at. Good modelling is full of these planes subtly fused together. Nothing is so characteristic of bad modelling as "gross roundnesses." The surface of a sphere is the surface with the least character, like the curve of a circle, and the one most to be avoided in good modelling.

In the search for form the knowledge of anatomy, and particularly the bony structures, is of the utmost importance. During the rage for realism and naturalism many hard things were said about the study of anatomy. And certainly, were it to be used to overstep the modesty of nature in these

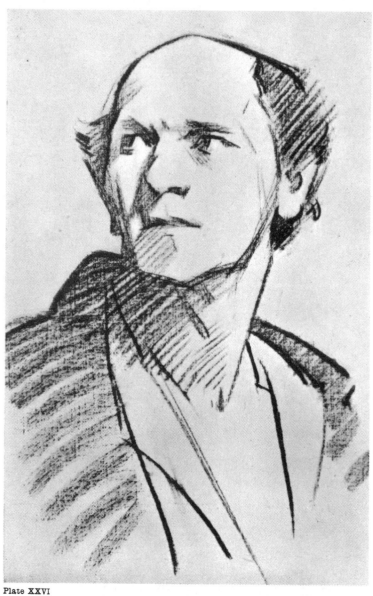

Plate XXVI

SET OF FOUR PHOTOGRAPHS OF THE SAME STUDY FROM THE LIFE
IN DIFFERENT STAGES

No. 1. Blocking out the spaces occupied by different masses in charcoal.

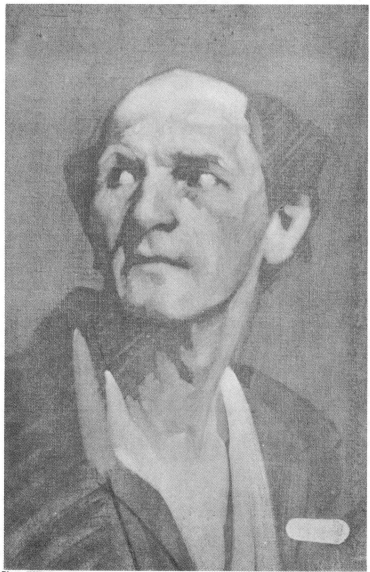

Plate **XXVII**

SET OF FOUR PHOTOGRAPHS OF THE SAME STUDY FROM THE LIFE
IN DIFFERENT STAGES

No. 2. A middle tone having been scrumbled over the whole, the lights are painted into it; variety being got by varying the thickness of the paint. The darks are due to the charcoal lines of initial drawing showing through middle tone.

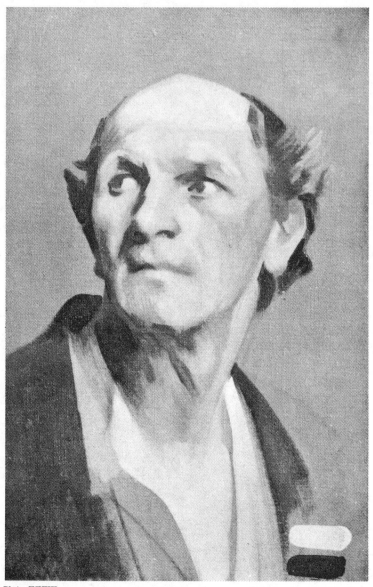

Plate XXVIII

SET OF FOUR PHOTOGRAPHS OF THE SAME STUDY FROM THE LIFE
IN DIFFERENT STAGES

No. 3.   The same as the last, but with the shadows added; variety being got
by varying thickness of paint as before.

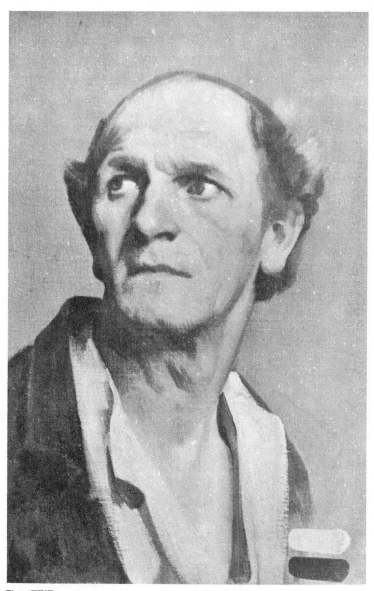

Plate XXIX

SET OF FOUR PHOTOGRAPHS OF THE SAME STUDY FROM THE LIFE
IN DIFFERENT STAGES

No. 4. The completed head.

respects and to be paraded to the exclusion of the charm and character of life, it would be as well left alone. But if we are to make a drawing that shall express something concrete, we must know something of its structure, whatever it is. In the case of the human figure it is impossible properly to understand its action and draw it in a way that shall give a powerful impression without a knowledge of the mechanics of its construction. But I hardly think the case for anatomy needs much stating at the present time. Never let anatomical knowledge tempt you into exaggerated statements of internal structure, unless such exaggeration helps the particular thing you wish to express. In drawing a figure in violent action it might, for instance, be essential to the drawing, whereas in drawing a figure at rest or a portrait, it would certainly be out of place.

In the chapter on line work it was stated that: "Lines of shading drawn across the forms suggest softness, lines drawn in curves fulness of form, lines drawn down the forms hardness, and lines crossing in every direction atmosphere," and these rules apply equally well to the direction of the brush strokes (the brush work) in a painting.

The brush swinging round the forms suggests fore-shortening, and fulness of form generally, and across the forms softness, while the brush following down the forms suggests toughness and hardness, and crossing in every direction atmosphere. A great deal of added force can be given to form expression in this way. In the foreshortened figure on the ground at the left of Tintoretto's "Finding of the Body of St. Mark," the foreshortened effect helped by the brush work swinging round can be seen (see illustration, page 236). The work of Henner in France is an extreme instance of the quality of softness and fleshiness got by painting across the form. The look of toughness and hardness given by the brush work following down the forms is well illustrated in much of the work of James Ward, the animal painter. In his picture in the National Gallery, "Harlech Castle," No. 1158, this can be seen in the painting of the tree-trunks, &c.

The crossing of the brush work in every direction, giving a look of atmosphere, is naturally often used in painting backgrounds and also such things as the plane surfaces of sky and mist, &c.

It is often inconvenient to paint across the form when softness is wanted. It is only possible to have one colour in your brush sweep, and the colour changes across, much more than down the form as a rule. For the shadows, half tones and lights, besides varying in tone, vary also in colour; so that it is not always possible to sweep across them with one colour. It is usually more convenient to paint down where the colours can be laid in overlapping bands of shadow, half tone and light, &c. Nevertheless, if this particular look of softness and fleshiness is desired, either the painting must be so thin or the tones so fused together that no brush strokes show, or a dry flat brush must afterwards be drawn lightly across when the painting is done, to destroy the downward brush strokes and substitute others going across, great care being taken to drag only from light to dark, and to wipe the brush carefully after each touch; and also never to go over the same place twice, or the paint will lose vitality. This is a method much employed by artists who delight in this particular quality.

MASS DRAWING: PRACTICAL

But when a strong, tough look is desired, such as one sees when a muscle is in violent action, or in the tendon above the wrist or above the heel in the leg, or generally where a bone comes to the surface, in all these cases the brush work should follow down the forms. It is not necessary and is often inadvisable for the brush work to show at all, in which case these principles will be of little account. But when in vigorously painted work they do, I think it will generally be found to create the effects named.

Drawing on toned paper with white chalk or Chinese white and black or red chalk is another form of mass drawing. And for studies it is intended to paint from, this is a quick and excellent manner. The rapidity with which the facts of an appearance can be noted makes it above all others the method for drapery studies. The lights are drawn with white, the toned paper being allowed to show through where a darker tone is needed, the white (either chalk or Chinese white) being put on thickly when a bright light is wanted and thinly where a quieter light is needed. So with the shadows, the chalk is put on heavily in the darks and less heavily in the lighter shadows. Since the days of the early Italians this has been a favourite method of drawing drapery studies (see illustrations, page 260).

Some artists have shaded their lights with gold and silver paint. The late Sir Edward Burne-Jones was very fond of this, and drawings with much decorative charm have been done this way. The principle is the same as in drawing with white chalk, the half tone being given by the paper.

Keep the lights separate from the shadows, let

the half tone paper always come as a buffer state between them. Get as much information into the drawing of your lights and shadows as possible; don't be satisfied with a smudge effect. Use the side of your white chalk when you want a mass, or work in parallel lines (hatching) on the principle described in the chapter on line drawing.

X

RHYTHM

THE subject of Rhythm in what are called the Fine Arts is so vague, and has received so little attention, that some courage, or perhaps foolhardiness, is needed to attack it. And in offering the following fragmentary ideas that have been stumbled on in my own limited practice, I want them to be accepted only for what they are worth, as I do not know of any proper authority for them. But they may serve as a stimulus, and offer some lines on which the student can pursue the subject for himself.

The word rhythm is here used to signify the power possessed by lines, tones, and colours, by their ordering and arrangement, to affect us, somewhat as different notes and combinations of sound do in music. And just as in music, where sounds affect us without having any direct relation with nature, but appeal directly to our own inner life; so in painting, sculpture, and architecture there is a music that appeals directly to us apart from any significance that may be associated with the representation of natural phenomena. There is, as it were, an abstract music of line, tone, and colour.

The danger of the naturalistic movement in painting in the nineteenth century has been that it has turned our attention away from this fundamental fact of art to the contemplation of interesting realisations of appearances—realisations often full of poetic suggestiveness due to associations connected with the objects painted as concrete things, but not always made directly significant as artistic expression; whereas it is the business of the artist to relate the form, colour, and tone of natural appearances to this abstract musical quality, with which he should never lose touch even in the most highly realised detail of his work. For only thus, when related to rhythm, do the form, tone, and colour of appearances obtain their full expressive power and become a means of vitally conveying the feeling of the artist.

Inquiry as to the origin of this power and of rhythm generally is a profoundly interesting subject; and now that recent advances in science tend to show that sound, heat, light, and possibly electricity and even nerve force are but different rhythmic forms of energy, and that matter itself may possibly be resolved eventually into different rhythmic motions, it does look as if rhythm may yet be found to contain even the secret of life itself. At any rate it is very intimately associated with life; and primitive man early began to give expression in some form of architecture, sculpture, or painting to the deeper feelings that were moving him; found some correspondence between the lines and colours of architecture, sculpture, and painting and the emotional life that was awakening within him. Thus, looking back at the remains of their work that have come down to us, we are enabled to judge of the nature of the people from the expression we find in hewn stone and on painted walls.

It is in primitive art generally that we see more clearly the direct emotional significance of line and form. Art appears to have developed from its most abstract position, to which bit by bit have been added the truths and graces of natural appearance, until as much of this naturalistic truth has been added as the abstract significance at the base of the expression could stand without loss of power. At this point, as has already been explained, a school is at the height of its development. The work after this usually shows an increased concern with naturalistic truth, which is always very popular, to the gradual exclusion of the backbone of abstract line and form significance that dominated the earlier work. And when these primitive conditions are lost touch with, a decadence sets in. At least, this is roughly the theory to which a study of the two great art developments of the past, in Greece and Italy, would seem to point.

And this theory is the excuse for all the attempts at primitivism of which we have lately seen so much. Art having lost touch with its primitive base owing to the over-doses of naturalism it has had, we must, these new apostles say, find a new primitive base on which to build the new structure of art. The theory has its attractions, but there is this difference between the primitive archaic Greek or early Italian and the modern primitive: the early men reverently clothed the abstract idea they started with in the most natural and beautiful form within their knowledge, ever seeking to discover new truths and graces from nature to enrich their work; while the modern artist, with the art treasures of all periods of the world before him, can never be in the position of these simple-minded men. It is therefore unlikely that the future development of art will be on lines similar to that of the past.

129

The same conditions of simple ignorance are never likely to occur again. Means of communication and prolific reproduction make it very unlikely that the art of the world will again be lost for a season, as was Greek art in the Middle Ages. Interesting intellectually as is the theory that the impressionist point of view (the accepting of the flat retina picture as a pattern of colour sensations) offers a new field from which to select material for a new basis of artistic expression, so far the evidence of results has not shown anything likely seriously to threaten the established principles of traditional design. And anything more different in spirit from the genuine primitive than the irreverent anarchy and flouting of all refinement in the work of some of these new primitives, it would be difficult to imagine. But much of the work of the movement has undoubted artistic vitality, and in its insistence on design and selection should do much to kill "realism" and the "copying nature" theory of a few years back.

Although it is perfectly true that the feelings and ideas that impel the artist may sooner or later find their own expression, there are a great many principles connected with the arranging of lines, tones, and colours in his picture that it is difficult to transgress without calamity. At any rate the knowledge of some of them will aid the artist in gaining experience, and possibly save him some needless fumbling.

But don't for one moment think that anything in the nature of rules is going to take the place of the initial artistic impulse which must come from within. This is not a matter for teaching, art training being only concerned with perfecting the means of its expression.

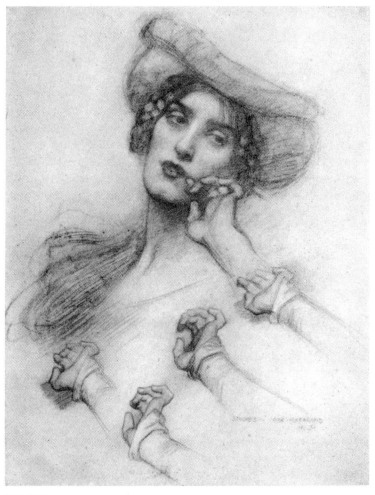

Plate **XXX**

A STUDY FOR A PICTURE OF " ROSALIND AND ORLANDO "

Ros. " He calls us back ; my pride fell with my fortunes."

RHYTHM

It is proposed to treat the subject from the material side of line and tone only, without any reference to subject matter, with the idea of trying to find out something about the expressive qualities line and tone are capable of yielding unassociated with visual things. What use can be made of any such knowledge to give expression to the emotional life of the artist is not our concern, and is obviously a matter for the individual to decide for himself.

There is at the basis of every picture a structure of lines and masses. They may not be very obvious, and may be hidden under the most broken of techniques, but they will always be found underlying the planning of any painting. Some may say that the lines are only the boundaries of the masses, and others that the masses are only the spaces between the lines. But whichever way you care to look at it, there are particular emotional qualities analogous to music that affect us in lines and line arrangements and also in tone or mass arrangements. And any power a picture may have to move us will be largely due to the rhythmic significance of this original planning. These qualities, as has already been stated, affect us quite apart from any association they may have with natural things : arrangements of mere geometrical lines are sufficient to suggest them. But of course other associations connected with the objects represented will largely augment the impression, when the line and tone arrangements and the sentiment of the object are in sympathy. And if they are not, it may happen that associations connected with the representation will cut in and obscure or entirely destroy this line and tone music. That is to say, if the line and tone arrangement in the abstract is expressive of the sublime, and the objects whose representation they support something ridiculous, say a donkey braying, the associations aroused by so ridiculous an appearance will override those connected with the line and tone arrangement. But it is remarkable how seldom this occurs in nature, the sentiment of the line and tone arrangements things present being usually in harmony with the sentiment of the object itself. As a matter of fact, the line effect of a donkey in repose is much more sublime than when he is braying.

There are two qualities that may be allowed to divide the consideration of this subject, two points of view from which the subject can be approached: **Unity** and **Variety,** qualities somewhat opposed to each other, as are harmony and contrast in the realm of colour. Unity is concerned with the relationship of all the parts to that oneness of conception that should control every detail of a work of art. All the more profound qualities, the deeper emotional notes, are on this side of the subject. On the other hand, variety holds the secrets of charm, vitality, and the picturesque, it is the "dither," the play between the larger parts, that makes for life and character. **Without variety there can be no life.**

In any conception of a perfect unity, like the perfected life of the Buddhist, Nirvana or Nibbāna (literally "dying out" or "extinction" as of an expiring fire), there is no room for variety, for the play of life; all such fretfulness ceases, to be replaced by an all-pervading calm, beautiful, if you like, but lifeless. There is this deadness about any conception of perfection that will always make it an un-

Unity and Variety.

attainable ideal in life. Those who, like the Indian fakir or the hermits of the Middle Ages, have staked their all on this ideal of perfection, have found it necessary to suppress life in every way possible, the fakirs often remaining motionless for long periods at a time, and one of the mediæval saints going so far as to live on the top of a high column where life and movement were well-nigh impossible.

And in art it is the same; all those who have aimed at an absolute perfection have usually ended in a deadness. The Greeks knew better than many of their imitators this vital necessity in art. In their most ideal work there is always that variety that gives character and life. No formula or canon of proportions or other mechanical device for the attainment of perfection was allowed by this vital people entirely to subdue their love of life and variety. And however near they might go towards a perfect type in their ideal heads and figures, they never went so far as to kill the individual in the type. It is the lack of this subtle distinction that, I think, has been the cause of the failure of so much art founded on so-called Greek ideals. Much Roman sculpture, if you except their portrait busts, illustrates this. Compared with Greek work it lacks that subtle variety in the modelling that gives vitality. The difference can be felt instinctively in the merest fragment of a broken figure. It is not difficult to tell Greek from Roman fragments, they pulsate with a life that it is impossible to describe but that one instinctively feels. And this vitality depends, I think it will be found, on the greater amount of life-giving variety in the surfaces of the modelling. In their architectural mouldings, the difference of which we are speaking can be more easily traced.

RHYTHM

The vivacity and brilliancy of a Greek moulding makes a Roman work look heavy and dull. And it will generally be found that the Romans used the curve of the circle in the sections of their mouldings, a curve possessing the least amount of variety, as is explained later, where the Greeks used the lines of conic sections, curves possessed of the greatest amount of variety.

But while unity must never exist without this life-giving variety, variety must always be under the moral control of unity, or it will get out of hand and become extravagant. In fact, the most perfect work, like the most perfect engine of which we spoke in a former chapter, has the least amount of variety, as the engine has the least amount of "dither," that is compatible with life. One does not hear so much talk in these days about a perfect type as was the fashion at one time; and certainly the pursuit of this ideal by a process of selecting the best features from many models and constructing a composite figure out of them, was productive of very dead and lifeless work. No account was taken of the variety from a common type necessary in the most perfect work, if life and individual interest are not to be lost, and the thing is not to become a dead abstraction. But the danger is rather the other way at the moment. Artists revel in the oddest of individual forms, and the type idea is flouted on all hands. An anarchy of individualism is upon us, and the vitality of disordered variety is more fashionable than the calm beauty of an ordered unity.

Excess of variations from a common type is what I think we recognise as ugliness in the objective world, whereas beauty is on the side of unity and conformity to type. Beauty possesses both variety and unity, and is never extreme, erring rather on the side of unity.

Burke in his essay on "The Sublime and the Beautiful" would seem to use the word beautiful where we should use the word pretty, placing it at the opposite pole from the sublime, whereas I think beauty always has some elements of the sublime in it, while the merely pretty has not. Mere prettiness is a little difficult to place, it does not come between either of our extremes, possessing little character or type, variety or unity. It is perhaps charm without either of these strengthening associates, and in consequence is always feeble, and the favourite diet of weak artistic digestions.

The sculpture of ancient Egypt is an instance of great unity in conception, and the suppression of variety to a point at which life scarcely exists. The lines of the Egyptian figures are simple and long, the surfaces smooth and unvaried, no action is allowed to give variety to the pose, the placing of one foot a little in front of the other being alone permitted in the standing figures; the arms, when not hanging straight down the sides, are flexed stiffly at the elbow at right angles; the heads stare straight before them. The expression of sublimity is complete, and this was, of course, what was aimed at. But how cold and terrible is the lack of that play and variety that alone show life. What a relief it is, at the British Museum, to go into the Elgin Marble room and be warmed by the noble life pulsating in the Greek work, after visiting the cold Egyptian rooms.

In what we call a perfect face it is not so much the perfect regularity of shape and balance in the features that charms us, not the things that belong to an ideal type, but rather the subtle variations

135

from this type that are individual to the particular head we are admiring. A perfect type of head, if such could exist, might excite our wonder, but would leave us cold. But it can never exist in life; the slightest movement of the features, which must always accompany life and expression, will mar it. And the influence of these habitual movements on the form of the features themselves will invariably mould them into individual shapes away from the so-called perfect type, whatever may have been nature's intention in the first instance.

If we call these variations from a common type in the features imperfections, as it is usual to do, it would seem to be the imperfections of perfection that charm and stir us; and that perfection without these so-called imperfections is a cold, dead abstraction, devoid of life: that unity without variety is lifeless and incapable of touching us.

On the other hand, variety without unity to govern it is a riotous exuberance of life, lacking all power and restraint and wasting itself in a madness of excess.

So that in art a balance has to be struck between these two opposing qualities. In good work unity is the dominating quality, all the variety being done in conformity to some large idea of the whole, which is never lost sight of, even in the smallest detail of the work. Good style in art has been defined as "variety in unity," and Hogarth's definition of composition as the art of "varying well" is similar. And I am not sure that "contrasts in harmony" would not be a suggestive definition of good colour.

Let us consider first variety and unity as they are related to line drawing, and afterwards to mass drawing.

CHAPTER XI

RHYTHM: VARIETY OF LINE

LINE rhythm or music depends on the shape of your lines, their relation to each other and their relation to the boundaries of your panel. In all good work this music of line is in harmony with the subject (the artistic intention) of your picture or drawing.

The two lines with the least variation are a perfectly straight line and a circle. A perfectly straight line has obviously no variety at all, while a circle, by curving at exactly the same ratio all along, has no variation of curvature, it is of all curves the one with the least possible variety. These two lines are, therefore, two of the dullest, and are seldom used in pictures except to enhance the beauty and variety of others. And even then, subtle variations, some amount of play, is introduced to relieve their baldness. But used in this way, vertical and horizontal lines are of the utmost value in rectangular pictures, uniting the composition to its bounding lines by their parallel relationship with them. And further, as a contrast to the richness and beauty of curves they are of great value, and are constantly used for this purpose. The group of mouldings cutting against the head in a portrait, or the lines of a column used to accentuate the curved forms of a face or figure, are well-known instances; and the portrait painter is always on the look out for an object in his background that will give him such straight lines. You may notice, too, how the lines drawn across a study in order to copy it (squaring it out, as it is called) improve the look of a drawing, giving a greater beauty to the variety of the curves by contrast with the variety lacking straight lines.

The perfect curve of the circle should always be avoided in the drawing of natural objects (even a full moon), and in vital drawings of any sort some variety should always be looked for. Neither should the modelling of the sphere ever occur in your work, the dullest of all curved surfaces.

Although the curve of the perfect circle is dull from its lack of variety, it is not without beauty, and this is due to its perfect unity. It is of all curves the most perfect example of static unity. Without the excitement of the slightest variation it goes on and on for ever. This is, no doubt, the reason why it was early chosen as a symbol of Eternity, and certainly no more perfect symbol could be found.

The circle seen in perspective assumes the more beautiful curve of the ellipse, a curve having much variety; but as its four quarters are alike, not so much as a symmetrical figure can have.

Perhaps the most beautiful symmetrically curved figure of all is the so-called egg of the well-known moulding from such a temple as the Erechtheum, called the egg and dart moulding. Here we have a perfect balance between variety and unity. The curvature is varied to an infinite degree, at no point is its curving at the same ratio as at any other point; perhaps the maximum amount of variety that can be got in a symmetrical figure, preserving, as it does, its almost perfect continuity, for it approaches the circle in the even flow of its curvature. This is, roughly, the line of the contour

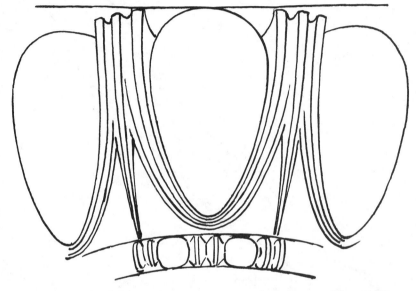

Diagram VII

EGG AND DART MOULDING FROM ONE OF THE CARYATIDES FROM THE ERECHTHEUM IN THE BRITISH MUSEUM

of a face, and you may note how much painters who have excelled in grace have insisted on it in their portraits. Gainsborough and Vandyke are striking instances.

The line of a profile is often one of great beauty, only here the variety is apt to overbalance the unity or run of the line. The most beautiful profiles are usually those in which variety is subordinated to the unity of the contour. I fancy the Greeks felt this when they did away with the hollow above the nose, making the line of the forehead run,

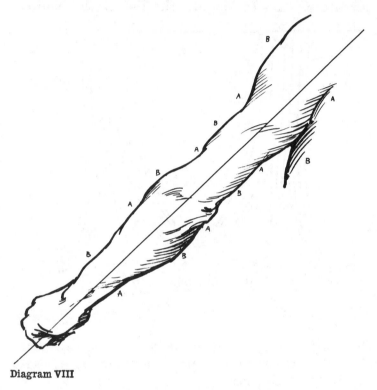

Diagram VIII

ILLUSTRATING VARIETY IN SYMMETRY

Note how the hollows marked A are opposed by fullnesses marked B.

with but little interruption, to the tip of the nose. The unity of line is increased, and the variety made more interesting. The idea that this was the common Greek type is, I should imagine, untrue, for their portrait statues do not show it.

VARIETY OF LINE

It does occur in nature at rare intervals, and in most Western nationalities, but I do not think there is much evidence of its ever having been a common type anywhere.

In drawing or painting a profile this run or unity of the line is the thing to feel, if you would express its particular beauty. This is best done in the case of a painting by finally drawing it with the brush from the background side, after having painted all the variety there is of tone and colour on the face side of the line. As the background usually varies little, the swing of the brush is not hampered on this side as it is on the other. I have seen students worried to distraction trying to paint the profile line from the face side, fearing to lose the drawing by going over the edge. With the edge blurred out from the face side, it is easy to come with a brush full of the colour the background is immediately against the face (a different colour usually from what it is further away), and draw it with some decision and conviction, care being taken to note all the variations on the edge, where the sharpnesses come and where the edge is more lost, &c.

The contours of the limbs illustrate another form of line variety—what may be called "Variety in Symmetry." While roughly speaking the limbs are symmetrical, each side not only has variety in itself, but there is usually *Variety in Symmetry.* variety of opposition. Supposing there is a convex curve on the one side, you will often have a concave form on the other. Always look out for this in drawing limbs, and it will often improve a poorly drawn part if more of this variation on symmetry is discovered.

The whole body, you may say, is symmetrical,

141

VARIETY OF LINE

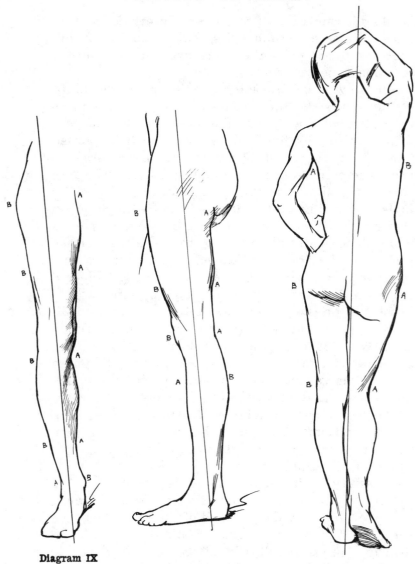

Diagram IX

ILLUSTRATING VARIETY IN SYMMETRY

Note how the hollows marked A are opposed by the fullnesses marked B.

142

but even here natural conditions make for variety. The body is seldom, except in soldiering, held in a symmetrical position. The slightest action produces the variety we are speaking about. The accompanying sketches will indicate what is meant.

Of course the student, if he has any natural ability, instinctively looks out for all these variations that give the play of life to his drawing. It is not for him in the full vigour of inspiration that books such as this are written. But there may come a time when things "won't come," and it is then that it is useful to know where to look for possible weak spots in your work.

A line of equal thickness is a very dead and inexpressive thing compared with one varied and stressed at certain points. If you observe any of the boundaries in nature we use a line to express, you will notice some points are accentuated, attract the attention, more

Variety of Thickness and Accent.

than others. The only means you have to express this in a line drawing is by darkening and sharpening the line. At other points, where the contour is almost lost, the line can be soft and blurred.

It is impossible to write of the infinite qualities of variety that a fine draughtsman will get into his line work; they must be studied at first hand. But on this play of thickness and quality of line much of the vitality of your drawing will depend.

XII

RHYTHM: UNITY OF LINE

UNITY of line is a bigger quality than variety, and
as it requires a larger mental grasp, is more rarely
met with. The bigger things in drawing and design
come under its consideration, including, as it does,
the relation of the parts to the whole. Its proper
consideration would take us into the whole field of
Composition, a subject needing far more consideration than can be given to it in this book.

In almost all compositions a rhythmic flow of
lines can be traced. Not necessarily a flow of actual
lines (although these often exist); they may be only
imaginary lines linking up or massing certain parts,
and bringing them into conformity with the rhythmic
conception of the whole. Or again, only a certain
stress and flow in the forms, suggesting line movements. But these line movements flowing through
your panel are of the utmost importance; they are
like the melodies and subjects of a musical symphony, weaving through and linking up the whole
composition.

Often, the line of a contour at one part of a
picture is picked up again by the contour of some
object at another part of the composition, and
although no actual line connects them, a unity is
thus set up between them. (See diagrams, pages
166 and 168, illustrating line compositions of pictures
144

UNITY OF LINE

by Botticelli and Paolo Veronese). This imaginary following through of contours across spaces in a composition should always be looked out for and sought after, as nothing serves to unite a picture like this relationship of remote parts. The flow of these lines will depend on the nature of the subject: they will be more gracious and easy, or more vigorous and powerful, according to the demands of your subject.

This linking up of the contours applies equally well to the drawing of a single figure or even a head or hand, and the student should always be on the look out for this uniting quality. It is a quality of great importance in giving unity to a composition.

When groups of lines in a picture occur parallel to each other they produce an accentuation of the particular quality the line may contain, a sort of sustained effect, like a sustained Parallelism. chord on an organ, the effect of which is much bigger than that of the same chord struck staccato. This sustained quality has a wonderful influence in steadying and uniting your work.

This parallelism can only be used successfully with the simplest lines, such as a straight line or a simple curve; it is never advisable except in decorative patterns to be used with complicated shapes. Blake is very fond of the sustained effect parallelism gives, and uses the repetition of curved and straight lines very often in his compositions. Note in Plate I of the Job series, page 146, the use made of this sustaining quality in the parallelism of the sheep's backs in the background and the parallel upward flow of the lines of the figures. In Plate II you see it used in the curved lines of the figures on either side of the throne above, and in the two angels with the scroll at the left-hand corner. Behind these two figures you again have its use accentuating by repetition the peaceful line of the backs of the sheep. The same thing can be seen in Plate IV, where the parallelism of the back lines of the sheep and the legs of the seated figures gives a look of peace contrasting with the violence of the messenger come to tell of the destruction of Job's sons. The emphasis that parallelism gives to the music of particular lines is well illustrated in all Blake's work. He is a mine of information on the subject of line rhythm. Compare Plate I with Plate XXI; note how the emotional quality is dependent in both cases on the parallelism of the upward flow of the lines. How also in Plate I he has carried the vertical feeling even into the sheep in the front, introducing little bands of vertical shading to carry through the vertical lines made by the kneeling figures. And in the last plate, "So the Lord blessed the latter end of Job more than the beginning," note how the greater completeness with which the parallelism has been carried out has given a much greater emphasis to the effect, expressing a greater exaltation and peace than in Plate I. Notice in Plate X, where "The just, upright man is laughed to scorn," how this power of emphasis is used to increase the look of scorn hurled at Job by the pointing fingers of his three friends.

Of the use of this principle in curved forms, the repetition of the line of the back in stooping figures is a favourite device with Blake. There will be found instances of this in Plates II and XVIII. (Further instances will be found on reference

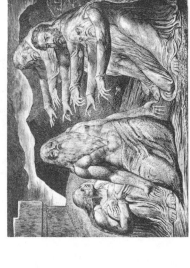

(Plate IV, Blake's Job)

And I only am escaped alone to tell thee.

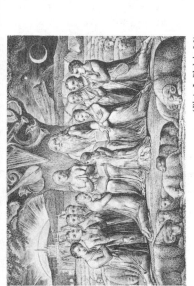

(Plate X, Blake's Job)

The just upright man is laughed to scorn.

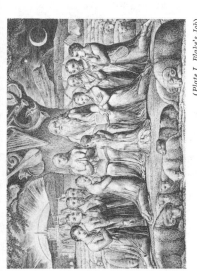

(Plate I, Blake's Job)

Thus did Job continually.

(Plate XXI, Blake's Job)

So the Lord blessed the latter end of Job more than
the beginning.

Plate XXXI

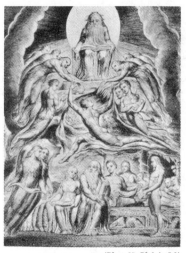

(Plate II, Blake's Job)

When the Almighty was yet with me, when my children were about me.

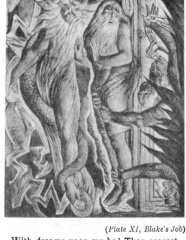

(Plate XI, Blake's Job)

With dreams upon my bed Thou scarest me, and affrightest me with visions.

Printed sideways up in order to show that the look of horror is not solely dependent on the things represented, but belongs to the rhythm, the pattern of the composition.

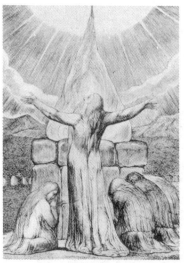

(Plate XVIII, Blake's Job)

And my servant Job shall pray for you.

Plate XXXII

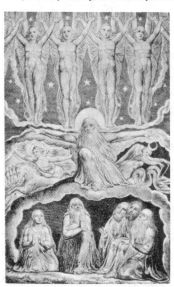

(Plate XIV, Blake's Job)

When the morning stars sang together, and all the sons of God shouted for joy.

to Plates VII, VIII, XIII, and XVIII, in Blake's Job.)
In the last instance it is interesting to note how he
has balanced the composition, which has three figures
kneeling on the right and only one on the left. By
losing the outline of the third figure on the right and
getting a double line out of the single figure on the
left by means of the outline of the mass of hair, and
also by shading this single figure more strongly, he
has contrived to keep a perfect balance. The head
of Job is also turned to the left, while he stands
slightly on that side, still further balancing the three
figures on the right. (This does not show so well in
the illustration here reproduced as in the original
print.)

Some rude things were said above about the
straight line and the circle, on account of their
lack of variety, and it is true that a mathematically
straight line, or a mathematically perfect circle,
are never found in good artistic drawing. For
without variety is no charm or life. But these
lines possess other qualities, due to their maximum
amount of unity, that give them great power in a
composition; and where the expression of sublimity
or any of the deeper and more profound sentiments
are in evidence, they are often to be found.

The rows of columns in a Greek temple, the
clusters of vertical lines in a Gothic cathedral interior, are instances of the sublimity and power
they possess. The necessary play that makes for
vitality—the "dither" as we called this quality in
a former chapter—is given in the case of the Greek
temple by the subtle curving of the lines of columns
and steps, and by the rich variety of the sculpture,
and in the case of the Gothic cathedral by a rougher
cutting of the stone blocks and the variety in the

147

colour of the stone. But generally speaking, in Gothic architecture this particular quality of "dither" or the play of life in all the parts is conspicuous, the balance being on the side of variety rather than unity. The individual workman was given a large amount of freedom and allowed to exercise his personal fancy. The capitals of columns, the cusping of windows, and the ornaments were seldom repeated, but varied according to the taste of the craftsman. Very high finish was seldom attempted, the marks of the chisel often being left showing in the stonework. All this gave a warmth and exuberance of life to a fine Gothic building that makes a classical building look cold by comparison. The freedom with which new parts were built on to a Gothic building is another proof of the fact that it is not in the conception of the unity of the whole that their chief charm consists.

On the other hand, a fine classic building is the result of one large conception to which every part has rigorously to conform. Any addition to this in after years is usually disastrous. A high finish is always attempted, no tool marks nor any individuality of the craftsman is allowed to mar the perfect symmetry of the whole. It may be colder, but how perfect in sublimity! The balance here is on the side of unity rather than variety.

The strength and sublimity of Norman architecture is due to the use of circular curves in the arches, combined with straight lines and the use of square forms in the ornaments—lines possessed of least variety.

All objects with which one associates the look of strength will be found to have straight lines in their composition. The look of strength in a strong man is due to the square lines of the contours, so different from the rounded forms of a fat man. And everyone knows the look of mental power a square forehead gives to a head and the look of physical power expressed by a square jaw. The look of power in a rocky landscape or range of hills is due to the same cause.

The horizontal and the vertical are two very important lines, the horizontal being associated with calm and contemplation and the vertical with a feeling of elevation. As was said above, their relation to the sides of the composition to which they are parallel in rectangular pictures is of great importance in uniting the subject to its bounding lines and giving it a well-knit look, conveying a feeling of great stability to a picture. *The Horizontal and the Vertical.*

How impressive and suggestive of contemplation is the long line of the horizon on a calm day at sea, or the long horizon line of a desert plain! The lack of variety, with all the energy and vitality that accompany it, gives one a sense of peace and rest, a touch of infinity that no other lines can convey. The horizontal lines which the breeze makes on still water, and which the sky often assumes at sunset, affect us from the same harmonic cause.

The pine and the cypress are typical instances of the sublime associated with the vertical in nature. Even a factory chimney rising above a distant town, in spite of its unpleasant associations, is impressive, not to speak of the beautiful spires of some of our Gothic cathedrals, pointing upwards. How well Constable has used the vertical sublimity of the spire of Salisbury Cathedral can be seen in his picture, at the Victoria and Albert Museum, where he has contrasted it with the gay tracery of an arch of elm trees. Gothic cathedrals generally depend much on this vertical feeling of line for their impressiveness.

The Romans knew the expressive power of the vertical when they set up a lonely column as a monument to some great deed or person. And a sense of this sublimity may be an unconscious explanation of the craze for putting towers and obelisks on high places that one comes across in different parts of the country, usually called someone's "folly."

In the accompanying diagrams, A, B, C and D, E, F, pages 152 and 153, are examples of the influence to be associated with horizontal and vertical lines. A is nothing but six straight lines drawn across a rectangular shape, and yet I think they convey something of the contemplative and peaceful sense given by a sunset over the sea on a calm evening. And this is entirely due to the expressive power straight lines possess, and the feelings they have the power to call up in the mind. In B a little more incident and variety has been introduced, and although there is a certain loss of calm, it is not yet enough to destroy the impression. The line suggesting a figure is vertical and so plays up to the same calm feeling as the horizontal lines. The circular disc of the sun has the same static quality, being the curve most devoid of variety. It is the lines of the clouds that give some excitement, but they are only enough to suggest the dying energy of departing day.

Now let us but bend the figure in a slight curve, as at C, and destroy its vertical direction, partly cover the disc of the sun so as to destroy the complete circle, and all this is immediately altered, our

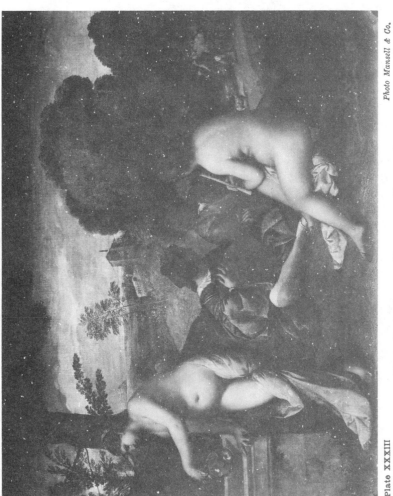

Plate **XXXIII**

FÊTE CHAMPÊTRE. GIORGIONI (LOUVRE)

Note the straight line introduced in seated female figure with flute to counteract rich forms

calm evening has become a windy one, our lines now being expressive of some energy.

To take a similar instance with vertical lines. Let D represent a row of pine trees in a wide plain. Such lines convey a sense of exaltation and infinite calm. Now if some foliage is introduced, as at E, giving a swinging line, and if this swinging line is carried on by a corresponding one in the sky, we have introduced some life and variety. If we entirely destroy the vertical feeling and bend our trees, as at F, the expression of much energy will be the result, and a feeling of the stress and struggle of the elements introduced where there was perfect calm.

It is the aloofness of straight lines from all the fuss and flurry of variety that gives them this calm, infinite expression. And their value as a steadying influence among the more exuberant forms of a composition is very great. The Venetians knew this and made great use of straight lines among the richer forms they so delighted in.

It is interesting to note how Giorgione in his "Fête Champêtre" of the Louvre (see illustration, page 150), went out of his way to get a straight line to steady his picture and contrast with the curves. Not wanting it in the landscape, he has boldly made the contour of the seated female figure conform to a rigid straight line, accentuated still further by the flute in her hand. If it were not for this and other straight lines in the picture, and a certain squareness of drawing in the draperies, the richness of the trees in the background, the full forms of the flesh and drapery would be too much, and the effect become sickly, if not positively sweet. Van Dyck, also, used to go out of his way to introduce a hard straight line near the head in his portraits for

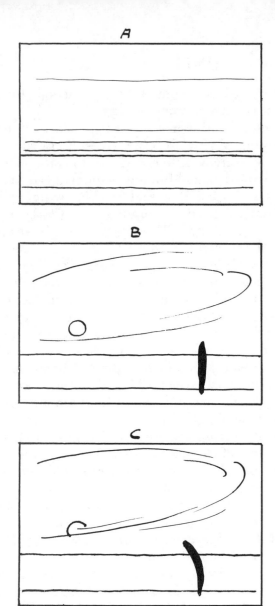

Diagram X

ILLUSTRATING, A, CALM RHYTHMIC INFLUENCE OF
HORIZONTAL LINES SUCH AS A SUNSET OVER THE
SEA MIGHT GIVE; B, INTRODUCTION OF LINES
CONVEYING SOME ENERGY; C, SHOWING DESTRUC-
TION OF REPOSE BY FURTHER CURVING OF LINES.
THE CALM EVENING HAS BECOME A WINDY ONE

152

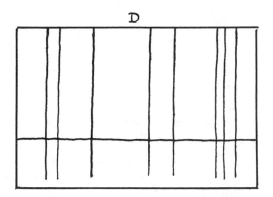

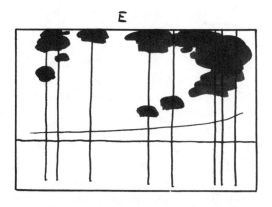

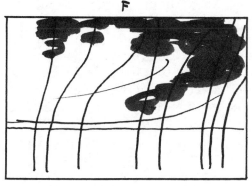

Diagram XI

ILLUSTRATING, D, RHYTHMIC INFLUENCE OF VERTICAL
LINES; E, THE INTRODUCTION OF SOME VARIETY;
F, THE DESTRUCTION OF THE VERTICAL AND
CONSEQUENT LOSS OF REPOSE

153

the same reason, often ending abruptly, without any apparent reason, a dark background in a hard line, and showing a distant landscape beyond in order to get a light mass to accentuate the straight line.

The rich modelling and swinging lines of the "Bacchus and Ariadne" of Titian in the National Gallery, reproduced on the opposite page, would be too gross, were it not for the steadying influence of the horizontal lines in the sky and the vertical lines of the tree-trunks.

While speaking of this picture, it might not be out of place to mention an idea that occurred to me as to the reason for the somewhat aggressive standing leg of the female figure with the cymbals leading the procession of revellers. I will not attempt any analysis of this composition, which is ably gone into in another book of this series. But the standing leg of this figure, given such prominence in the composition, has always rather puzzled me. I knew Titian would not have given it that vigorous stand without a good reason. It certainly does not help the run of the composition, although it may be useful in steadying it, and it is not a particularly beautiful thing in itself, as the position is one better suited to a man's leg than to a woman's. But if you cover it over with your finger and look at the composition without it, I think the reason of its prominence becomes plainer. Titian evidently had some trouble, as well he might have, with the forward leg of the Bacchus. He wished to give the look of his stepping from the car lightly treading the air, as gods may be permitted to do. But the wheel of the car that comes behind the foot made it difficult to evade the idea that he was stepping on it, which would be the way an ordinary mortal

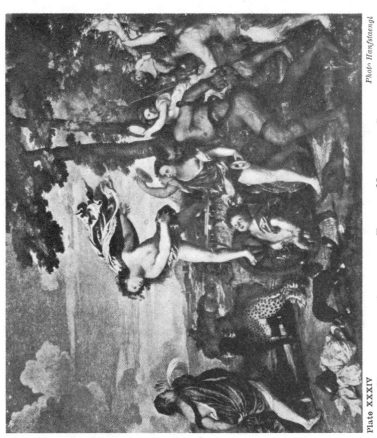

Photo Hanfstaengl

Plate XXXIV   BACCHUS AND ARIADNE.   TITIAN (NATIONAL GALLERY)

would alight. I think the duty of the aggressive standing leg of the leading Bacchante, with its great look of weight, is to give a look of lightness to this forward leg of Bacchus, by contrast—which it certainly does. On examining the picture closely in a good light, you will see that he has had the foot of Bacchus in several positions before he got it right. Another foot can distinctly be seen about a couple of inches or so above the present one. The general vertical direction of this leg is also against its look of lightness and motion, tending rather to give it a stationary, static look. I could not at first see why he did not bring the foot further to the right, which would have aided the lightness of the figure and increased its movement. But you will observe that this would have hurled the whole weight of the mass of figures on the right, forward on to the single figure of Ariadne, and upset the balance; as you can see by covering this leg with your finger and imagining it swinging to the right. So that Titian, having to retain the vertical position for Bacchus' forward leg, used the aggressive standing leg of the cymbal lady to accentuate its spring and lightness.

A feeling of straight-up-ness in a figure or of the horizontal plane in anything will produce the same effect as a vertical or horizontal line without any actual line being visible. Blake's "Morning Stars Singing Together" is an instance of the vertical chord, although there is no actual upright line in the figures. But they all have a vigorous straight-up-ness that gives them the feeling of peace and elevation coupled with a flame-like line running through them that gives them their joyous energy. (See page 147.)

The combination of the vertical with the horizontal produces one of the strongest and most arrest-

ing chords that you can make, and it will be found to exist in most pictures and drawings where there is the expression of dramatic power.
The Right Angle. The cross is the typical example of this. It is a combination of lines that instantly rivets the attention, and has probably a more powerful effect upon the mind —quite apart from anything symbolised by it—than any other simple combinations that could have been devised. How powerful is the effect of a vertical figure, or even a post, seen cutting the long horizontal line of the horizon on the sea-shore. Or a telegraph post by the side of the road, seen against the long horizontal line of a hill at sunset. The look of power given by the vertical lines of a contracted brow is due to the same cause. The vertical furrows of the brow continuing the lines of the nose, make a continuous vertical which the horizontal lines of the brow cross (see Fig. A in the illustration). The same cause gives the profile a powerful look when the eyebrows make a horizontal line contrasting with the vertical line of the forehead (Fig. B). Everybody knows the look of power associated with a square brow: it is not that the square forehead gives the look of a larger brain capacity, for if the forehead protrudes in a curved line, as at C, the look of power is lost, although there is obviously more room for brains.

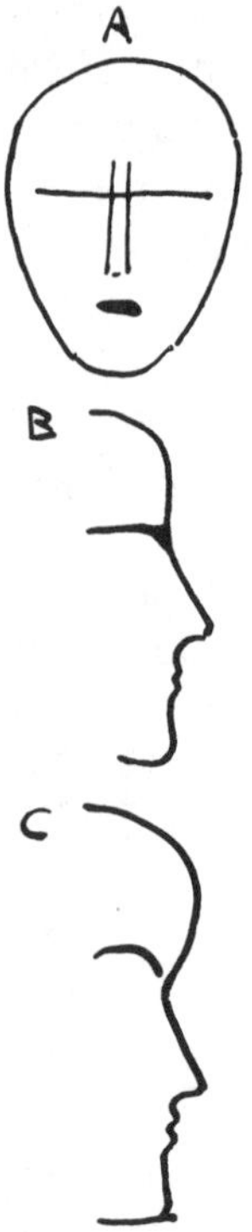

Diagram XII

This power of the right angle is well exemplified in Watts' "Love and Death," here reproduced, page 158.

In this noble composition, in the writer's opinion one of the most sublime expressions produced by nineteenth-century art, the irresistible power and majesty of the slowly advancing figure of Death is largely due to the right angle felt through the pose. Not getting it in the contour, Watts has boldly introduced it by means of shading the farther arm and insisting on the light upper edge of the outstretched arm and hand, while losing somewhat the outline of the head beyond. Note also the look of power the insistence on square forms in the drapery gives this figure. The expression is still further emphasised by the hard square forms of the steps, and particularly by the strong horizontal line of the first step, so insisted on, at right angles to the vertical stand of the figure; and also the upright lines of the doorway above. In contrast with the awful sublimity of this figure of Death, how touching is the expression of the little figure of Love, trying vainly to stop the inevitable advance. And this expression is due to the curved lines on which the action of the figure is hung, and the soft undulating forms of its modelling. Whereas the figure of Death is all square lines and flat crisp planes, the whole hanging on a dramatic right angle; this figure is all subtle fullness both of contour and modelling melting one into the other, the whole hung upon a rich full curve starting at the standing foot of the advancing figure. And whereas the expression of Death is supported and emphasised by the hard, square forms and texture of the stone steps, the expression of Love is supported and emphasised by the rounded forms and soft texture of the clustering roses. On this contrast of line and form, so in sympathy with the

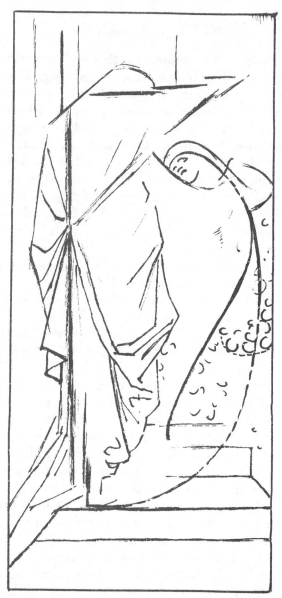

Diagram XIII

ILLUSTRATING SOME OF THE LINES ON WHICH THE
RHYTHMIC POWER OF THIS PICTURE DEPENDS

158

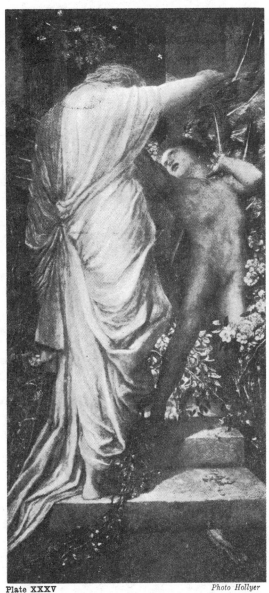

Photo Hollyer

LOVE AND DEATH. BY G. F. WATTS

A noble composition, founded on the power of the right angle in the figure of Death, in contrast with the curved lines in the figure of Love. (See diagram opposite.)

profound sentiment to which this picture owes its origin, the expressive power of this composition will be found to depend.

In the diagram accompanying the reproduction of this picture I have tried to indicate in diagrammatical form some of the chief lines of its anatomy.

In these diagrams of the anatomy of compositions the lines selected are not always very obvious in the originals and are justly much broken into by truths of natural appearance. But an emotional significance depending on some arrangement of abstract lines is to be found underlying the expression in every good picture, carefully hidden as it is by all great artists. And although some apology is perhaps necessary for the ugliness of these diagrams, it is an ugliness that attends all anatomy drawings. If the student will trace them and put his tracing over the reproductions of the originals, they will help him to see on what things in the arrangement the rhythmic force of the picture depends.

Other lines, as important as those selected, may have been overlooked, but the ones chosen will suffice to show the general character of them all.

There is one condition in a composition, that is laid down before you begin, and that is the shape of your panel or canvas. This is usually a rectangular form, and all the lines of your design will have to be considered in relation to this shape. Vertical and horizontal lines being parallel to the boundaries of rectangular pictures, are always right and immediately set up a relationship, as we have seen.

The arresting power of the right angle exists at each corner of a rectangular picture, where the vertical sides meet the horizontal base, and this presents a difficulty, because you do not wish the spectator's attention drawn to the corners, and this dramatic combination of lines always attracts the eye. A favourite way of getting rid of this is to fill them with some dark mass, or with lines swinging round and carrying the eye past them, so that the attention is continually swung to the centre of the picture. For lines have a power of directing the attention, the eye instinctively running with them, and this power is of the greatest service in directing the spectator to the principal interest.

It is this trouble with the corners that makes the problem of filling a square so exacting. In an ordinary rectangular panel you have a certain amount of free space in the middle, and the difficulty of filling the corners comfortably does not present itself until this space is arranged for. But in a square, the moment you leave the centre you are in one or other of the corners, and the filling of them governs the problem much more than in the case of other shapes. It is a good exercise for students to give themselves a square to fill, in order to understand this difficulty and learn to overcome it.

Other lines that possess a direct relation to a rectangular shape are the diagonals. Many compositions that do not hang on a vertical or horizontal basis are built on this line, and are thus related to the bounding shape.

When vertical, horizontal, or diagonal lines are referred to, it must not be assumed that one means in all cases naked lines. There is no pure vertical line in a stone pine or cypress tree, nor pure hori-

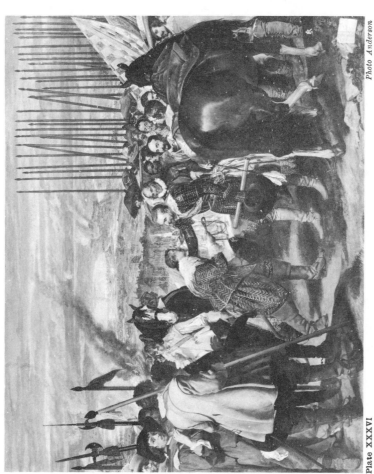

Plate XXXVI   THE SURRENDER OF BREDA.   VELAZQUEZ (PRADO)

zontal line in a stretch of country, but the whole swing of their lines is vertical or horizontal. And in the same way, when one speaks of a composition being hung upon a diagonal, it is seldom that a naked diagonal line exists in the composition, but the general swing is across the panel in harmony with one or other diagonal. And when this is so, there is a unity set up between the design and its boundaries. A good instance of vertical, horizontal, and diagonal lines to unite a picture is Velazquez's "The Surrender of Breda," here reproduced. Note the vertical chord in the spears on the left, continued in the leg of the horse and front leg of the figure receiving the key, and the horizontal line made by the dark mass of distant city, to be continued by the gun carried over the shoulder of the figure with the slouch hat behind the principal group. Velazquez has gone out of his way to get this line, as it could hardly have been the fashion to carry a gun in this position, pointing straight at the head of the man behind. Horizontal lines also occur in the sky and distant landscape, one running right through the group of spears. The use of the diagonal is another remarkable thing in the lines of this picture. If you place a ruler on the slanting line of the flag behind the horse's head to the right, you find it is exactly parallel to a diagonal drawn from the top right-hand corner to the lower left-hand corner. Another line practically parallel to this diagonal is the line of the sword belonging to the figure offering the key, the feeling of which is continued in the hand and key of this same figure. It may be noted also that the back right leg of the horse in the front is parallel to the other diagonal, the under side of it being actually on the diagonal and thus brought into relation with the bounding lines of the picture. And all these lines, without the artifice being too apparent, give that well-knit, dignified look so in harmony with the nature of the subject.

Curved lines have not the moral integrity of straight lines. Theirs is not so much to minister to the expression of the sublime as to **Curved Lines.** woo us to the beauteous joys of the senses. They hold the secrets of charm. But without the steadying power of straight lines and flatnesses, curves get out of hand and lose their power. In architecture the rococo style is an example of this excess. While all expressions of exuberant life and energy, of charm and grace depend on curved lines for their effect, yet in their most refined and beautiful expression they err on the side of the square forms rather than the circle. When the uncontrolled use of curves approaching the circle and volute are indulged in, unrestrained by the steadying influence of any straight lines, the effect is gross. The finest curves are full of restraint, and excessive curvature is a thing to be avoided in good drawing. We recognise this integrity of straight lines when we say anybody is "an upright man" or is "quite straight," wishing to convey the impression of moral worth.

Rubens was a painter who gloried in the unrestrained expression of the zeal to live and drink deeply of life, and glorious as much of his work is, and wonderful as it all is, the excessive use of curves and rounded forms in his later work robs it of much of its power and offends us by its grossness. His best work is full of squarer drawing and planes.

162

UNITY OF LINE

Always be on the look out for straightnesses in curved forms and for planes in your modelling.

Let us take our simplest form of composition again, a stretch of sea and sky, and apply curved lines where we formerly had straight lines. You will see how the lines at A, page 164, although but slightly curved, express some energy, where the straight lines of our former diagram expressed repose, and then how in B and C the increasing curvature of the lines increases the energy expressed, until in D, where the lines sweep round in one vigorous swirl, a perfect hurricane is expressed. This last, is roughly the rhythmic basis of Turner's "Hannibal Crossing the Alps" in the Turner Gallery.

One of the simplest and most graceful forms the tying lines of a composition may take is a continuous flow, one line evolving out of another in graceful sequence, thus leading the eye on from one part to another and carrying the attention to the principal interests.

Two good instances of this arrangement are Botticelli's "Birth of Venus" and the "Rape of Europa," by Paolo Veronese, reproduced on pages 166 and 168. The Venetian picture does not depend so much on the clarity of its line basis as the Florentine. And it is interesting to note how much nearer to the curves of the circle the lines of Europa approach than do those of the Venus picture. Were the same primitive treatment applied to the later work painted in the oil medium as has been used by Botticelli in his tempera picture, the robustness of the curves would have offended and been too gross for the simple formula; whereas overlaid and hidden under such a rich abundance of natural truth as it is in this gorgeous picture, we are too

A

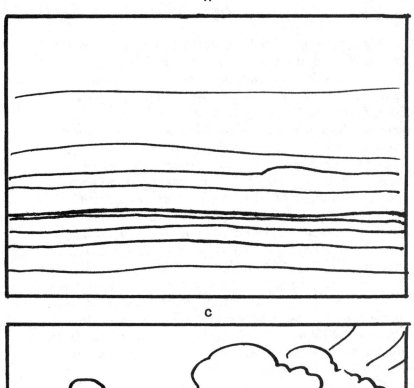

C

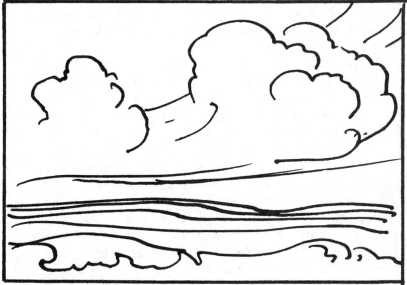

Diagram XIV (1)

ILLUSTRATING POWER OF CURVED
164

B

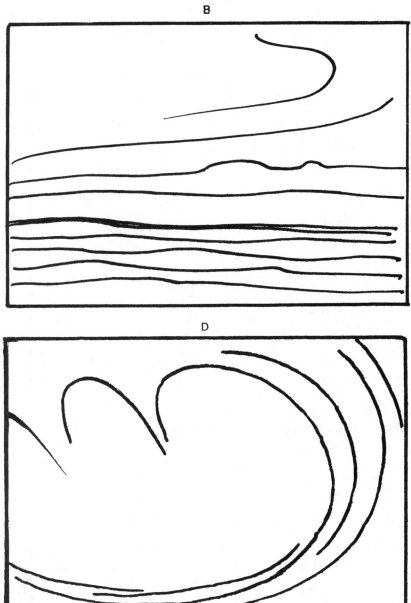

D

Diagram XIV (2)

LINES TO CONVEY ENERGY

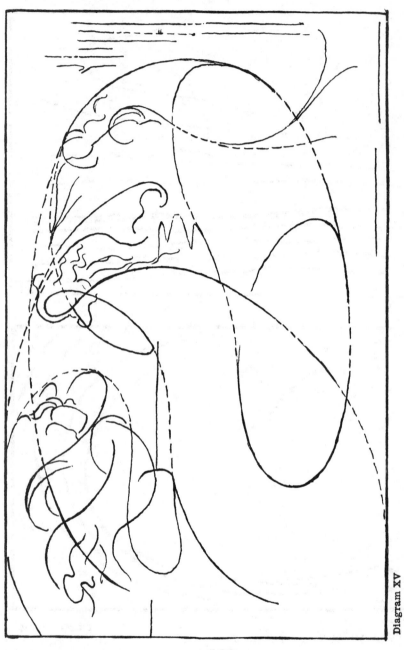

Diagram XV

ILLUSTRATING THE FLOW OF LINES ON WHICH THE RHYTHMIC UNITY OF THIS PICTURE DEPENDS

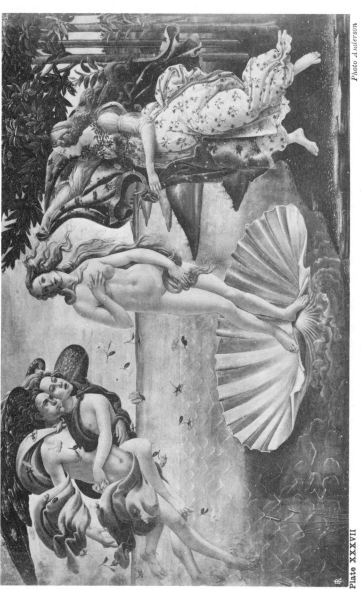

Plate XXXVII

THE BIRTH OF VENUS. BOTTICELLI (FLORENCE)

A beautiful example of Botticelli's refined line rhythm. (See diagram on opposite page for analysis.)

much distracted and entertained by such wealth to have time to dwell on the purity of the line arrangement at its base. And the rich fullness of line arrangement, although rather excessive, seen detached, is in keeping with the sumptuous luxuriance the Venetian loved so well to express. But for pure line beauty the greater restraint of the curves in Botticelli's picture is infinitely more satisfying, though here we have not anything like the same wealth and richness of natural appearance to engage our attention, and the innocent simplicity of the technique leaves much more exposed the structure of lines, which in consequence play a greater part in the effect of the picture.

In both cases note the way the lines lead up to the principal subject, and the steadying power introduced by means of horizontal, vertical, and other straight lines. Veronese has contented himself with keeping a certain horizontal feeling in the sky, culminating in the straight lines of the horizon and of the sea edge. And he has also introduced two pyramids, giving straight lines in among the trees, the most pronounced of which leads the eye straight on to the principal head.

Botticelli has first the long line of the horizon echoed in the ground at the right-hand lower corner. And then he has made a determined stand against the flow of lines carrying you out of the picture on the right, by putting straight, upright trees and insisting upon their straightness.

Another rhythmic form the lines at the basis of a composition may take is a flame-like flow of lines ; curved lines meeting and parting and meeting again, or even crossing in one continual movement onwards. A striking instance of the use of this

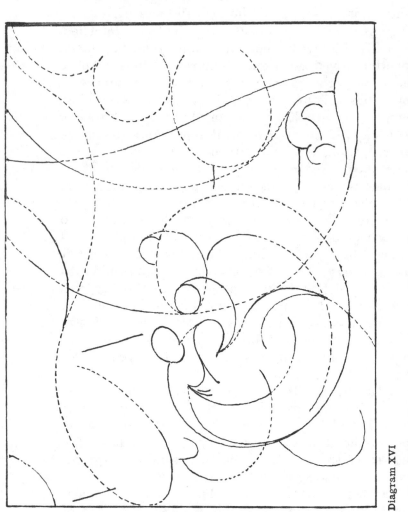

Diagram XVI

ILLUSTRATING SOME OF THE MAIN LINES ON WHICH THE RHYTHMIC
UNITY OF THIS PICTURE DEPENDS

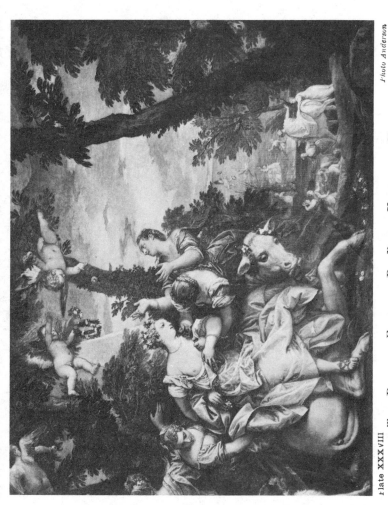

Photo Anderson

Plate XXXVIII The Rape of Europa. By Paolo Veronese (Venice)

A composition of rich full forms and rich full colour. (See diagram on opposite page
for analysis of line rhythm.)

quality is the work of the remarkable Spanish painter usually called El Greco, two of whose works are here shown (page 172). Whatever may be said by the academically minded as to the incorrectness of his drawing, there can be no two opinions as to the remarkable rhythmic vitality of his work. The upward flow of his lines and the flame-like flicker of his light masses thrills one in much the same way as watching a flaring fire. There is something exalting and stimulating in it, although, used to excess as he sometimes uses it, it is apt to suffer from lack of repose. Two examples of his pictures are reproduced here, and illustrate his use of this form of movement in the lines and masses of his compositions. Nowhere does he let the eye rest, but keeps the same flickering movement going throughout all his masses and edges. The extraordinary thing about this remarkable painter is that while this restless, unrestrained form of composition makes his work akin to the rococo work of a later period, there is a fiery earnestness and sincerity in all he does, only to be matched among the primitive painters of the fourteenth and fifteenth centuries, and very different from the false sentiment of the later school.

Blake was also fond of this flame line, but usually used it in combination with more straight lines than the energetic Spaniard allowed himself. Plates III and V in the Job series are good examples of his use of this form. In both cases it will be seen that he uses it in combination with the steadying influence of straight lines, which help to keep the balance and repose necessary in the treatment of even the most violent subjects in art.

A continual interruption in the flow of lines, and

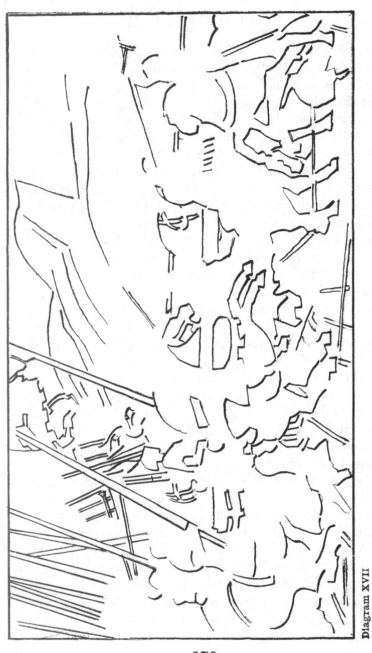

Diagram XVII

SHOWING THE CLASH OF LINES IN SYMPATHY WITH THE MARTIAL NATURE OF THIS SUBJECT

170

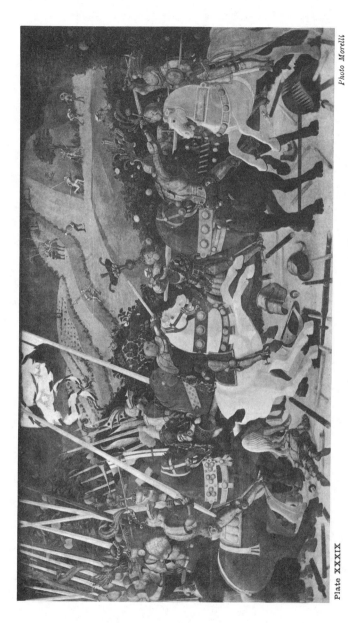

Plate XXXIX

BATTLE OF ST. EGIDIO. PAOLO UCCELLO (NATIONAL GALLERY)

Illustrating the effect of jarring lines in composition. (See diagram on opposite page.)

a harsh jarring of one against another in an angular, jagged fashion, produces a feeling of terror and horror. A streak of fork lightning is a natural example of this. The plate of Blake's No. XI, p. 147, reproduced here, is also a good example. I have had it put sideways on so that you may see that the look of horror is not only in the subject but belongs to the particular music of line in the picture. The effect of the harsh contrasts in the lines is further added to by the harsh contrasts of tone: everywhere hard lights are brought up against hard darks. Harsh contrasts of tone produce much the same look of terror as harsh contrasts of line. Battle pictures are usually, when good, full of these clashes of line and tone, and thrilling dramatic effects in which a touch of horror enters are usually founded on the same principle. In the picture by Paolo Uccello in the National Gallery, reproduced on page 170, a milder edition of this effect is seen. The artist has been more interested in the pageantry of war and a desire to show off his newly-acquired knowledge of perspective, than anything very terrible. The contrasts of line are here but confined to the smaller parts, and there are no contrasts of light and shade, chiaroscuro not being yet invented. However, it will be seen by the accompanying diagram how consistently the harsh contrasts of line were carried out in the planning of this picture. Notice the unconscious humour of the foreshortened spears and figure carefully arranged on the ground to vanish to the recently discovered vanishing point.

Lines radiating in smooth curves from a common centre are another form employed to give unity in pictorial design. The point from which they radiate need not necessarily be within the picture, and is often considerably outside it. But the feeling that they would meet if produced gives them a unity that brings them into harmonious relationship.

There is also another point about radiating lines, and that is their power of setting up a relationship between lines otherwise unrelated. Let us try and explain this. In Panel A, page 174, some lines are drawn at random, with the idea of their being as little related to each other as possible. In B, by the introduction of radiating lines in sympathy with them, they have been brought into some sort of relationship. The line 1–2 has been selected as the dominating line, and an assortment of radiating ones drawn about it. Now, by drawing 7–8, we have set up a relationship between lines 3–4, 5–6, and 1–2, for this line radiates with all of them. Line 9–10 accentuates this relationship with 1–2. The others echo the same thing. It is this echoing of lines through a composition that unites the different parts and gives unity to the whole.

The crossing of lines at angles approaching the right angle is always harsh and somewhat discordant, useful when you want to draw attention dramatically to a particular spot, but to be avoided or covered up at other times. There is an ugly clash of crossing lines in our original scribble, and at C we have introduced a mass to cover this up, and also the angles made by line 3–4 as it crosses the radiating lines above 1–2. With a small mass at 11 to make the balance right, you have a basis for a composition, Diagram C, not at all unpleasing in arrangement, although based on a group of discordant lines drawn at random, but brought into harmony by means of sympathetic radiation.

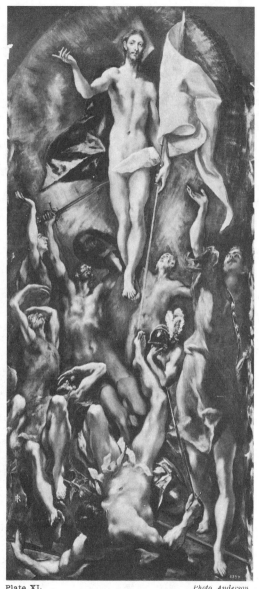

Plate XL   *Photo Anderson*

THE ASCENSION OF CHRIST. BY DOMINICO THEOTOCÓPULI CALLED EL GRECO

Note the flame-like form and flow of the light masses, and the exalted feeling this conveys.

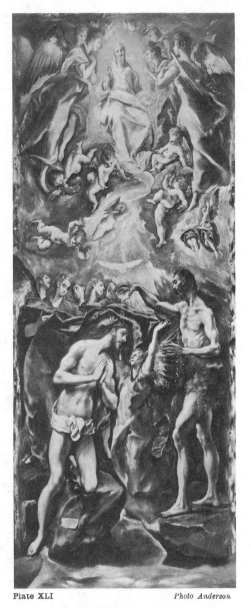

Plate XLI   *Photo Anderson*

THE BAPTISM OF CHRIST. BY DOMINICO THEOTOCÓPULI
CALLED EL GRECO

Another example of his restless flame-like composition.

UNITY OF LINE

In Panel D the same group is taken, but this time line 3-4 is used as the dominant one. Line 7-8 introduces 3-4 to 1-2, as it is related to both. Lines 9-10 and 11-12 introduce 3-4 to 5-6, as they are related to both, and the others follow on the same principle. By introducing some masses covering up the crossings, a rhythmic basis for a composition (Diagram E) entirely different from C is obtained, based on the same random group.

In Panel F, 5-6 has been taken as the dominant line, and sympathetic lines drawn on the same principle as before. By again covering the crossings and introducing balancing masses we obtain yet another arrangement from the same random scribble.

I would suggest this as a new game to students, one giving another two or three lines drawn in a panel at random, the problem being to make harmonious arrangements by the introduction of others radiating in sympathy.

Often in a picture certain conditions are laid down to start with; something as ugly as our original group of lines drawn at random has to be treated pictorially, and it is by means such as here suggested that its discordancy can be subdued and the whole brought into harmony with the shape of your panel. The same principles apply in colour, discordant notes can be brought into harmony by the introduction of others related to both the original colours, thus leading the eye from one to the other by easy stages and destroying the shock. Somewhat in the way a musician will take you from one key into another very remote by means of a few chords leading from the one to the other; whereas, had he taken you straight there, the shock would have

173

UNITY OF LINE

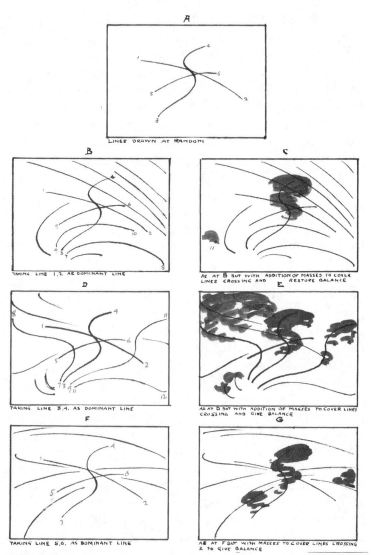

Diagram XVIII

SHOWING HOW LINES UNRELATED CAN BE BROUGHT
INTO HARMONY BY THE INTRODUCTION OF OTHERS
IN SYMPATHY WITH THEM

174

UNITY OF LINE

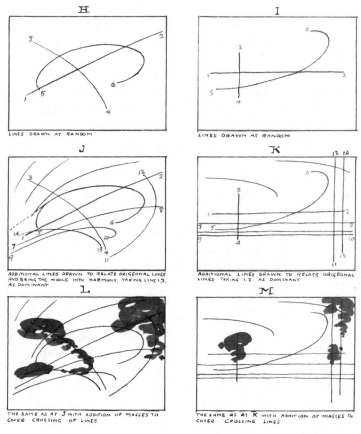

H

LINES DRAWN AT RANDOM

I

LINES DRAWN AT RANDOM

J

ADDITIONAL LINES DRAWN TO RELATE ORIGEONAL LINES
AND BRING THE WHOLE INTO HARMONY, TAKING LINE 1,2,
AS DOMINANT

K

ADDITIONAL LINES DRAWN TO RELATE ORIGEONAL
LINES TAKING 1.2. AS DOMINANT

L

THE SAME AS AT J WITH ADDITION OF MASSES TO
COVER CROSSING OF LINES

M

THE SAME AS AT K WITH ADDITION OF MASSES TO
COVER CROSSING LINES

Diagram XIX

SHOWING HOW LINES UNRELATED CAN BE BROUGHT
INTO HARMONY BY THE INTRODUCTION OF OTHERS
IN SYMPATHY WITH THEM

been terrible. As it is, these transitions from one
key into another please and surprise one, and are
very effective.

In H, I have introduced a straight line into our

175

initial scribble, and this somewhat increases the difficulties of relating them. But by drawing 7–8 and 9–10 radiating from 1–2, we have introduced this straight line to 5–6. For although 5–6 and 9–10 do not radiate from the same point, they are obviously in sympathy. It is only a short part of the line at the end marked 5 that is out of sympathy, and had 5–6 taken the course of the dotted line, it would have radiated from the same point as 9–10. We still have line 3–4 to account for. But by drawing 11–12 we bring it into relationship with 5–6, and so by stages through 9–10 and 7–8 to the original straight line 1–2. Line 13–14, by being related to 3–4, 11–12, and also 5–6, still further harmonises the group, and the remainder echo 5–6 and increase the dominant swing. At L masses have been introduced, covering crossing lines, and we have a basis for a composition.

In Diagram I lines have been drawn as before, at random, but two of them are straight and at right angles, the longer being across the centre of the panel. The first thing to do is to trick the eye out of knowing that this line is in the centre by drawing others parallel to it, leading the eye downwards to line 9–10, which is now much more important than 1–2 and in better proportion with the height of the panel. The vertical line 3–4 is rather stark and lonely, and so we introduce two more verticals at 11–12 and 13–14, which modify this, and with another two lines in sympathy with 5–6 and leading the eye back to the horizontal top of the panel, some sort of unity is set up, the introduction of some masses completing the scheme at M.

There is a quality of sympathy set up by certain line relationships about which it is important to say

something. Ladies who have the instinct for choos-
ing a hat or doing their hair to suit their face
instinctively know something of this; know that
certain things in their face are emphasised by certain
forms in their hats or hair, and the care that has
to be taken to see that the things thus drawn
attention to are their best and not their worst
points.

The principle is more generally understood in
relation to colour; everybody knows how the
blueness of blue eyes is emphasised by a sympathetic
blue dress or touch of blue on a hat, &c. But the
same principle applies to lines. The qualities of
line in beautiful eyes and eyebrows are emphasised
by the long sympathetic curve of a picture hat, and
the becoming effect of a necklace is partly due to
the same cause, the lines being in sympathy with
the eyes or the oval of the face, according to how
low or high it hangs. The influence of long lines
is thus to "pick out" from among the lines of a
face those with which they are in sympathy, and
thus to accentuate them.

To illustrate this, on page 178 is reproduced "The
Portrait of the Artist's Daughter," by Sir Edward
Burne-Jones, Bart.

The two things that are brought out by the line
arrangement in this portrait are the beauty of the
eyes and the shape of the face. Instead of the
picture hat you have the mirror, the widening circles
of which swing round in sympathy with the eyes
and concentrate the attention on them. That on
the left (looking at the picture) has the greatest
attention concentrated upon it, the lines of the
mirror being more in sympathy with this than the
other eye, as it is nearer the centre. If you care

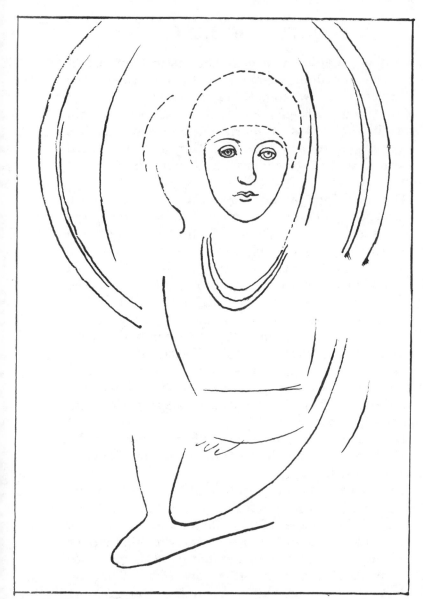

Diagram **XX**

INDICATING THE SYMPATHETIC FLOW OF LINES THAT GIVE
UNITY TO THIS COMPOSITION

178

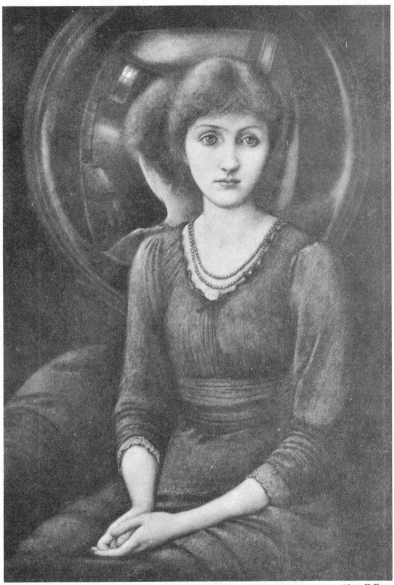

Photo Hollyer

PORTRAIT OF THE ARTIST'S DAUGHTER
SIR EDWARD BURNE-JONES, BART.

An example of sympathetic rhythm. (See diagram on opposite page.)

to take the trouble, cut a hole in a piece of opaque paper the size of the head and placing it over the illustration look at the face without the influence of these outside lines; and note how much more equally divided the attention is between the two eyes without the emphasis given to the one by the mirror. This helps the unity of impression, which with both eyes realised to so intense a focus might have suffered. This mirror forms a sort of echo of the pupil of the eye with its reflection of the window in the left-hand corner corresponding to the high light, greatly helping the spell these eyes hold.

The other form accentuated by the line arrangement is the oval of the face. There is first the necklace, the lines of which lead on to those on the right in the reflection. It is no mere accident that this chain is so in sympathy with the line of the face: it would hardly have remained where it is for long, and must have been put in this position by the artist with the intention (conscious or instinctive) of accentuating the face line. The line of the reflection on the left and the lines of the mirror are also sympathetic. Others in the folds of the dress, and those forming the mass of the hands and arms, echo still further this line of the face and bring the whole canvas into intense sympathetic unity of expression.

The influence that different ways of doing the hair may have on a face is illustrated in the accompanying scribbles. The two profiles are exactly alike—I took great trouble to make them so. It is quite remarkable the difference the two ways of doing the hair make to the look of the faces. The upward swing of the lines in A sympathise with the line of the one and the sharper projections of the face gener-

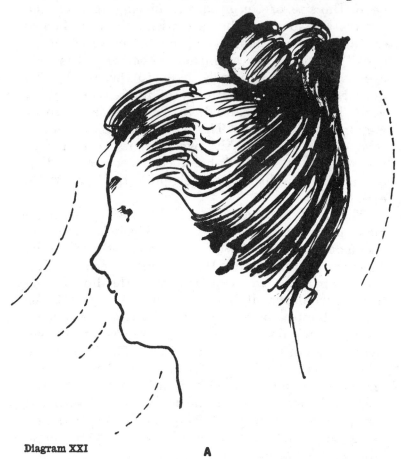

Diagram XXI   **A**

ILLUSTRATING THE EFFECT ON THE FACE OF PUTTING
THE HAIR UP AT THE BACK. HOW THE UPWARD
FLOW OF LINES ACCENTUATES THE SHARPNESSES
OF THE FEATURES

ally (see dotted lines), while the full downward
curves of B sympathise with the fuller curves of

180

the face and particularly emphasise the fullness
under the chin so dreaded by beauty past its

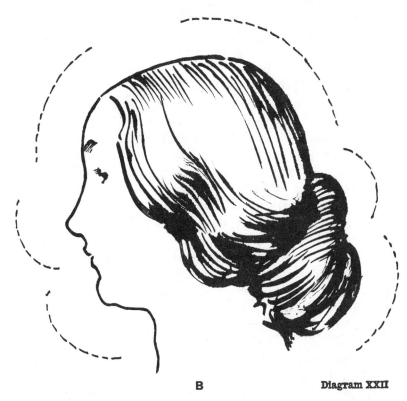

B Diagram XXII

ILLUSTRATING THE EFFECT ON THE SAME FACE AS
DIAGRAM XXI, OF PUTTING THE HAIR LOW AT
THE BACK. HOW THE FULLER LINES THUS GIVEN
ACCENTUATE THE FULLNESSES OF THE FEATURES

first youth (see dotted lines). It is only a very
sharply-cut face that can stand this low knot at
the back of the head, in which case it is one of the
simplest and most beautiful ways of doing the hair.

181

The hair dragged up high at the back sharpens the lines of the profile as the low knot blunts them.

The illustrations to this chapter have been drawn in diagrammatical form in order to try and show that the musical quality of lines and the emotions they are capable of calling up are not dependent upon truth to natural forms but are inherent in abstract arrangements themselves. That is to say, whenever you get certain arrangements of lines, no matter what the objects in nature may be that yield them, you will always get the particular emotional stimulus belonging to such arrangements. For instance, whenever you get long uninterrupted horizontal lines running through a picture not opposed by any violent contrast, you will always get an impression of intense quiet and repose; no matter whether the natural objects yielding these lines are a wide stretch of country with long horizontal clouds in the sky, a pool with a gentle breeze making horizontal bars on its surface, or a pile of wood in a timber yard. And whenever you get long vertical lines in a composition, no matter whether it be a cathedral interior, a pine forest, or a row of scaffold poles, you will always have the particular feeling associated with rows of vertical lines in the abstract. And further, whenever you get the swinging lines of the volute, an impression of energy will be conveyed, no matter whether it be a breaking wave, rolling clouds, whirling dust, or only a mass of tangled hoop iron in a wheelwright's yard. As was said above, these effects may be greatly increased, modified, or even destroyed by associations connected with the things represented. If in painting the timber yard the artist is thinking more about making it look like a stack of real wood with its commercial associations and less about using the artistic material its appearance presents for the making of a picture, he may miss the harmonic impression the long lines of the stacks of wood present. If real wood is the first thing you are led to think of in looking at his work, he will obviously have missed the expression of any artistic feeling the subject was capable of producing. And the same may be said of the scaffold poles or the hoop iron in the wheelwright's yard.

This structure of abstract lines at the basis of a picture will be more or less overlaid with the truths of nature, and all the rich variety of natural forms, according to the requirements of the subject. Thus, in large decorative work, where the painting has to take its place as part of an architectural scheme, the severity of this skeleton will be necessary to unite the work to the architectural forms around it, of which it has to form a part; and very little indulgence in the realisation of natural truth should be permitted to obscure it. But in the painting of a small cabinet picture that exists for close inspection, the supporting power of this line basis is not nearly so essential, and a full indulgence in all the rich variety of natural detail is permissible. And this is how it happens that painters who have gloried in rich details have always painted small pictures, and painters who have preferred larger truths pictures of bigger dimensions. It sounds rather paradoxical to say the smaller the picture the more detail it should contain, and the larger the less, but it is nevertheless true. For although a large picture has not of necessity got to be part of an architectural scheme, it has to be looked at from a distance at which small detail could not be seen, and where such detail would greatly weaken its expressive power.

And further, the small picture easily comes within the field of vision, and the whole impression can be readily grasped without the main lines being, as it were, underlined. But in a big picture one of the greatest difficulties is to get it to read simply, to strike the eye as one impression. Its size making it difficult for it to be got comfortably within the field of vision, every artifice has to be used to give it "breadth of treatment," as it is called, and nothing interferes with this like detail.

XIII

VARIETY OF MASS

THE masses that go to make up a picture have variety in their **shape**, their **tone values**, their **edges**, in **texture or quality**, and in **gradation**. Quite a formidable list, but each of these particulars has some rhythmic quality of its own about which it will be necessary to say a word.

As to variety of shape, many things that were said about lines apply equally to the spaces enclosed by them. It is impossible to write of the rhythmic possibilities that the infinite variety of shapes possessed by natural objects contain, except to point out how necessary the study of nature is for this. Variety of shape is one of the most difficult things to invent, and one of the commonest things in nature. However imaginative your conception, and no matter how far you may carry your design, working from imagination, there will come a time when studies from nature will be necessary if your work is to have the variety that will give life and interest. Try and draw from imagination a row of elm trees of about the same height and distance apart, and get the variety of nature into them; and you will see how difficult it is to invent. On examining your work you will probably discover two or three pet forms repeated, or there may be only one. Or try and draw some cumulus clouds from imagination, several groups of them

Variety of Shape.

185

across a sky, and you will find how often again
you have repeated unconsciously the same forms.
How tired one gets of the pet cloud or tree of a
painter who does not often consult nature in his
pictures. Nature is the great storehouse of variety;
even a piece of coal will suggest more interesting
rock-forms than you can invent. And it is fascinating to watch the infinite variety of graceful
forms assumed by the curling smoke from a cigar-
ette, full of suggestions for beautiful line arrangements. If this variety of form in your work is
allowed to become excessive it will overpower
the unity of your conception. It is in the larger
unity of your composition that the imaginative
faculty will be wanted, and variety in your forms
should always be subordinated to this idea.

Nature does not so readily suggest a scheme
of unity, for the simple reason that the first condition of your picture, the four bounding lines, does
not exist in nature. You may get infinite suggestions for arrangements, and should always be on
the look out for them, but your imagination will
have to relate them to the rigorous conditions of
your four bounding lines, and nature does not
help you much here. But when variety in the
forms is wanted, she is pre-eminent, and it is never
advisable to waste inventive power where it is so
unnecessary.

But although nature does not readily suggest
a design fitting the conditions of a panel her tendency is always towards unity of arrangement.
If you take a bunch of flowers or leaves and
haphazard stuff them into a vase of water, you
will probably get a very chaotic arrangement. But
if you leave it for some time and let nature have

VARIETY OF MASS

a chance you will find that the leaves and flowers have arranged themselves much more harmoniously. And if you cut down one of a group of trees, what a harsh discordant gap is usually left; but in time nature will, by throwing a bough here and filling up a gap there, as far as possible rectify matters and bring all into unity again. I am prepared to be told this has nothing to do with beauty but is only the result of nature's attempts to seek for light and air. But whatever be the physical cause, the fact is the same, that nature's laws tend to pictorial unity of arrangement.

It will be as well to try and explain what is meant by tone values. All the masses or tones (for the terms are often used interchangeably) that go to the making of a visual impression can be considered in relation to an imagined scale from white, to represent the lightest, to black, to represent the darkest tones. This scale of values does not refer to light and shade only, but light and shade, colour, and the whole visual impression are considered as one mosaic of masses of different degrees of darkness or lightness. A dark object in strong light may be lighter than a white object in shadow, or the reverse: it will depend on the amount of reflected light. Colour only matters in so far as it affects the position of the tone in this imagined scale of black and white. The correct observation of these tone values is a most important matter, and one of no little difficulty.

The word tone is used in two senses, in the first place when referring to the individual masses as to their relations in the scale of "tone values"; and secondly when referring to the musical relationship of these values to a oneness of tone idea

Variety of Tone Values.

187

governing the whole impression. In very much the same way you might refer to a single note in music as a tone, and also to the tone of the whole orchestra. The word values always refers to the relationship of the individual masses or tones in our imagined scale from black to white. We say a picture is out of value or out of tone when some of the values are darker or lighter than our sense of harmony feels they should be, in the same way as we should say an instrument in an orchestra was out of tone or tune when it was higher or lower than our sense of harmony allowed. Tone is so intimately associated with the colour of a picture that it is a little difficult to treat of it apart, and it is often used in a sense to include colour in speaking of the general tone. We say it has a warm tone or a cold tone.

There is a particular rhythmic beauty about a well-ordered arrangement of tone values that is a very important part of pictorial design. This music of tone has been present in art in a rudimentary way since the earliest time, but has recently received a much greater amount of attention, and much new light on the subject has been given by the impressionist movement and the study of the art of China and Japan, which is nearly always very beautiful in this respect.

This quality of tone music is most dominant when the masses are large and simple, when the contemplation of them is not disturbed by much variety, and they have little variation of texture and gradation. A slight mist will often improve the tone of a landscape for this reason. It simplifies the tones, masses them together, obliterating many smaller varieties. I have even heard of the tone

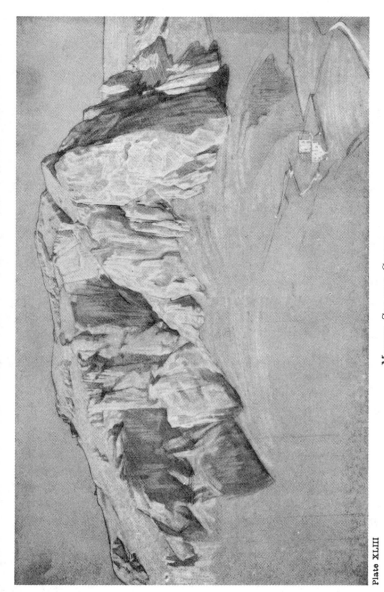

MONTE SOLARO CAPRI

Study on brown paper in charcoal and white chalk.

of a picture being improved by such a mist scrambled or glazed over it.

The powder on a lady's face, when not over-done, is an improvement for the same reason. It simplifies the tones by destroying the distressing shining lights that were cutting up the masses; and it also destroys a large amount of half tone, broadening the lights almost up to the commence-ment of the shadows.

Tone relationships are most sympathetic when the middle values of your scale only are used, that is to say, when the lights are low in tone and the darks high.

They are most dramatic and intense when the con-trasts are great and the jumps from dark to light sudden.

The sympathetic charm of half-light effects is due largely to the tones being of this middle range only; whereas the striking dramatic effect of a storm clearing, in which you may get a landscape brilliantly lit by the sudden appearance of the sun, seen against the dark clouds of the retreating storm, owes its dramatic quality to contrast. The strong contrasts of tone values coupled with the strong colour contrast between the warm sunlit land and the cold angry blue of the retreating storm, gives such a scene much dramatic effect and power.

The subject of values will be further treated in dealing with unity of tone.

Variety in quality and texture is almost too subtle to write about with any prospect of being understood. The play of different qualities and textures in the masses that go to form a picture must be appreciated at first hand, and little can be written about it. Oil paint is capable of almost unlimited variety in this

Variety in Quality and Tex-ture.

way. But it is better to leave the study of such qualities until you have mastered the medium in its more simple aspects.

The particular tone music of which we were speaking is not helped by any great use of this variety. A oneness of quality throughout the work is best suited to exhibit it. Masters of tone, like Whistler, preserve this oneness of quality very carefully in their work, relying chiefly on the grain of a rough canvas to give the necessary variety and prevent a deadness in the quality of the tones.

But when more force and brilliancy are wanted, some use of your paint in a crumbling, broken manner is necessary, as it catches more light, thus increasing the force of the impression. Claude Monet and his followers in their search for brilliancy used this quality throughout many of their paintings, with new and striking results. But it is at the sacrifice of many beautiful qualities of form, as this roughness of surface does not lend itself readily to any finesse of modelling. In the case of Claude Monet's work, however, this does not matter, as form with all its subtleties is not a thing he made any attempt at exploiting. Nature is sufficiently vast for beautiful work to be done in separate departments of vision, although one cannot place such work on the same plane with successful pictures of wider scope. And the particular visual beauty of sparkling light and atmosphere, of which he was one of the first to make a separate study, could hardly exist in a work that aimed also at the significance of beautiful form, the appeal of form, as was explained in an earlier chapter, not being entirely due to a visual but to a mental perception, into which the sense of touch enters by association. The scintillation and glitter of light destroys this touch idea, which is better preserved in quieter lightings.

There is another point in connection with the use of thick paint, that I don't think is sufficiently well known, and that is, its greater readiness to be discoloured by the oil in its composition coming to the surface. Fifteen years ago I did what it would be advisable for every student to do as soon as possible, namely, make a chart of the colours he is likely to use. Get a good white canvas, and set upon it in columns the different colours, very much as you would do on your palette, writing the names in ink beside them. Then take a palette-knife, an ivory one by preference, and drag it from the individual masses of paint so as to get a gradation of different thicknesses, from the thinnest possible layer where your knife ends to the thick mass where it was squeezed out of the tube. It is also advisable to have previously ruled some pencil lines with a hard point down the canvas in such a manner that the strips of paint will cross the lines. This chart will be of the greatest value to you in noting the effect of time on paint. To make it more complete, the colours of several makers should be put down, and at any rate the whites of several different makes should be on it. As white enters so largely into your painting it is highly necessary to use one that does not change.

The two things that I have noticed are that the thin ends of the strips of white have invariably kept whiter than the thick end, and that all the paints have become a little more transparent with time. The pencil lines here come in useful, as they can be seen through the thinner portion, and show to what extent this transparency has occurred. But the point I wish to emphasise is that at the thick end the larger body of oil in the paint, which always comes to the surface as it dries, has darkened and yellowed the surface greatly; while the small amount of oil at the thin end has not darkened it to any extent.

Claude Monet evidently knew this, and got over the difficulty by painting on an absorbent canvas, which sucks the surplus oil out from below and thus prevents its coming to the surface and discolouring the work in time. When this thick manner of painting is adopted, an absorbent canvas should always be used. It also has the advantage of giving a dull dry surface of more brilliancy than a shiny one.

Although not so much as with painting, varieties of texture enter into drawings done with any of the mediums that lend themselves to mass drawing; charcoal, conté crayon, lithographic chalk, and even red chalk and lead pencil are capable of giving a variety of textures, governed largely by the surface of the paper used. But this is more the province of painting than of drawing proper, and charcoal, which is more painting than drawing, is the only medium in which it can be used with much effect.

There is a very beautiful rhythmic quality in the play from softness to sharpness on the edges of masses. A monotonous sharpness of edge **Variety of Edges.** is hard, stern, and unsympathetic. This is a useful quality at times, particularly in decorative work, where the more intimate sympathetic qualities are not so much wanted, and where the harder forms go better with the architectural surroundings of which your painted decoration should form a part. On the other hand, a monotonous softness of edge is very weak and feeble-looking, and too entirely lacking in power to be desirable. If you find any successful work done with this quality of edge unrelieved by any sharpnesses, it will depend on colour, and not form, for any qualities it may possess.

Some amount of softness makes for charm, and is extremely popular: " I do like that because it's so nice and soft " is a regular show-day remark in the studio, and is always meant as a great compliment, but is seldom taken as such by the suffering painter. But a balance of these two qualities playing about your contours produces the most delightful results, and the artist is always on the look out for such variations. He seldom lets a sharpness of edge run far without losing it occasionally. It may be necessary for the hang of the composition that some leading edges should be much insisted on. But even here a monotonous sharpness is too dead a thing, and although a firmness of run will be allowed to be felt, subtle variations will be introduced to prevent deadness. The Venetians from Giorgione's time were great masters of this music of edges. The structure of lines surrounding the masses on which their compositions are built were fused in the most mysterious and delightful way. But although melting into the surrounding mass, they are always firm and never soft and feeble. Study the edge in such a good example of the Venetian manner as the " Bacchus and Ariadne" at the National Gallery, and note where they are hard and where lost.

There is one rather remarkable fact to be observed in this picture and many Venetian works, and this is that the **most accented edges are reserved for unessential parts,** like the piece of white drapery on the lower arm of the girl with the cymbals, and the little white flower on the boy's head in front. The edges on the flesh are everywhere fused and soft, the draperies being much sharper. You may notice the same thing in many pictures of the later Venetian schools. The greatest accents on the edges are rarely in the head, except it may be occasionally in the eyes. But they love to get some strongly-accented feature, such as a crisply-painted shirt coming against the soft modelling of the neck, to balance the fused edges in the flesh. In the head of Philip IV in our National Gallery the only place where Velazquez has allowed himself anything like a sharp edge is in the high lights on the chain hanging round the neck. The softer edges of the principal features in such compositions give a largeness and mystery to these parts, and to restore the balance, sharpnesses are introduced in non-essential accessories.

In the figure with the white tunic from Velazquez's "Surrender of Breda," here reproduced, note the wonderful variety on the edges of the white masses of the coat and the horse's nose, and also that the sharpest accents are reserved for such non-essentials as the bows on the tunic and the loose hair on the horse's forehead. Velazquez's edges are wonderful, and cannot be too carefully studied. He worked largely in flat tones or planes; but this richness and variety of his edges keeps his work from looking flat and dull, like that of some of his followers. I am sorry to say this variety does not come out so well in the reproduction on page 194 as I could have wished, the half-tone process having a tendency to sharpen edges rather monotonously.

This quality is everywhere to be found in

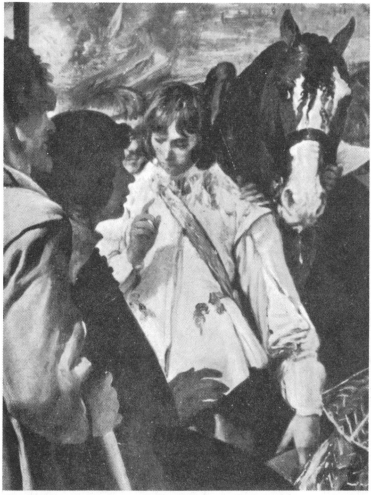

Plate XLIV   *Photo Anderson*

PART OF THE SURRENDER OF BREDA. BY VELAZQUEZ

Note the varied quantity of the edge in white mass of tunic. (The reproduction does
not unfortunately show this as well as the original.)

nature. If you regard any scene pictorially, looking at it as a whole and not letting your eye focus on individual objects wandering from one to another while being but dimly conscious of the whole, but regarding it as a beautiful ensemble; you will find that the boundaries of the masses are not hard continuous edges but play continually along their course, here melting imperceptibly into the surrounding mass, and there accentuated more sharply. Even a long continuous line, like the horizon at sea, has some amount of this play, which you should always be on the look out for. But when the parts only of nature are regarded and each is separately focussed, hard edges will be found to exist almost everywhere, unless there is a positive mist enveloping the objects. And this is the usual way of looking at things. But a picture that is a catalogue of many little parts separately focussed will not hang together as one visual impression.

In naturalistic work the necessity for painting to one focal impression is as great as the necessity of painting in true perspective. What perspective has done for drawing, the impressionist system of painting to one all-embracing focus has done for tone. Before perspective was introduced, each individual object in a picture was drawn with a separate centre of vision fixed on it in turn. What perspective did was to insist that all objects in a picture should be drawn in relation to one fixed centre of vision. And whereas formerly each object was painted to a hard focus, whether it was in the foreground or the distance, impressionism teaches that you cannot have the focus in a picture at the same time on the foreground and the distance.

195

VARIETY OF MASS

Of course there are many manners of painting with more primitive conventions in which the consideration of focus does not enter. But in all painting that aims at reproducing the impressions directly produced in us by natural appearances, this question of focus and its influence on the quality of your edges is of great importance.

Something should be said about the serrated edges of masses, like those of trees seen against the sky. These are very difficult to treat, and almost every landscape painter has a different formula. The hard, fussy, cut-out, photographic appearance of trees misses all their beauty and sublimity.

There are three principal types of treatment that may serve as examples. In the first place there are the trees of the early Italian painters, three examples of which are illustrated on page 197. A thin tree is always selected, and a rhythmic pattern of leaves against the sky painted. This treatment of a dark pattern on a light ground is very useful as a contrast to the softer tones of flesh. But the treatment is more often applied nowadays to a spray of foliage in the foreground, the pattern of which gives a very rich effect. The poplar trees in Millais' " Vale of Rest " are painted in much the same manner as that employed by the Italians, and are exceptional among modern tree paintings, the trees being treated as a pattern of leaves against the sky. Millais has also got a raised quality of paint in his darks very similar to that of Bellini and many early painters.

Giorgione added another tree to landscape art: the rich, full, solidly-massed forms that occur in his " Concert Champêtre " of the Louvre, reproduced on page 150. In this picture you may see both types of treatment. There are the patterns of leaves variety on the left and the solidly-massed treatment on the right.

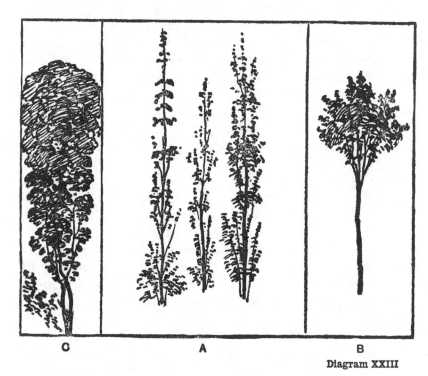

C   A   B

Diagram XXIII

EXAMPLES OF EARLY ITALIAN TREATMENT OF TREES

A. From pictures in Oratorio di S. Ansano. "Il trionfo dell' Amore," attributed to Botticelli.
B. From "L'Annunziazione," by Botticelli, Uffizi, Florence.
C. From "La Vergine," by Giovanni Bellini in the Accademia, Venice.

Corot in his later work developed a treatment that has been largely followed since. Looking at trees with a very wide focus, he ignored individual leaves, and resolved them into masses of tone, here lost and here found more sharply against the sky. The subordinate masses of foliage within these main boundaries are treated in the same way, resolved into masses of infinitely varying edges. This play, this lost-and-foundness at his edges is one of the great distinguishing charms of Corot's trees. When they have been painted from this mass point of view, a suggestion of a few leaves here and a bough there may be indicated, coming sharply against the sky, but you will find this basis of tone music, this crescendo and diminuendo throughout all his later work (see illustration, page 215).

These are three of the more extreme types of trees to be met with in art, but the variations on these types are very numerous. Whatever treatment you adopt, the tree must be considered as a whole, and some rhythmic form related to this large impression selected. And this applies to all forms with serrated edges: some large order must be found to which the fussiness of the edges must conform.

The subject of edges generally is a very important one, and one much more worried over by a master than by the average student. It is interesting to note how all the great painters have begun with a hard manner, with edges of little variety, from which they have gradually developed a looser manner, learning to master the difficulties of design that hard contours insist on your facing, and only when this is thoroughly mastered letting themselves develop freely this play on the edges, this looser handling.

For under the freest painting, if it be good, there will be found a bed-rock structure of well-constructed masses and lines. They may never be insisted on but their steadying influence will always be felt. So err in your student work on the side of hardness rather than looseness, if you would discipline yourself to design your work well. Occasionally only let yourself go at a looser handling.

Variety of gradation will naturally be governed largely by the form and light and shade of the objects in your composition. But while studying the gradations of tone that express form and give the modelling, you should never neglect to keep the mind fixed upon the relation the part you are painting bears to the whole picture. And nothing should be done that is out of harmony with this large conception. It is one of the most difficult things to decide the amount of variety and emphasis allowable for the smaller parts of a picture, so as to bring all in harmony with that oneness of impression that should dominate the whole; how much of your scale of values it is permissible to use for the modelling of each individual part. In the best work the greatest economy is exercised in this respect, so that as much power may be kept in reserve as possible. You have only the one scale from black to white to work with, only one octave within the limits of which to compose your tone symphonies. There are no higher and lower octaves as in music to extend your effect. So be very sparing with your tone values when modelling the different parts.

Variety of Gradation.

XIV

UNITY OF MASS

WHAT has been said about unity of line applies obviously to the outlines bounding the masses, so that we need not say anything further on that subject. The particular quality of which something should be said, is the unity that is given to a picture by means of a well-arranged and rhythmically considered scheme of tone values.

The modifications in the relative tone values of objects seen under different aspects of light and atmosphere are infinite and ever varying; and this is quite a special study in itself. Nature is the great teacher here, her tone arrangements always possessing unity. How kind to the eye is her attempt to cover the ugliness of our great towns in an envelope of atmosphere, giving the most wonderful tone symphonies; thus using man's desecration of her air by smoke to cover up his other desecration of her country-side, a manufacturing town.

This study of values is a distinguishing feature of modern art. But schemes taken from nature are not the only harmonious ones. The older masters were content with one or two well-tried arrangements of tone in their pictures, which were often not at all true to natural appearances but nevertheless harmonious. The chief instance of this is the low-toned sky. The painting of flesh higher in tone than the sky was almost universal at many periods of art, and in portraits is still often seen. Yet it is only in strong sunlight that this is ever so in nature, as you can easily see by holding your hand up against a sky background. The possible exception to this rule is a dark storm-cloud, in which case your hand would have to be strongly lit by some bright light in another part of the sky to appear light against it.

This high tone of the sky is a considerable difficulty when one wishes the interest centred on the figures. The eye instinctively goes to the light masses in a picture, and if these masses are sky, the figures lose some importance. The fashion of lowering its tone has much to be said for it on the score of the added interest it gives to the figures. But it is apt to bring a heavy stuffy look into the atmosphere, and is only really admissible in frankly conventional treatment, in which one has not been led to expect implicit truth to natural effect. If truth to natural appearances is carried far in the figures, the same truth will be expected in the background; but if only certain truths are selected in the figures, and the treatment does not approach the naturalistic, much more liberty can be taken with the background without loss of verisimilitude.

But there is a unity about nature's tone arrangements that it is very difficult to improve upon; and it is usually advisable, if you can, to base the scheme of tone in your picture on a good study of values from nature.

Such effects as twilight, moonlight, or even sunlight were seldom attempted by the older painters, at any rate in their figure subjects. All the lovely tone arrangements that nature presents in these more unusual aspects are a new study, and offer unlimited new material to the artist. Many artists are content to use this simply for itself, the beauty of a rare tone effect being sufficient with the simplest accessories to make a picture. But in figure composition, what new and wonderful things can be imagined in which some rare aspect of nature's tone-music is combined with a fine figure design.

These values are not easily perceived with accuracy, although their influence may be felt by many. A true eye for the accurate perception of subtle tone arrangements is a thing you should study very diligently to acquire. How then is this to be done? It is very difficult, if not impossible, to teach anybody to see. Little more can be said than has already been written about this subject in the chapter on variety in mass. Every mass has to be considered in relation to an imagined tone scale, taking black for your darkest and white for your highest light as we have seen. A black glass, by reducing the light, enables you to observe these relationships more accurately; the dazzling quality of strong light making it difficult to judge them. But this should only be used to correct one's eye, and the comparison should be made between nature seen in the glass and your work seen also in the glass. To look in a black glass and then compare what you saw with your work looked at direct is not a fair comparison, and will result in low-toned work with little brilliancy.

Now, to represent this scale of tones in painting we have white paint as our highest and black paint as our lowest notes. It is never advisable to play either of these extremes, although you may go very near to them. That is to say, there should never be pure white or pure black masses in a picture. There is a kind of screaminess set up when one goes the whole gamut of tone, that gives a look of unrestraint and weakness; somewhat like the feeling experienced when a vocalist sings his or her very highest or very lowest note. In a good singer one always feels he could have gone still higher or still lower, as the case may be, and this gives an added power to the impression of his singing. And in art, likewise, it is always advisable to keep something of this reserve power. Also, the highest lights in nature are never without colour, and this will lower the tone; neither are the deepest darks colourless, and this will raise their tone. But perhaps this is dogmatising, and it may be that beautiful work is to be done with all the extremes you can "clap on," though I think it very unlikely.

In all the quieter aspects of lighting this range from black to white paint is sufficient. But where strong, brilliantly lit effects are wanted, something has to be sacrificed, if this look of brilliancy is to be made telling.

In order to increase the relationship between some of the tones others must be sacrificed. There are two ways of doing this. The first, which was the method earliest adopted, is to begin from the light end of the scale, and, taking something very near pure white as your highest light, to get the relationships between this and the next most brilliant tone, and to proceed thus, tone by tone, from the lightest to the darkest. But working in this way you will find that you arrive at the greatest dark you can make in paint before you have completed the scale of relationships as in nature, if the subject happens to be brilliantly lit.

Another method is to put down the highest light and the darkest dark, and then work your scale of tone relatively between them. But it will be found that working in this way, unless the subject in nature is very quietly lit, you will not get anything like the forceful impression of tone that nature gives.

The third way, and this is the more modern, is to begin from the dark end of the scale, getting the true relationship felt between the greatest dark and the next darkest tone to it, and so on, proceeding towards the light. By this method you will arrive at your highest light in paint before the highest light in nature has been reached. All variety of tone at the light end of the scale will have to be modified in this case, instead of at the dark end as in the other case. In the painting of sunlight the latter method is much the more effective, a look of great brilliancy and light being produced, whereas in the earlier method, the scale being commenced from the light end, so much of the picture was dark that the impression of light and air was lost and a dark gloomy land took its place, a gloom accentuated rather than dispelled by the streaks of lurid light where the sun struck.

Rembrandt is an example of beginning the tone relationships from the light side of the scale, and a large part of his canvas is in consequence always dark

Bastien Lepage is an example of the second method, that of fixing upon two extremes and working relatively between them. And it will be noticed that he confined himself chiefly to quiet grey day effects of lighting, the rendering of which was well within the range of his palette.

UNITY OF MASS

The method of beginning from the dark side, getting the true relations of tones on this side of the scale, and letting the lights take care of themselves, was perhaps first used by Turner. But it is largely used now whenever a strong impression of light is desired. The light masses instead of the dark masses dominate the pictures, which have great brilliancy.

These tone values are only to be perceived in their true relationship by the eye contemplating a wide field of vision. With the ordinary habit of looking only at individual parts of nature, the general impression being but dimly felt, they are not observed. The artist has to acquire the habit of generalising his visual attention over a wide field if he would perceive the true relation of the parts to this scale of values. Half closing the eyes, which is the usual method of doing this, destroys the perception of a great deal of colour. Another method of throwing the eyes out of focus and enabling one to judge of large relationships, is to dilate them widely. This rather increases than diminishes the colour, but is not so safe a method of judging subtle tone relationships.

It is easier in approaching this study out of doors to begin with quiet effects of light. Some of those soft grey days in this country are very beautiful in tone, and change so little that careful studies can be made. And with indoor work, place your subject rather away from the direct light and avoid much light and shade ; let the light come from behind you.

If very strong light effects, such as sunlight, or a dark interior lit by one brilliant window, are attempted, the values will be found to be much simpler and more harsh, often resolving themselves into two masses, a brilliant light contrasted with a dark shadow. This tone arrangement of strong light in contrast with dark shadow was a favourite formula with many schools of the past, since Leonardo da Vinci first used it. Great breadth and splendour is given by it to design, and it is one of the most impressive of tone arrangements. Leonardo da Vinci's "Our Lady of the Rocks," in the National Gallery, is an early example of this treatment. And Correggio's "Venus, Mercury, and Cupid," here reproduced, is another particularly fine example. Reynolds and many of the eighteenth-century men used this scheme in their work almost entirely. This strong light and shade, by eliminating to a large extent the half tones, helps to preserve in highly complete work a simplicity and directness of statement that is very powerful. For certain impressions it probably will never be bettered, but it is a very well-worn convention. Manet among the moderns has given new life to this formula, although he did not derive his inspiration directly from Correggio but through the Spanish school. By working in a strong, rather glaring, **direct light,** he eliminated still further the half tones, and got rid to a great extent of light and shade. Coming at a time when the realistic and plain air movements were destroying simple directness, his work was of great value, bringing back, as it did with its insistence on large, simple masses, a sense of frank **design.** His influence has been very great in recent years, as artists have felt that it offered a new formula for design and colour. Light and shade and half tone are the great enemies of colour, sullying, as they do, its purity; and to some extent to design also, destroying, as they do, the flatness of the picture. But with the strong direct

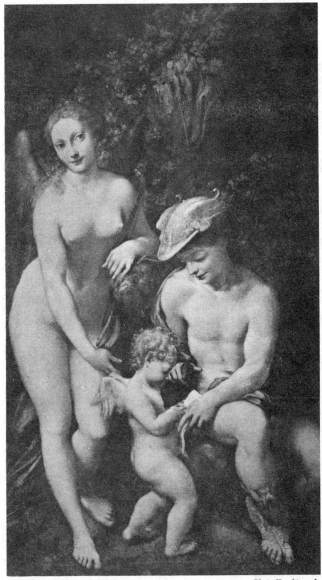

Plate XLV   *Photo Haufstaengl*

CORREGGIO.   VENUS, MERCURY, AND CUPID (NATIONAL GALLERY)

A fine example of one of the most effective tone arrangements; a brilliantly-lit,
richly-modelled light mass on a dark background.

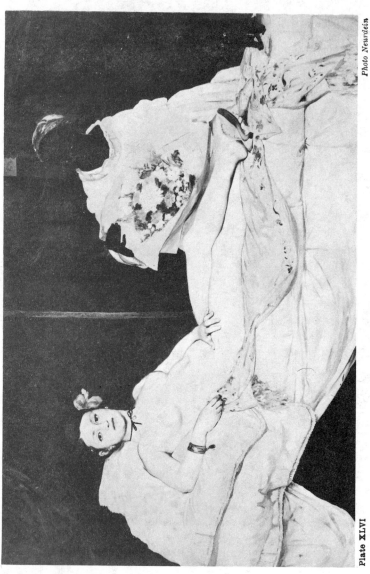

Plate XLVI

OLYMPIA. MANET (LOUVRE)

A further development of the composition formula illustrated by Correggio's "Venus. Added force is given by lighting with low direct light eliminating half-tones.

light, the masses are cut out as simply as possible, and their colour is little sullied by light and shade. The picture of Manet's reproduced is a typical example of his manner. The aggressive shape of the pattern made by the light mass against the dark background is typical of his revolutionary attitude towards all accepted canons of beauty. But even here it is interesting to note that many principles of composition are conformed to. The design is united to its boundaries by the horizontal line of the couch and the vertical line of the screen at the back, while the whole swing hangs on the diagonal from top left-hand corner to right lower corner, to which the strongly marked edge of the bedclothes and pillow at the bottom of the picture is parallel.

Large flat tones give a power and simplicity to a design, and a largeness and breadth of expression that are very valuable, besides showing up every little variety in the values used for your modelling; and thus enabling you to model with the least expenditure of tones. Whatever richness of variation you may ultimately desire to add to your values, see to it that in planning your picture you get a good basic structure of simply designed, and as far as possible flat, tones.

In speaking of variety in mass we saw how the nearer these tones are in the scale of values, the more reserved and quiet the impression created, and the further apart or greater the contrast, the more dramatic and intense the effect. And the sentiment of tone in a picture, like the sentiment of line and colour, should be in harmony with the nature of your subject.

Generally speaking more variety of tone and shape

in the masses of your composition is permissible when a smaller range of values is used than when your subject demands strong contrasts. When strong contrasts of tone or what are called black and white effects are desired, the masses must be very simply designed. Were this not so, and were the composition patterned all over with smaller masses in strong contrast, the breadth and unity of the effect would be lost. While when the difference of relative values between one tone and another is slight, the oneness of effect is not so much interfered with by there being a large number of them. Effects of strong contrasts are therefore far the most difficult to manage, as it is not easy to reduce a composition of any complexity to a simple expressive pattern of large masses.

This principle applies also in the matter of colour. Greater contrasts and variety of colour may be indulged in where the middle range only of tones is used, and where there is little tone contrast, than where there is great contrast. In other words, you cannot with much hope of success have strong contrasts of colour and strong contrasts of tone in the same picture: it is too violent.

If you have strong contrasts of colour, the contrasts of tone between them must be small. The Japanese and Chinese often make the most successful use of violent contrasts of colour by being careful that they shall be of the same tone value.

And again, where you have strong contrasts of tone, such as Rembrandt was fond of, you cannot successfully have strong contrasts of colour as well. Reynolds, who was fond both of colour and strong tone contrast, had to compromise, as he tells us in his lectures, by making the shadows all the same brown colour, to keep a harmony in his work.

There is some analogy between straight lines and flat tones, and curved lines and gradated tones. And a great deal that was said about the rhythmic significance of these lines will apply equally well here. What was said about long vertical and horizontal lines conveying a look of repose and touching the serious emotional notes, can be said of large flat tones. The feeling of infinity suggested by a wide blue sky without a cloud, seen above a wide bare plain, is an obvious instance of this. And for the same harmonic cause, a calm evening has so peaceful and infinite an expression. The waning light darkens the land and increases the contrast between it and the sky, with the result that all the landscape towards the west is reduced to practically one dark tone, cutting sharply against the wide light of the sky.

And the graceful charm of curved lines swinging in harmonious rhythm through a composition has its analogy in gradated tones. Watteau and Gainsborough, those masters of charm, knew this, and in their most alluring compositions the tone-music is founded on a principle of tone-gradations, swinging and interlacing with each other in harmonious rhythm throughout the composition. Large, flat tones, with their more thoughtful associations are out of place here, and are seldom if ever used. In their work we see a world where the saddening influences of profound thought and its expression are far away. No deeper notes are allowed to mar the gaiety of this holiday world. Watteau created a dream country of his own, in which a tired humanity has delighted ever since, in which all serious thoughts are far away and the mind takes

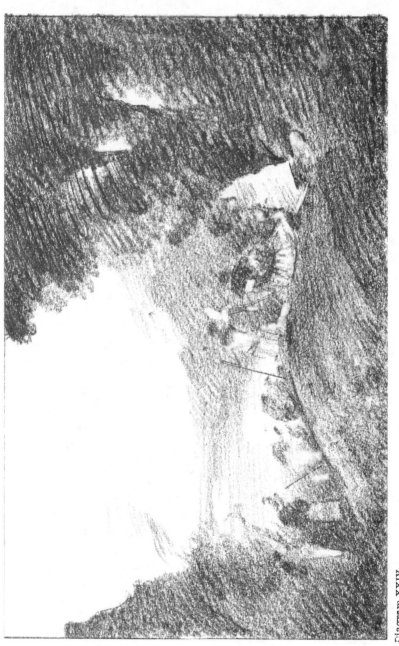

Diagram XXIV

SHOWING THE PRINCIPLE ON WHICH THE MASS OR TONE RHYTHM OF THE
COMPOSITION REPRODUCED ON THE OPPOSITE PAGE IS ARRANGED

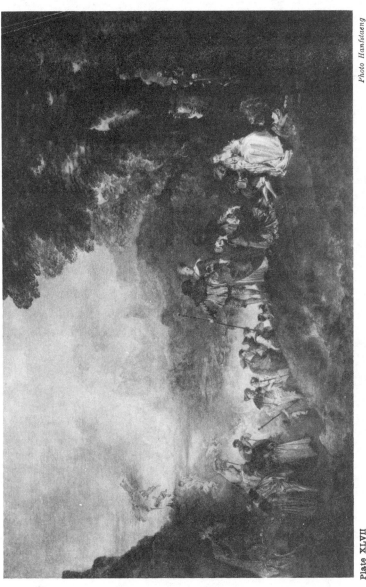

Plate XLVII

L'Embarquement pour Cythère. Watteau (Louvre)

A typical example of composition founded on gradated tones.   (See analysis on opposite page.)

refreshment in the contemplation of delightful things. And a great deal of this charm is due to the pretty play from a crescendo to a diminuendo in the tone values on which his compositions are based—so far removed from the simple structure of flat masses to which more primitive and austere art owes its power.

But Watteau's great accomplishment was in doing this without degenerating into feeble prettiness, and this he did by an insistence on character in his figures, particularly his men. His draperies also are always beautifully drawn and full of variety, never feeble and characterless. The landscape backgrounds are much more lacking in this respect, nothing ever happened there, no storms have ever bent his graceful tree-trunks, and the incessant gradations might easily become wearisome. But possibly the charm in which we delight would be lost, did the landscape possess more character. At any rate there is enough in the figures to prevent any sickly prettiness, although I think if you removed the figures the landscape would not be tolerable.

But the followers of Watteau seized upon the prettiness and gradually got out of touch with the character, and if you compare Boucher's heads, particularly his men's heads, with Watteau's you may see how much has been lost.

The following are three examples of this gradated tone composition (see pages 210, 213, 215):

Watteau: "Embarquement pour l'Île de Cythère."

This is a typical Watteau composition, founded on a rhythmic play of gradated tones and gradated edges. Flat tones and hard edges are avoided. Beginning at the centre of the top with a strongly accented note of contrast, the dark tone of the mass of trees gradates into the ground and on past the lower right-hand corner across the front of the picture, until, when nearing the lower left-hand corner, it reverses the process and from dark to light begins gradating light to dark, ending somewhat sharply against the sky in the rock form to the left. The rich play of tone that is introduced in the trees and ground, &c., blinds one at first to the perception of this larger tone motive, but without it the rich variety would not hold together. Roughly speaking the whole of this dark frame of tones from the accented point of the trees at the top to the mass of the rock on the left, may be said to gradate away into the distance; cut into by the wedge-shaped middle tone of the hills leading to the horizon.

Breaking across this is a graceful line of figures, beginning on the left where the mass of rock is broken by the little flight of cupids, and continuing across the picture until it is brought up sharply by the light figure under the trees on the right. Note the pretty clatter of spots this line of figures brings across the picture, introducing light spots into the darker masses, ending up with the strongly accented light spot of the figure on the right; and dark spots into the lighter masses, ending up with the figures of the cupids dark against the sky.

Steadying influences in all this flux of tone are introduced by the vertical accent of the tree-stem and statue in the dark mass on the right, by the horizontal line of the distance on the left, the outline of the ground in the front, and the straight staffs held by some of the figures.

In the charcoal scribble illustrating this composition I have tried carefully to avoid any drawing in the figures or trees to show how the tone-music depends not so much on truth to natural appear-

212

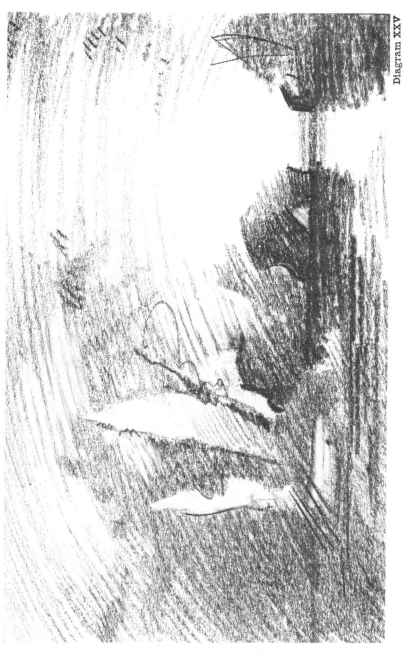

Diagram XXV

SHOWING THE PRINCIPLE ON WHICH THE MASS OR TONE RHYTHM IS ARRANGED IN TURNER'S PICTURE IN THE NATIONAL GALLERY OF BRITISH ART, "ULYSSES DERIDING POLYPHEMUS"

213

ances as on the abstract arrangement of tone values and their rhythmic play.

Of course nature contains every conceivable variety of tone-music, but it is not to be found by unintelligent copying except in rare accidents. Emerson says, "Although you search the whole world for the beautiful you'll not find it unless you take it with you," and this is true to a greater extent of rhythmic tone arrangements.

Turner: "Ulysses deriding Polyphemus."

Turner was very fond of these gradated tone compositions, and carried them to a lyrical height to which they had never before attained. His "Ulysses deriding Polyphemus," in the National Gallery of British Art, is a splendid example of his use of this principle. A great unity of expression is given by bringing the greatest dark and light together in sharp contrast, as is done in this picture by the dark rocks and ships' prows coming against the rising sun. From this point the dark and light masses gradate in different directions until they merge above the ships' sails. These sails cut sharply into the dark mass as the rocks and ship on the extreme right cut sharply into the light mass. Note also the edges where they are accented and come sharply against the neighbouring mass, and where they are lost, and the pleasing quality this play of edges gives.

Stability is given by the line of the horizon and waves in front, and the masts of the ships, the oars, and, in the original picture, a feeling of radiating lines from the rising sun. Without these steadying influences these compositions of gradated masses would be sickly and weak.

Corot: 2470 Collection Chauchard, Louvre.

This is a typical example of Corot's tone scheme,

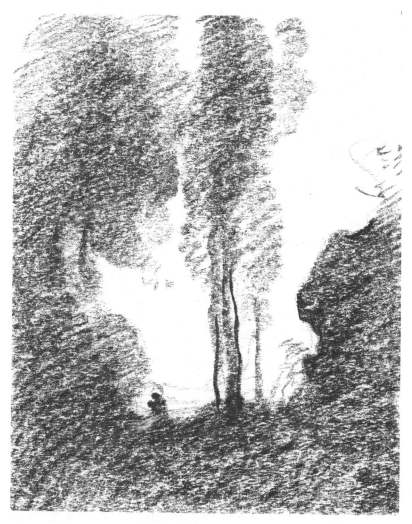

Diagram XXVI

TYPICAL EXAMPLE OF COROT'S SYSTEM OF MASS RHYTHM,
AFTER THE PICTURE IN THE LOUVRE, PARIS

and little need be added to the description already given. Infinite play is got with the simplest means. A dark silhouetted mass is seen against a light sky, the perfect balance of the shapes and the infinite play of lost-and-foundness in the edges giving to this simple structure a richness and beauty effect that is very satisfying. Note how Corot, like Turner, brings his greatest light and dark together in sharp contrast where the rock on the right cuts the sky.

Stability is given by the vertical feeling in the central group of trees and the suggestion of horizontal distance behind the figure.

It is not only in the larger disposition of the masses in a composition that this principle of gradated masses and lost and found edges can be used. Wherever grace and charm are your motive they should be looked for in the working out of the smallest details.

In concluding this chapter I must again insist that knowledge of these matters will not make you compose a good picture. A composition may be perfect as far as any rules or principles of composition go, and yet be of no account whatever. The life-giving quality in art always defies analysis and refuses to be tabulated in any formula. This vital quality in drawing and composition must come from the individual artist himself, and nobody can help him much here. He must ever be on the look out for those visions his imagination stirs within him, and endeavour, however haltingly at first, to give them some sincere expression. Try always when your mind is filled with some pictorial idea to get something put down, a mere fumbled expression possibly, but it may contain the germ. Later on the same idea may occur to you again, only it will be less vague this time, and a process of development will have taken place. It may be years before it takes sufficiently definite shape to justify a picture; the process of germination in the mind is a slow one. But try and acquire the habit of making some record of what pictorial ideas pass in the mind, and don't wait until you can draw and paint well to begin. Qualities of drawing and painting don't matter a bit here, it is the sensation, the feeling for the picture, that is everything.

If knowledge of the rhythmic properties of lines and masses will not enable you to compose a fine picture, you may well ask what is their use? There may be those to whom they are of no use. Their artistic instincts are sufficiently strong to need no direction. But such natures are rare, and it is doubtful if they ever go far, while many a painter might be saved a lot of worry over something in his picture that " won't come " did he but know more of the principle of pictorial design his work is transgressing. I feel certain that the old painters, like the Venetians, were far more systematic and had far more hard and fast principles of design than ourselves. They knew the science of their craft so well that they did not so often have to call upon their artistic instinct to get them out of difficulties. Their artistic instinct was free to attend to higher things, their knowledge of the science of picture-making keeping them from many petty mistakes that a modern artist falls into. The desire of so many artists in these days to cut loose from tradition and start all over again puts a very severe strain upon their intuitive faculties, and keeps them occupied correcting things that more knowledge of some of the fundamental principles that don't really alter and that are the same in all schools would have saved them. Knowledge in art is like a railway built behind the pioneers who have gone before; it offers a point of departure for those who come after, further on into the unknown country of nature's secrets—a help not lightly to be discarded.

But all artifice in art must be concealed, **a picture obviously composed is badly composed.** In a good composition it is as though the parts had been carefully placed in rhythmic relation and then the picture jarred a little, so that everything is slightly shifted out of place, thus introducing our "dither" or play of life between the parts. Of course no mechanical jogging will introduce the vital quality referred to, which must come from the vitality of the artist's intuition; although I have heard of photographers jogging the camera in an endeavour to introduce some artistic "play" in its mechanical renderings. But one must say something to show how in all good composition the mechanical principles at the basis of the matter are subordinate to a vital principle on which the life in the work depends.

This concealment of all artifice, this artlessness and spontaneity of appearance, is one of the greatest qualities in a composition, any analysis of which is futile. It is what occasionally gives to the work of the unlettered genius so great a charm. But the artist in whom the true spark has not been quenched by worldly success or other enervating influence, keeps the secret of this freshness right on, the culture of his student days being used only to give it splendour of expression, but never to stifle or suppress its native charm.

XV

BALANCE

THERE seems to be a strife between opposing forces at the basis of all things, a strife in which a perfect balance is never attained, or life would cease. The worlds are kept on their courses by such opposing forces, the perfect equilibrium never being found, and so the vitalising movement is kept up. States are held together on the same principle, no State seeming able to preserve a balance for long; new forces arise, the balance is upset, and the State totters until a new equilibrium has been found. It would seem, however, to be the aim of life to strive after balance, any violent deviation from which is accompanied by calamity.

And in art we have the same play of opposing factors, straight lines and curves, light and dark, warm and cold colour oppose each other. Were the balance between them perfect, the result would be dull and dead. But if the balance is very much out, the eye is disturbed and the effect too disquieting. It will naturally be in pictures that aim at repose that this balance will be most perfect. In more exciting subjects less will be necessary, but some amount should exist in every picture, no matter how turbulent its motive; as in good tragedy the horror of the situation is never allowed to overbalance the beauty of the treatment.

BALANCE

Let us consider in the first place the balance between straight lines and curves. The richer and fuller the curves, the more severe should be the straight lines that balance them, if perfect repose is desired. But if the subject demands excess of movement and life, of course there will be less necessity for the balancing influence of straight lines. And on the other hand, if the subject demands an excess of repose and contemplation, the bias will be on the side of straight lines. But a picture composed entirely of rich, rolling curves is too disquieting a thing to contemplate, and would become very irritating. Of the two extremes, one composed entirely of straight lines would be preferable to one with no squareness to relieve the richness of the curves. For straight lines are significant of the deeper and more permanent things of life, of the powers that govern and restrain, and of infinity; while the rich curves (that is, curves the farthest removed from the straight line) seem to be expressive of uncontrolled energy and the more exuberant joys of life. Vice may be excess in any direction, but asceticism has generally been accepted as a nobler vice than voluptuousness. The rococo art of the eighteenth century is an instance of the excessive use of curved forms, and, like all excesses in the joys of life, it is vicious and is the favourite style of decoration in vulgar places of entertainment. The excessive use of straight lines and square forms may be seen in some ancient Egyptian architecture, but this severity was originally, no doubt, softened by the use of colour, and in any case it is nobler and finer than the vicious cleverness of rococo art.

Between Straight Lines and Curves.

BALANCE

We have seen how the Greeks balanced the straight lines of their architectural forms with the rich lines of the sculpture which they used so lavishly on their temples. But the balance was always kept on the side of the square forms and never on the side of undue roundness. And it is on this side that the balance would seem to be in the finest art. Even the finest curves are those that approach the straight line rather than the circle, that err on the side of flatnesses rather than roundnesses.

What has been said about the balance of straight lines and curves applies equally well to tones, if for straight lines you substitute flat tones, and for curved lines gradated tones. The deeper, more permanent things find expression in the wider, flatter tones, while an excess of gradations makes for prettiness, if not for the gross roundnesses of vicious modelling.

Between Flat and Gradated Tones.

Often when a picture is hopelessly out of gear and "mucked up," as they say in the studio, it can be got on the right road again by reducing it to a basis of flat tones, going over it and painting out the gradations, getting it back to a simpler equation from which the right road to completion can be more readily seen. Overmuch concern with the gradations of the smaller modelling is a very common reason of pictures and drawings getting out of gear. The less expenditure of tone values you can express your modelling with, the better, as a general rule. The balance in the finest work is usually on the side of flat tones rather than on the side of gradated tones. Work that errs on the side of gradations, like that of Greuze, however popular its appeal, is much poorer stuff

221

than work that errs on the side of flatness in tone, like Giotto and the Italian primitives, or Puvis de Chavannes among the moderns.

There is a balance of tone set up also between light and dark, between black and white in the scale of tone. Pictures that do not go **Between Light and** far in the direction of light, starting from **Dark Tones.** a middle tone, should not go far in the direction of dark either. In this respect note the pictures of Whistler, a great master in matters of tone; his lights seldom approach anywhere near white, and, on the other hand, his darks never approach black in tone. When the highest lights are low in tone, the darkest darks should be high in tone. Painters like Rembrandt, whose pictures when fresh must have approached very near white in the high lights, also approach black in the darks, and nearer our own time, Frank Holl forced the whites of his pictures very high and correspondingly the darks were very heavy. And when this balance is kept there is a rightness about it that is instinctively felt. We do not mean that the **amount** of light tones in a picture should be balanced by the **amount** of dark tones, but that there should be some balance between the extremes of light and dark used in the tone scheme of a picture. The old rule was, I believe, that a picture should be two-thirds light and one-third dark. But I do not think there is any rule to be observed here: there are too many exceptions, and no mention is made of half tones.

Like all so-called laws in art, this rule is capable of many apparent exceptions. There is the white picture in which all the tones are high. But in some of the most successful of these you will generally find spots of intensely dark pigment. Turner was fond of these light pictures in his later manner, but he usually put in some dark spot, such as the black gondolas in some of his Venetian pictures, that illustrate the law of balance we are speaking of, and are usually put in excessively dark in proportion as the rest of the picture is excessively light.

The successful one-tone pictures are generally painted in the middle tones, and thus do not in any way contradict our principle of balance.

One is tempted at this point to wander a little into the province of colour, where the principle of balance of which we are speaking is much felt, the scale here being between warm Between Warm and and cold colours. If you divide the solar Cold Colours. spectrum roughly into half, you will have the reds, oranges, and yellows on one side, and the purples, blues, and greens on the other, the former being roughly the warm and the latter the cold colours. The clever manipulation of the opposition between these warm and cold colours is one of the chief means used in giving vitality to colouring. But the point to notice here is that the further your colouring goes in the direction of warmth, the further it will be necessary to go in the opposite direction, to right the balance. That is how it comes about that painters like Titian, who loved a warm, glowing, golden colouring, so often had to put a mass of the coldest blue in their pictures. Gainsborough's " Blue Boy," although done in defiance of Reynolds' principle, is no contradiction of our rule, for although the boy has a blue dress all the rest of the picture is **warm** brown and so the balance is kept. It is the failure to observe this balance that makes so many of the red-coated huntsmen and soldiers' portraits in our exhibitions so objectionable. They are too often painted on a dark, hot, burnt sienna and black background, with nothing but warm colours in the flesh, &c., with the result that the screaming heat is intolerable. With a hot mass of red like a huntsman's coat in your picture, the coolest colour should be looked for everywhere else. Seen in a November landscape, how well a huntsman's coat looks, but then, how cold and grey is the colouring of the landscape. The right thing to do is to support your red with as many cool and neutral tones as possible and avoid hot shadows. With so strong a red, blue might be too much of a contrast, unless your canvas was large enough to admit of its being introduced at some distance from the red.

Most painters, of course, are content to keep to middle courses, never going very far in the warm or cold directions. And, undoubtedly, much more freedom of action is possible here, although the results may not be so powerful. But when beauty and refinement of sentiment rather than force are desired, the middle range of colouring (that is to say, all colours partly neutralised by admixture with their opposites) is much safer.

There is another form of balance that must be mentioned, although it is connected more with the

Between Interest and Mass.   subject matter of art, as it concerns the mental significance of objects rather than the rhythmic qualities possessed by lines and masses; I refer to the balance there is between interest and mass. The all-absorbing interest of the human figure makes it often when quite minute in scale balance the weight and interest of a great mass. Diagram XXVII is a rough instance of what is meant. Without the little figure the composition would be out of balance. But the weight of interest centred upon that lonely little person is enough to right the balance occasioned by the great mass of trees on the left. Figures are largely used by landscape painters in this way, and are of great use in restoring balance in a picture.

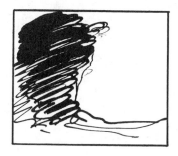 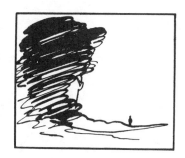

Diagram XXVII

ILLUSTRATING HOW INTEREST MAY BALANCE MASS

And lastly, there must be a balance struck between variety and unity. A great deal has already been said about this, and it will only be necessary to recapitulate here that *Between Variety and Unity.* to variety is due all the expression of the picturesque, of the joyous energy of life, and all that makes the world such a delightful place, but that to unity belongs the relating of this variety to the underlying bed-rock principles that support it in nature and in all good art. It will depend on the nature of the artist and on the nature of his theme how far this underlying unity will dominate the expression in his work; and how far it will be overlaid and hidden behind a rich garment of variety.

BALANCE

But both ideas must be considered in his work. If the unity of his conception is allowed to exclude variety entirely, it will result in a dead abstraction, and if the variety is to be allowed none of the restraining influences of unity, it will develop into a riotous extravagance.

XVI

RHYTHM: PROPORTION

RULES and canons of proportion designed to reduce to a mathematical formula the things that move us in beautiful objects, have not been a great success; the beautiful will always defy such clumsy analysis. But however true it is that beauty of proportion must ever be the result of the finer senses of the artist, it is possible that canons of proportion, such as those of the human body, may be of service to the artist by offering some standard from which he can depart at the dictates of his artistic instinct. There appears to be no doubt that the ancient sculptors used some such system. And many of the renaissance painters were interested in the subject, Leonardo da Vinci having much to say about it in his book.

Like all scientific knowledge in art, it fails to trap the elusive something that is the vital essence of the whole matter, but such scientific knowledge does help to bring one's work up to a high point of mechanical perfection, from which one's artistic instinct can soar with a better chance of success than if no scientific scaffolding had been used in the initial building up. Yet, however perfect your system, don't forget that the life, the "dither," will still have to be accounted for, and no science will help you here.

The idea that certain mathematical proportions

227

or relationships underlie the phenomena we call beauty is very ancient, and too abstruse to trouble us here. But undoubtedly proportion, the **quantitative** relation of the parts to each other and to the whole, forms a very important part in the impression works of art and objects give us, and should be a subject of the greatest consideration in planning your work. The mathematical relationship of these quantities is a subject that has always fascinated scholars, who have measured the antique statues accurately and painstakingly to find the secret of their charm. Science, by showing that different sounds and different colours are produced by waves of different lengths, and that therefore different colours and sounds can be expressed in terms of numbers, has certainly opened the door to a new consideration of this subject of beauty in relation to mathematics. And the result of such an inquiry, if it is being or has been carried on, will be of much interest.

But there is something chilling to the artist in an array of dead figures, for he has a consciousness that the life of the whole matter will never be captured by such mechanical means.

The question we are interested to ask here is: are there particular sentiments connected with the different relations of quantities, their proportions, as we found there were in connection with different arrangements of lines and masses? Have abstract proportions any significance in art, as we found abstract line and mass arrangements had? It is a difficult thing to be definite about, and I can only give my own feeling on the matter; but I think in some degree they have.

Proportion can be considered from our two points of view of unity and variety. In so far as the proportions of any picture or object resolve themselves into a simple, easily grasped unity of relationship, a sense of repose and sublimity is produced. In so far as the variety of proportion in the different parts is assertive and prevents the eye grasping the arrangement as a simple whole, a sense of the lively restlessness of life and activity is produced. In other words, as we found in line arrangements, unity makes for sublimity, while variety makes for the expression of life. Of course the scale of the object will have something to do with this. That is to say, the most sublimely proportioned dog-kennel could never give us the impression of sublimity produced by a great temple. In pictures the scale of the work is not of so great importance, a painting or drawing having the power of giving the impression of great size on a small scale.

The proportion that is most easily grasped is the half—two equal parts. This is the most devoid of variety, and therefore of life, and is only used when an effect of great repose and aloofness from life is wanted ; and even then, never without some variety in the minor parts to give vitality. The third and the quarter, and in fact any equal proportions, are others that are easily grasped and partake in a lesser degree of the same qualities as the half. So that equality of proportion should be avoided except on those rare occasions when effects remote from nature and life are desired. Nature seems to abhor equalities, never making two things alike or the same proportion if she can help it. All systems founded on equalities, as are so many modern systems of social reform, are man's work, the products of a machine-made age. For this is the difference between nature and the machine: nature never produces two things alike, the machine never produces two things different. Man could solve the social problem to-morrow if you could produce him equal units. But if all men were alike and equal, where would be the life and fun of existence? it would depart with the variety. And in proportion, as in life, variety is the secret of vitality, only to be suppressed where a static effect is wanted. In architecture equality of proportion is more often met with, as the static qualities of repose are of more importance here than in painting. One meets it on all fine buildings in such things as rows of columns and windows of equal size and distances apart, or the continual repetition of the same forms in mouldings, &c. But even here, in the best work, some variety is allowed to keep the effect from being quite dead, the columns on the outside of a Greek pediment being nearer together and leaning slightly inwards, and the repeated forms of windows, columns, and mouldings being infinitely varied in themselves. But although you often find repetitions of the same forms equidistant in architecture, it is seldom that equality of proportion is observable in the main distribution of the large masses.

Let us take our simple type of composition, and in Diagram XXVIII, A, put the horizon across the centre and an upright post cutting it in the middle of the picture. And let us introduce two spots that may indicate the position of birds in the upper spaces on either side of this.

Here we have a maximum of equality and the deadest and most static of results.

To see these diagrams properly it is necessary to cover over with some pieces of notepaper all but

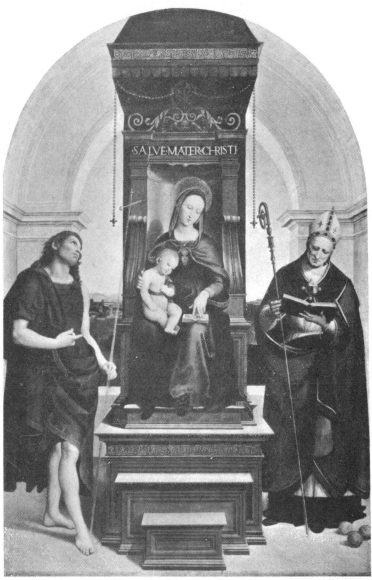

Plate XLVIII *Photo Hanfstaengl*

THE ANSIDEI MADONNA. BY RAPHAEL (NATIONAL GALLERY)

A typical example of static balance in composition.

the one being considered, as they affect each other
when seen together, and the quality of their proportion is not so readily observed.

In many pictures of the Madonna, when a hush
and reverence are desired rather than exuberant
life, the figure is put in the centre of the canvas,
equality of proportion existing between the spaces
on either side of her. But having got the repose
this centralisation gives, everything is done to con-
ceal this equality, and variety in the contours on
either side, and in any figures there may be, is carefully sought. Raphael's "Ansidei Madonna," in the
National Gallery, is an instance of this (p. 230). You
have first the centralisation of the figure of the
Madonna with the throne on which she sits, exactly
in the middle of the picture. Not only is the throne
in the centre of the picture, but its width is exactly
that of the spaces on either side of it, giving us
three equal proportions across the picture. Then
you have the circular lines of the arches behind,
curves possessed of the least possible amount of
variety and therefore the calmest and most reposeful; while the horizontal lines of the steps and the
vertical lines of the throne and architecture, and
also the rows of hanging beads give further emphasis to this infinity of calm. But when we come
to the figures this symmetry has been varied everywhere. All the heads swing towards the right,
while the lines of the draperies swing freely in
many directions. The swing of the heads towards
the right is balanced and the eye brought back to
equilibrium by the strongly-insisted-upon staff of
St. Nicholas on the right. The staff of St. John
necessary to balance this line somewhat, is very
slightly insisted on, being represented transparent

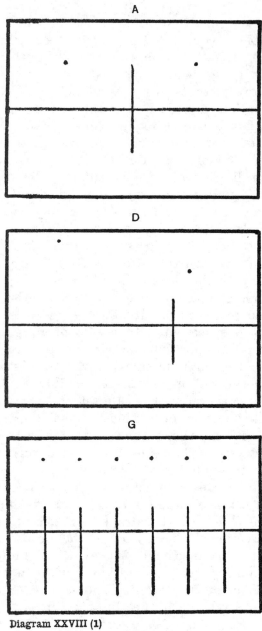

Diagram XXVIII (1)

232

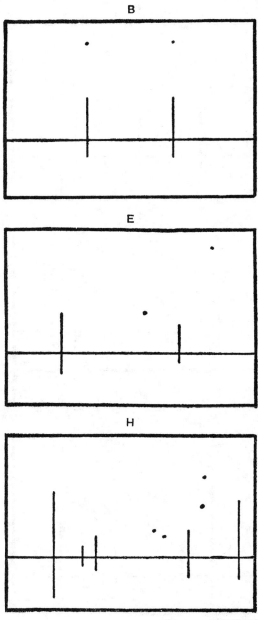

Diagram XXVIII (2)

233

C

F

I

Diagram XXVIII (3)

234

PROPORTION

as if made of glass, so as not to increase the swing
to the right occasioned by the heads. It is interesting to note the fruit introduced at the last moment
in the right-hand lower corner, dragged in, as it
were, to restore the balance occasioned by the figure
of the Christ being on the left. In the writer's
humble opinion the extremely obvious artifice
with which the lines have been balanced, and the
severity of the convention of this composition generally, are out of harmony with the amount of naturalistic detail and particularly of solidity allowed in the
treatment of the figures and accessories. The small
amount of truth to visual nature in the work of
earlier men went better with the formality of such
compositions. With so little of the variety of life
in their treatment of natural appearances, one was
not led to demand so much of the variety of life
in the arrangement. It is the simplicity and re-
moteness from the full effect of natural appearances
in the work of the early Italian schools that made
their painting such a ready medium for the expression of religious subjects. This atmosphere of
other-worldliness where the music of line and colour
was uninterrupted by any aggressive look of real
things is a better convention for the expression
of such ideas and emotions.

In B and C the proportions of the third and
the quarter are shown, producing the same static
effect as the half, although not so completely.

At D, E, F the same number of lines and spots
as we have at A, B, C have been used, but varied
as to size and position, so that they have no obvious
mechanical relationship. The result is an expression of much more life and character.

At G, H, I more lines and spots have been
235

added. At G they are equidistant and dead from lack of variety, while at H and I they are varied to a degree that prevents the eye grasping any obvious relationship between them. They have consequently a look of liveliness and life very different from A, B, C, or G. It will be observed that as the amount of variety increases so does the life and liveliness of the impression.

In these diagrams a certain static effect is kept up throughout, on account of our lines being vertical and horizontal only, which lines, as we saw in an earlier chapter, are the calmest we have. But despite this, I think the added life due to the variety in the proportions is sufficiently apparent in the diagrams to prove the point we wish to make.

As a contrast to the infinite calm of Raphael's "Madonna," we have reproduced Tintoretto's "Finding of the Body of St. Mark," in the Brera Gallery, Milan. Here all is life and movement. The proportions are infinitely varied, nowhere does the eye grasp any obvious mathematical relationship. We have the same semi-circular arches as in the Raphael, but not symmetrically placed, and their lines everywhere varied, and their calm effect destroyed by the flickering lights playing about them. Note the great emphasis given to the outstretched hand of the powerful figure of the Apostle on the left by the lines of the architecture and the line of arm of the kneeling figure in the centre of the picture converging on this hand and leading the eye immediately to it. There is here no static symmetry, all is energy and force. Starting with this arresting arm, the eye is led down the majestic figure of St. Mark, past the recumbent figure, and across the picture by means of the band of light on the ground, to the

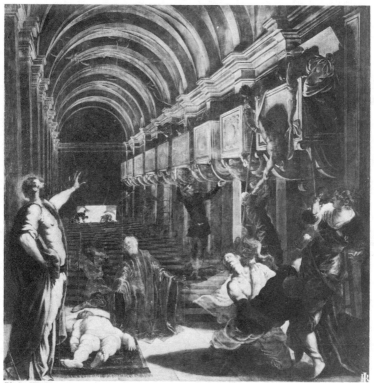

Plate **XLIX**

Photo Anderson

The Finding of the Body of St. Mark
Tintoretto (Brera. Milan)

Compare with Raphael's Ansidei Madonna, and note how energy and movement take
the place of static calm in the balance of this composition.

important group of frightened figures on the right. And from them on to the figures engaged in lowering a corpse from its tomb. Or, following the direction of the outstretched arm of St. Mark, we are led by the lines of the architecture to this group straight away, and back again by means of the group on the right and the band of light on the ground. The quantities are not placed in reposeful symmetry about the canvas, as was the case in the Raphael, but are thrown off apparently haphazard from lines leading the eye round the picture. Note also the dramatic intensity given by the strongly contrasted light and shade, and how Tintoretto has enjoyed the weird effect of the two figures looking into a tomb with a light, their shadows being thrown on the lid they hold open, at the far end of the room. This must have been an amazingly new piece of realism at the time, and is wonderfully used, to give an eerie effect to the darkened end of the room. With his boundless energy and full enjoyment of life, Tintoretto's work naturally shows a strong leaning towards variety, and his amazing compositions are a liberal education in the innumerable and unexpected ways in which a panel can be filled, and should be carefully studied by students.

A pleasing proportion that often occurs in nature and art is one that may be roughly stated in figures as that between 5 and 8. In such a proportion the eye sees no mathematical relationship. Were it less than 5, it would be too near the proportion of 4 to 8 (or one-third the total length), a dull proportion; or were it more, it would be approaching too near equality of proportion to be quite satisfactory.

I have seen a proportional compass, imported from Germany, giving a relationship similar to this

PROPORTION

and said to contain the secret of good proportion. There is certainly something remarkable about it, and in the Appendix, page 289, you will find some further interesting facts about this.

The variety of proportions in a building, a picture, or a piece of sculpture should always be under the control of a few simple, dominant quantities that simplify the appearance and give it a unity which is readily grasped except where violence and lack of repose are wanted. The simpler the proportion is, the more sublime will be the impression, and the more complicated, the livelier and more vivacious the effect. From a few well-chosen large proportions the eye may be led on to enjoy the smaller varieties. But in good proportion the lesser parts are not allowed to obtrude, but are kept in subordination to the main dispositions on which the unity of the effect depends.

XVII

PORTRAIT DRAWING

THERE is something in every individual that is likely
for a long time to defy the analysis of science.
When you have summed up the total of atoms or
electrons or whatever it is that goes to the making
of the tissues and also the innumerable complex
functions performed by the different parts, you have
not yet got on the track of the individual that
governs the whole performance. The effect of this
personality on the outward form, and the influence
it has in modifying the aspect of body and features,
are the things that concern the portrait draughtsman: the seizing on and expressing forcefully the
individual character of the sitter, as expressed by
his outward appearance.

This character expression in form has been
thought to be somewhat antagonistic to beauty,
and many sitters are shy of the particular characteristics of their own features. The fashionable
photographer, knowing this, carefully stipples out
of his negative any striking characteristics in the
form of his sitter the negative may show. But
judging by the result, it is doubtful whether any
beauty has been gained, and certain that interest
and vitality have been lost in the process. Whatever may be the nature of beauty, it is obvious that
what makes one object more beautiful than another

is something that is characteristic of the appearance of the one and not of the other: so that some close study of individual characteristics must be the aim of the artist who would seek to express beauty, as well as the artist who seeks the expression of character and professes no interest in beauty.

Catching the likeness, as it is called, is simply seizing on the essential things that belong only to a particular individual and differentiate that individual from others, and expressing them in a forceful manner. There are certain things that are common to the whole species, likeness to a common type; the individual likeness is not in this direction but at the opposite pole to it.

It is one of the most remarkable things connected with the amazing subtlety of appreciation possessed by the human eye, that of the millions of heads in the world, and probably of all that have ever existed in the world, no two look exactly alike. When one considers how alike they are, and how very restricted is the range of difference between them, is it not remarkable how quickly the eye recognises one person from another? It is more remarkable still how one sometimes recognises a friend not seen for many years, and whose appearance has changed considerably in the meantime. And this likeness that we recognise is not so much as is generally thought a matter of the individual features. If one sees the eye alone, the remainder of the face being covered, it is almost impossible to recognise even a well-known friend, or tell whether the expression is that of laughing or crying. And again, how difficult it is to recognise anybody when the eyes are masked and only the lower part of the face visible.

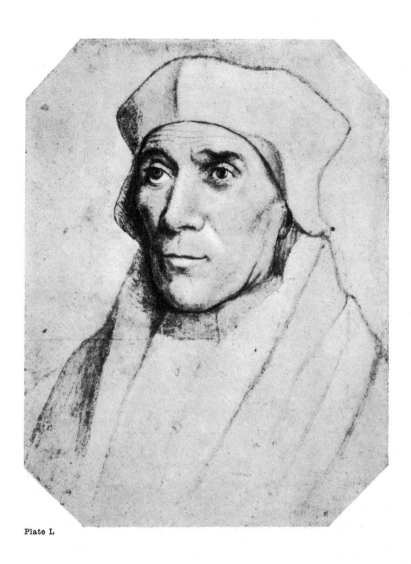

Plate L

FROM A DRAWING IN RED CHALK BY HOLBEIN IN
THE BRITISH MUSEUM PRINT ROOM

Note how every bit of variety is sought for, the difference in the eyes and on
either side of the mouth, etc.

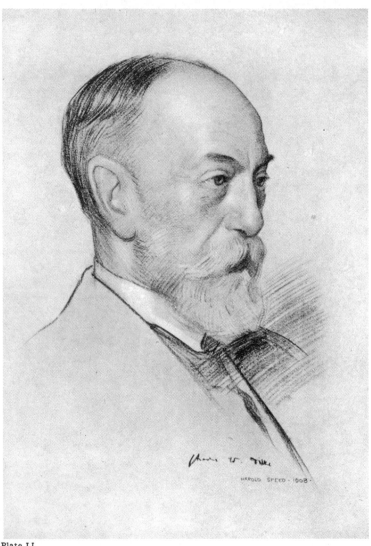

Plate LI

SIR CHARLES DILKE, BART.

From the drawing in the collection of Sir **Walter Essex**, M.P., in red conté chalk rubbed, the high lights being picked out with rubber.

PORTRAIT DRAWING

If you try and recall a well-known head it will not be the shape of the features that will be recollected so much as an impression, the result of all these combined, a sort of chord of which the features will be but the component elements. It is the relation of the different parts to this chord, this impression of the personality of a head, that is the all-important thing in what is popularly called " catching the likeness." In drawing a portrait the mind must be centred on this, and all the individual parts drawn in relation to it. The moment the eye gets interested solely in some individual part and forgets the consideration of its relationship to this whole impression, the likeness suffers.

Where there is so much that is similar in heads, it is obvious that what differences there are must be searched out and seized upon forcefully, if the individuality of the head is to be made telling. The drawing of portraits should therefore be approached from the direction of these differences ; that is to say, the things in general disposition and proportion in which your subject differs from a common type, should be first sought for, the things common to all heads being left to take care of themselves for a bit. The reason for this is that the eye, when fresh, sees these differences much more readily than after it has been working for some time. The tendency of a tired eye is to see less differentiation, and to hark back to a dull uniformity ; so get in touch at once with the vital differences while your eye is fresh and your vision keen.

Look out first for the character of the disposition of the features, note the proportions down an imagined centre line, of the brows, the base of the nose, the mouth and chin, and get the character of the shape of the enclosing line of the face blocked out in square lines. The great importance of getting these proportions right early cannot be over-emphasised, as any mistake may later on necessitate completely shifting a carefully drawn feature. And the importance of this may be judged from the fact that you recognise a head a long way off, before anything but the general disposition of the masses surrounding the features can be seen. The shape of the skull, too, is another thing of which to get an early idea, and its relation to the face should be carefully noted. But it is impossible to lay down hard and fast rules for these things.

Some artists begin in point drawing with the eyes, and some leave the eyes until the very last. Some draughtsmen are never happy until they have an eye to adjust the head round, treating it as the centre of interest and drawing the parts relatively to it. While others say, with some truth, that there is a mesmeric effect produced when the eye is drawn that blinds one to the cold-blooded technical consideration of a head as line and tone in certain relationships; that it is as well to postpone until the last, that moment when the shapes and tones that represent form in your drawing shall be lit up by the introduction of the eye, to the look of a live person. One is freer to consider the accuracy of one's form before this disturbing influence is introduced. And there is a good deal to be said for this.

Although in point drawing you can, without serious effect, begin at any part that interests you, in setting out a painting I think there can be no two opinions as to the right way to go about it. The character of the general disposition of the masses must be first constructed. And if this general blocking in has been well done, the character of the sitter will be apparent from the first even in this early stage; and you will be able to judge of the accuracy of your blocking out by whether or not it **does** suggest the original. If it does not, correct it before going any further, working, as it were, from the general impression of the masses of the head as seen a long way off, adding more and more detail, and gradually bringing the impression nearer, until the completed head is arrived at, thus getting in touch from the very first with the likeness which should dominate the work all along.

There are many points of view from which a portrait can be drawn—I mean, **mental** points of view. And, as in a biography, the value of the work will depend on the insight and distinction of the author or artist. The valet of a great man might write a biography of his master that could be quite true to his point of view; but, assuming him to be an average valet, it would not be a great work. I believe the gardener of Darwin when asked how his master was, said, "Not at all well. You see, he moons about all day. I've seen him staring at a flower for five or ten minutes at a time. Now, if he had some work to do, he would be much better." A really great biography cannot be written except by a man who can comprehend his subject and take a wide view of his position among men, sorting what is trivial from what is essential, what is common to all men from what is particular to the subject of his work. And it is very much the same in portraiture. It is only the painter who possesses the intuitive faculty for seizing on the significant things in the form expression of his subject, of disentangling what is trivial from what is important; and who can convey this forcibly to the beholder on his canvas, more forcibly than a casual sight of the real person could do—it is only this painter who can hope to paint a really fine portrait.

It is true, the honest and sincere expression of any painter will be of some interest, just as the biography written by Darwin's gardener might be; but there is a vast difference between this point of view and that of the man who thoroughly comprehends his subject.

Not that it is necessary for the artist to grasp the mind of his sitter, although that is no disadvantage. But this is not his point of view, his business is with the effect of this inner man on his outward appearance. And it is necessary for him to have that intuitive power that seizes instinctively on those variations of form that are expressive of this inner man. The habitual cast of thought in any individual affects the shape and moulds the form of the features, and, to the discerning, the head is expressive of the person; both the bigger and the smaller person, both the larger and the petty characteristics everybody possesses. And the fine portrait will express the larger and subordinate the petty individualities, will give you what is of value, and subordinate what is trivial in a person's appearance.

The pose of the head is a characteristic feature about people that is not always given enough attention in portraits. The habitual cast of thought affects its carriage to a very large degree. The two extreme types of what we mean are the strongly emotional man who carries his head high, drinking in impressions as he goes through the world; and the man of deep thought who carries his head bent forward, his back bent in sympathy with it. Everybody has some characteristic action in the way that should be looked out for and that is usually absent when a sitter first appears before a painter on the studio throne. A little diplomacy and conversational humouring is necessary to produce that unconsciousness that will betray the man in his appearance.

How the power to discover these things can be acquired, it is, of course, impossible to teach. All the student can do is to familiarise himself with the best examples of portraiture, in the hope that he may be stimulated by this means to observe finer qualities in nature and develop the best that is in him. But he must never be insincere in his work. If he does not appreciate fine things in the work of recognised masters, let him stick to the honest portrayal of what he does see in nature. The only distinction of which he is capable lies in this direction. It is not until he awakens to the sight in nature of qualities he may have admired in others' work that he is in a position honestly to introduce them into his own performances.

Probably the most popular point of view in portraiture at present is the one that can be described as a " striking presentment of the live person." This is the portrait that arrests the crowd in an exhibition. You cannot ignore it, vitality bursts from it, and everything seems sacrificed to this quality of striking lifelikeness. And some very wonderful modern portraits have been painted from this point of view. But have we not sacrificed too much to this quality of vitality? Here is a lady hurriedly getting up from a couch, there a gentle-man stepping out of the frame to greet you, violence and vitality everywhere. But what of repose, harmony of colour and form, and the wise ordering and selecting of the materials of vision that one has been used to in the great portraiture of the past? While the craftsman in one is staggered and amazed at the brilliant virtuosity of the thing, the artist in one resents the sacrifice of so much for what is, after all, but a short-lived excitement. Age may, no doubt, improve some of the portraits of this class by quieting them in colour and tone. And those that are good in design and arrangement will stand this without loss of distinction, but those in which everything has been sacrificed to this striking lifelike quality will suffer considerably. This par-ticular quality depends so much on the freshness of the paint that when this is mellowed and its vividness is lost, nothing will remain of value, if the quieter qualities of design and arrangement have been sacrificed for it.

Frans Hals is the only old master I can think of with whom this form of portrait can be compared. But it will be noticed that besides designing his canvases carefully, he usually balanced the vigour and vitality of his form with a great sobriety of colour. In fact, in some of his later work, where this restless vitality is most in evidence, the colour is little more than black and white, with a little yellow ochre and Venetian red. It is this extreme reposefulness of colour that opposes the unrest in the form and helps to restore the balance and neces-sary repose in the picture. It is interesting to note the restless variety of the edges in Frans Hal's work, how he never, if he can help it, lets an edge

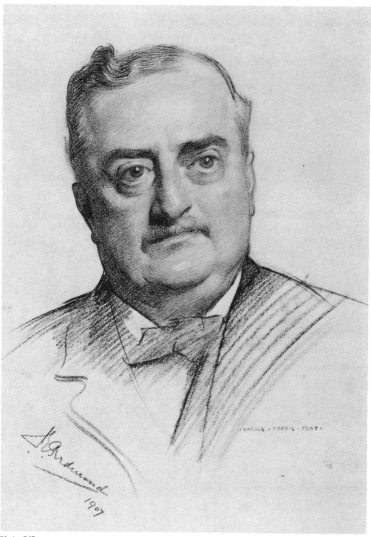

Plate LII

John Redmond, M.P.

From the drawing in the collection of Sir Robert Essex, M.P., in red conté chalk
rubbed, the high lights being picked out with rubber.

run smoothly, but keeps it constantly on the move, often leaving it quite jagged, and to compare this with what was said about vitality depending on variety.

Another point of view is that of the artist who seeks to give a significant and calm view of the exterior forms of the sitter, an expressive map of the individuality of those forms, leaving you to form your own intellectual judgments. A simple, rather formal, attitude is usually chosen, and the sitter is drawn with searching honesty. There is a great deal to be said for this point of view in the hands of a painter with a large appreciation of form and design. But without these more inspiring qualities it is apt to have the dulness that attends most literal transcriptions. There are many instances of this point of view among early portrait painters, one of the best of which is the work of Holbein. But then, to a very distinguished appreciation of the subtleties of form characterisation he added a fine sense of design and colour arrangement, qualities by no means always at the command of some of the lesser men of this school.

Every portrait draughtsman should make a pilgrimage to Windsor, armed with the necessary permission to view the wonderful series of portrait drawings by this master in the library of the castle. They are a liberal education in portrait drawing. It is necessary to see the originals, for it is only after having seen them that one can properly understand the numerous and well-known reproductions. A study of these drawings will, I think, reveal the fact that they are not so literal as is usually thought. Unflinchingly and unaffectedly honest they are, but honest not to a cold, mechanically accurate record of the sitter's appearance, but honest and accurate to the vital impression of the live sitter made on the mind of the live artist. This is the difference we were trying to explain that exists between the academic and the vital drawing, and it is a very subtle and elusive quality, like all artistic qualities, to talk about. The record of a vital impression done with unflinching accuracy, but under the guidance of intense mental activity is a very different thing from a drawing done with the cold, mechanical accuracy of a machine. The one will instantly grip the attention and give one a vivid sensation in a way that no mechanically accurate drawing could do, and in a way that possibly the sight of the real person would not always do. We see numbers of faces during a day, but only a few with the vividness of which I am speaking. How many faces in a crowd are passed indifferently—there is no vitality in the impression they make on our mind; but suddenly a face will rivet our attention, and although it is gone in a flash, the memory of the impression will remain for some time.

The best of Holbein's portrait drawings give one the impression of having been seen in one of these flashes and rivet the attention in consequence. Drawings done under this mental stimulus present subtle differences from drawings done with cold accuracy. The drawing of the Lady Audley, here reproduced, bears evidence of some of this subtle variation on what are called the facts, in the left eye of the sitter. It will be noticed that the pupil of this eye is larger than the other. Now I do not suppose that as a matter of mechanical accuracy this was so,

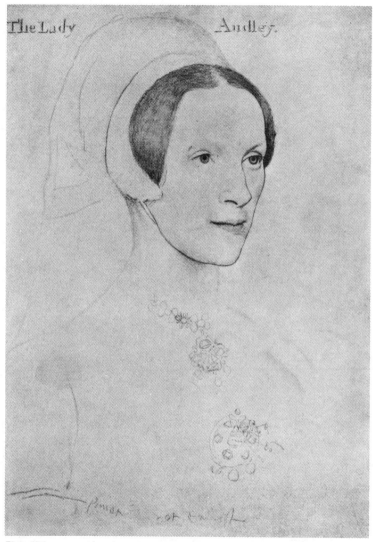

The Lady Audley.

THE LADY AUDLEY. HOLBEIN (WINDSOR)

Note the different sizes of pupils in the eyes, and see letterpress on the opposite page.

but the impression of the eyes seen as part of a vivid impression of the head is seldom that they are the same size. Holbein had in the first instance in this very carefully wrought drawing made them so, but when at the last he was vitalising the impression, "pulling it together" as artists say, he has deliberately put a line outside the original one, making this pupil larger. This is not at all clearly seen in the reproduction, but **is distinctly visible in the original.** And to my thinking it was done at the dictates of the vivid mental impression he wished his drawing to convey. Few can fail to be struck in turning over this wonderful series of drawings by the vividness of their portraiture, and the vividness is due to their being severely accurate to the vital impression on the mind of Holbein, not merely to the facts coldly observed.

Another point of view is that of seeking in the face a symbol of the person within, and selecting those things about a head that express this. As has already been said, the habitual attitude of mind has in the course of time a marked influence on the form of the face, and in fact of the whole body, so that—to those who can see—the man or woman is a visible symbol of themselves. But this is by no means apparent to all.

The striking example of this class is the splendid series of portraits by the late G. F. Watts. Looking at these heads one is made conscious of the people in a fuller, deeper sense than if they were before one in the flesh. For Watts sought to discover the person in their appearance and to paint a picture that should be a living symbol of them. He took pains to find out all he could about the mind of

PORTRAIT DRAWING

his sitters before he painted them, and sought in
the appearance the expression of this inner man.
So that whereas with Holbein it was the vivid
presentation of the impression as one might see a
head that struck one in a crowd, with Watts it is
the spirit one is first conscious of. The thunders
of war appear in the powerful head of Lord
Lawrence, the music of poetry in the head of
Swinburne, and the dry atmosphere of the higher
regions of thought in the John Stuart Mill, &c.

In the National Portrait Gallery there are two
paintings of the poet Robert Browning, one by
Rudolph Lehmann and one by Watts. Now the
former portrait is probably much more "like" the
poet as the people who met him casually saw him.
But Watts's portrait is like the man who wrote the
poetry, and Lehmann's is not. Browning was a
particularly difficult subject in this respect, in that
to a casual observer there was much more about
his external appearance to suggest a prosperous man
of business, than the fiery zeal of the poet.

These portraits by Watts will repay the closest
study by the student of portraiture. They are full
of that wise selection by a great mind that lifts
such work above the triviality of the commonplace
to the level of great imaginative painting.

Another point of view is that of treating the
sitter as part of a symphony of form and colour,
and subordinating everything to this artistic consideration. This is very fashionable at the present
time, and much beautiful work is being done with
this motive. And with many ladies who would not,
I hope, object to one's saying that their principal
characteristic was the charm of their appearance

250

this point of view offers, perhaps, one of the best opportunities of a successful painting. A pose is selected that makes a good design of line and colour —a good pattern—and the character of the sitter is not allowed to obtrude or mar the symmetry of the whole considered as a beautiful panel. The portraits of J. M'Neill Whistler are examples of this treatment, a point of view that has very largely influenced modern portrait painting in England.

Then there is the official portrait in which the dignity of an office held by the sitter, of which occasion the portrait is a memorial, has to be considered. The more intimate interest in the personal character of the sitter is here subordinated to the interest of his public character and attitude of mind towards his office. Thus it happens that much more decorative pageantry symbolic of these things is permissible in this kind of portraiture than in that of plain Mr. Smith; a greater stateliness of design as befitting official occasions.

It is not contended that this forms anything like a complete list of the numerous aspects from which a portrait can be considered, but they are some of the more extreme of those prevalent at the present time. Neither is it contended that they are incompatible with each other: the qualities of two or more of these points of view are often found in the same work. And it is not inconceivable that a single portrait might contain all and be a striking lifelike presentment, a faithful catalogue of all the features, a symbol of the person and a symphony of form and colour. But the chances are against such a composite affair being a success. One or other quality will dominate in a successful work; and it is not advisable to try and combine too many different points of view as, in the confusion of ideas, directness of expression is lost. But no good portrait is without some of the qualities of all these points of view, whichever may dominate the artist's intention.

The camera, and more particularly the instantaneous camera, has habituated people to expect in a portrait a momentary expression, and of these momentary expressions the faint smile, as we all know, is an easy first in the matter of popularity. It is no uncommon thing for the painter to be asked in the early stages of his work when he is going to put in the smile, it never being questioned that this is the artist's aim in the matter of expression.

Expression.

The giving of lifelike expression to a painting is not so simple a matter as it might appear to be. Could one set the real person behind the frame and suddenly fix them for ever with one of those passing expressions on their faces, however natural it might have been at the moment, fixed for ever it is terrible, and most unlifelike. As we have already said, a few lines scribbled on a piece of paper by a consummate artist would give a greater sense of life than this fixed actuality. It is not ultimately by the pursuit of the actual realisation that expression and life are conveyed in a portrait. Every face has expression of a far more interesting and enduring kind than these momentary disturbances of its form occasioned by laughter or some passing thought, &c. And it must never be forgotten that a portrait is a panel painted to remain for centuries without movement. So that a large amount of the quality of repose must enter into its composition. Portraits in which this has not been borne in mind, however entertaining at a picture exhibition, where they are seen for a few moments only, pall on one if constantly seen, and are finally very irritating.

But the real expression in a head is something more enduring than these passing movements: one that belongs to the forms of a head, and the marks left on that form by the life and character of the person. This is of far more interest than those passing expressions, the results of the contraction of certain muscles under the skin, the effect of which is very similar in most people. It is for the portrait painter to find this more enduring expression and give it noble expression in his work.

It is a common idea among sitters that if they are painted in modern clothes the picture will look old-fashioned in a few years. If the sitter's appearance were fixed upon the canvas exactly as they stood before the artist in his studio, without any selection on the part of the painter, this might be the result, and *is* the result in the case of painters who have no higher aim than this. **Treatment of Clothes.**

But there are qualities in dress that do not belong exclusively to the particular period of their fashion. Qualities that are the same in all ages. And when these are insisted upon, and the frivolities of the moment in dress not troubled about so much, the portrait has a permanent quality, and will never in consequence look old-fashioned in the offensive way that is usually meant. In the first place, the drapery and stuffs of which clothes are made follow laws in the manner in which they fold and drape over the figure, that are the same in all times. If the expression of the figure through the draperies is sought by the painter, a permanent quality will be given in his work, whatever fantastic shapes the cut of the garments may assume.

And further, the artist does not take whatever comes to hand in the appearance of his sitter, but works to a thought-out arrangement of colour and form, to a design. This he selects from the moving and varied appearance of his sitter, trying one thing after another, until he sees a suggestive arrangement, from the impression of which he makes his design. It is true that the extremes of fashion do not always lend themselves so readily as more reasonable modes to the making of a good pictorial pattern. But this is not always so, some extreme fashions giving opportunities of very piquant and interesting portrait designs. So that, however extreme the fashion, if the artist is able to select some aspect of it that will result in a good arrangement for his portrait, the work will never have the offensive old-fashioned look. The principles governing good designs are the same in all times; and if material for such arrangement has been discovered in the most modish of fashions, it has been lifted into a sphere where nothing is ever out of date.

It is only when the painter is concerned with the trivial details of fashion for their own sake, for the making his picture look like the real thing, and has not been concerned with transmuting the appearance of fashionable clothes by selection into the permanent realms of form and colour design, that his work will justify one in saying that it will look stale in a few years.

PORTRAIT DRAWING

The fashion of dressing sitters in meaningless, so-called classical draperies is a feeble one, and usually argues a lack of capacity for selecting a good arrangement from the clothes of the period in the artist who adopts it. Modern women's clothes are full of suggestions for new arrangements and designs quite as good as anything that has been done in the past. The range of subtle colours and varieties of texture in materials is amazing, and the subtlety of invention displayed in some of the designs for costumes leads one to wonder whether there is not something in the remark attributed to an eminent sculptor that "designing ladies' fashions is one of the few arts that is thoroughly vital to-day."

XVIII

THE VISUAL MEMORY

THE memory is the great storehouse of artistic material, the treasures of which the artist may know little about until a chance association lights up some of its dark recesses. From early years the mind of the young artist has been storing up impressions in these mysterious chambers, collected from nature's aspects, works of art, and anything that comes within the field of vision. It is from this store that the imagination draws its material, however fantastic and remote from natural appearances the forms it may assume.

How much our memory of pictures colours the impressions of nature we receive is probably not suspected by us, but who could say how a scene would appear to him, had he never looked at a picture? So sensitive is the vision to the influence of memory that, after seeing the pictures of some painter whose work has deeply impressed us, we are apt, while the memory of it is still fresh in our minds, to see things as he would paint them. On different occasions after leaving the National Gallery I can remember having seen Trafalgar Square as Paolo Veronese, Turner, or whatever painter may have impressed me in the Gallery, would have painted it, the memory of their work colouring the impression the scene produced.

THE VISUAL MEMORY

But, putting aside the memory of pictures, let us consider the place of direct visual memory from nature in our work, pictures being indirect or second-hand impressions.

We have seen in an earlier chapter how certain painters in the nineteenth century, feeling how **very** second-hand and far removed from nature painting had become, started a movement to discard studio traditions and study nature with a single eye, taking their pictures out of doors, and endeavouring to wrest nature's secrets from her on the spot. The Pre-Raphaelite movement in England and the Impressionist movement in France were the results of this impulse. And it is interesting, by the way, to contrast the different manner in which this desire for more truth to nature affected the French and English temperaments. The intense individualism of the English sought out every detail, every leaf and flower for itself, painting them with a passion and intensity that made their painting a vivid medium for the expression of poetic ideas; while the more synthetic mind of the Frenchman approached this search for visual truth from the opposite point of view of the whole effect, finding in the large, generalised impression a new world of beauty. And his more logical mind led him to inquire into the nature of light, and so to invent a technique founded on scientific principles.

But now the first blush of freshness has worn off the new movement, painters have begun to see that if anything but very ordinary effects are to be attempted, this painting on the spot must give place to more reliance on the memory.

Memory has this great advantage over direct vision: it retains more vividly the essential things,

257

and has a habit of losing what is unessential to the pictorial impression.

But what is the essential in a painting? What is it makes one want to paint at all? Ah! Here we approach very debatable and shadowy ground, and we can do little but ask questions, the answer to which will vary with each individual temperament. What is it that these rays of light striking our retina convey to our brain, and from our brain to whatever is ourselves, in the seat of consciousness above this? What is this mysterious correspondence set up between something within and something without, that at times sends such a clamour of harmony through our whole being? Why do certain combinations of sound in music and of form and colour in art affect us so profoundly? What are the laws governing harmony in the universe, and whence do they come? It is hardly trees and sky, earth, or flesh and blood, as such, that interest the artist; but rather that through these things in memorable moments he is permitted a consciousness of deeper things, and impelled to seek utterance for what is moving him. It is the record of these rare moments in which one apprehends truth in things seen that the artist wishes to convey to others. But these moments, these flashes of inspiration which are at the inception of every vital picture, occur but seldom. What the painter has to do is to fix them vividly in his memory, to snapshot them, as it were, so that they may stand by him during the toilsome procedure of the painting, and guide the work.

This initial inspiration, this initial flash in the mind, need not be the result of a scene in nature, but may of course be purely the work of the imagination; a composition, the sense of which flashes across the mind. But in either case the difficulty is to preserve vividly the sensation of this original artistic impulse. And in the case of its having been derived from nature direct, as is so often the case in modern art, the system of painting continually on the spot is apt to lose touch with it very soon. For in the continual observation of anything you have set your easel before day after day, comes a series of impressions, more and more commonplace, as the eye becomes more and more familiar with the details of the subject. And ere long the original emotion that was the reason of the whole work is lost sight of, and one of those pictures or drawings giving a catalogue of tired objects more or less ingeniously arranged (that we all know so well) is the result—work utterly lacking in the freshness and charm of true inspiration. For however commonplace the subject seen by the artist in one of his "flashes," it is clothed in a newness and surprise that charm us, be it only an orange on a plate.

Now a picture is a thing of paint upon a flat surface, and a drawing is a matter of certain marks upon a paper, and how to translate the intricacies of a visual or imagined impression to the prosaic terms of masses of coloured pigment or lines and tones is the business with which our technique is concerned. The ease, therefore, with which a painter will be able to remember an impression in a form from which he can work, will depend upon his power to analyse vision in this technical sense. The more one knows about what may be called the anatomy of picture-making—how certain forms produce cer-

THE VISUAL MEMORY

tain effects, certain colours or arrangements other effects, &c.—the easier will it be for him to carry away a visual memory of his subject that will stand by him during the long hours of his labours at the picture. The more he knows of the expressive powers of lines and tones, the more easily will he be able to observe the vital things in nature that convey the impression he wishes to memorise.

It is not enough to drink in and remember the emotional side of the matter, although this must be done fully, but if a memory of the subject is to be carried away that will be of service technically, the scene must be committed to memory in terms of whatever medium you intend to employ for reproducing it—in the case of a drawing, lines and tones. And the impression will have to be analysed into these terms as if you were actually drawing the scene on some imagined piece of paper in your mind. The faculty of doing this is not to be acquired all at once, but it is amazing of how much development it is capable. Just as the faculty of committing to memory long poems or plays can be developed, so can the faculty of remembering visual things. This subject has received little attention in art schools until just recently. But it is not yet so systematically done as it might be. Monsieur Lecoq de Boisbaudran in France experimented with pupils in this memory training, beginning with very simple things like the outline of a nose, and going on to more complex subjects by easy stages, with the most surprising results. And there is no doubt that a great deal more can and should be done in this direction than is at present attempted. What students should do is to form a habit of making every day in their sketch-book

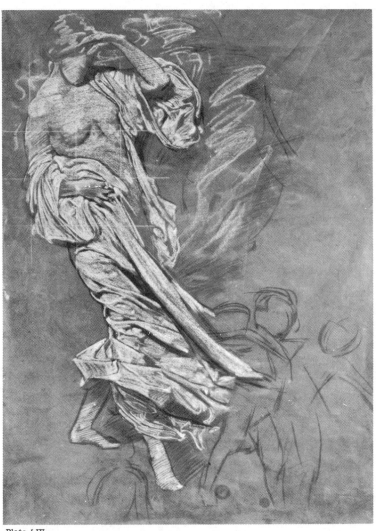

Plate LIV

STUDY ON BROWN PAPER IN BLACK AND WHITE CONTÉ CHALK

Illustrating a simple method of studying drapery forms.

a drawing of something they have seen that has interested them, and that they have made some attempt at memorising. Don't be discouraged if the results are poor and disappointing at first—you will find that by persevering your power of memory will develop and be of the greatest service to you in your after work. Try particularly to remember the spirit of the subject, and in this memory-drawing some scribbling and fumbling will necessarily have to be done. You cannot expect to be able to draw definitely and clearly from memory, at least at first, although your aim should always be to draw as frankly and clearly as you can.

Let us assume that you have found a subject that moves you and that, being too fleeting to draw on the spot, you wish to commit to memory. Drink a full enjoyment of it, let it soak in, for the recollection of this will be of the utmost use to you afterwards in guiding your memory-drawing. This mental impression is not difficult to recall; it is the visual impression in terms of line and tone that is difficult to remember. Having experienced your full enjoyment of the artistic matter in the subject, you must next consider it from the material side, as a flat, visual impression, as this is the only form in which it can be expressed on a flat sheet of paper. Note the proportions of the main lines, their shapes and disposition, as if you were drawing it, in fact do the whole drawing in your mind, memorising the forms and proportions of the different parts, and fix it in your memory to the smallest detail.

If only the emotional side of the matter has been remembered, when you come to draw it you will be hopelessly at sea, as it is remarkable how

THE VISUAL MEMORY

little the memory retains of the appearance of things constantly seen, if no attempt has been made to memorise their visual appearance.

The true artist, even when working from nature, works from memory very largely. That is to say, he works to a scheme in tune to some emotional enthusiasm with which the subject has inspired him in the first instance. Nature is always changing, but he does not change the intention of his picture. He always keeps before him the initial impression he sets out to paint, and only selects from nature those things that play up to it. He is a feeble artist, who copies individually the parts of a scene with whatever effect they may have at the moment he is doing them, and then expects the sum total to make a picture. If circumstances permit, it is always as well to make in the first instance a rapid sketch that shall, whatever it may lack, at least contain the main disposition of the masses and lines of your composition seen under the influence of the enthusiasm that has inspired the work. This will be of great value afterwards in freshening your memory when in the labour of the work the original impulse gets dulled. It is seldom that the vitality of this first sketch is surpassed by the completed work, and often, alas! it is far from equalled.

In portrait painting and drawing the memory must be used also. A sitter varies very much in the impression he gives on different days, and the artist must in the early sittings, when his mind is fresh, select the aspect he means to paint and afterwards work largely to the memory of this.

Always work to a scheme on which you have decided, and do not flounder on in the hope of some-

262

thing turning up as you go along. Your faculties are never so active and prone to see something interesting and fine as when the subject is first presented to them. This is the time to decide your scheme; this is the time to take your fill of the impression you mean to convey. This is the time to learn your subject thoroughly and decide on what you wish the picture to be. And having decided this, work straight on, using nature to support your original impression, but don't be led off by a fresh scheme because others strike you as you go along. New schemes will do so, of course, and every new one has a knack of looking better than your original one. But it is not often that this is so; the fact that they are new makes them appear to greater advantage than the original scheme to which you have got accustomed. So that it is not only in working away from nature that the memory is of use, but actually when working directly in front of nature.

To sum up, there are two aspects of a subject, the one luxuriating in the sensuous pleasure of it, with all of spiritual significance it may consciously or unconsciously convey, and the other concerned with the lines, tones, shapes, &c., and their rhythmic ordering, by means of which it is to be expressed—the matter and manner, as they may be called. And, if the artist's memory is to be of use to him in his work, both these aspects must be memorised, and of the two the second will need the most attention. But although there are these two aspects of the subject, and each must receive separate attention when memorising it, they are in reality only two aspects of the same thing, which in the act of painting or drawing must be united if a work of art is to result. When a subject first flashes upon an artist he delights in it as a painted or drawn thing, and feels instinctively the treatment it will require. In good draughtsmanship the thing felt will guide and govern everything, every touch will be instinct with the thrill of that first impression. The craftsman mind, so laboriously built up, should by now have become an instinct, a second nature, at the direction of a higher consciousness. At such times the right strokes, the right tones come naturally and go on the right place, the artist being only conscious of a fierce joy and a feeling that things are in tune and going well for once. It is the thirst for this glorious enthusiasm, this fusing of matter and manner, this act of giving the spirit within outward form, that spurs the artist on at all times, and it is this that is the wonderful thing about art.

XIX

PROCEDURE

In commencing a drawing, don't, as so many students do, start carelessly floundering about with your chalk or charcoal in the hope that something will turn up. It is seldom if ever that an artist puts on paper anything better than he has in his mind before he starts, and usually it is not nearly so good.

Don't spoil the beauty of a clean sheet of paper by a lot of scribble. Try and see in your mind's eye the drawing you mean to do, and then try and make your hand realise it, making the paper more beautiful by every touch you give instead of spoiling it by a slovenly manner of procedure.

To know what you want to do and then to do it is the secret of good style and technique. This sounds very commonplace, but it is surprising how few students make it their aim. You may often observe them come in, pin a piece of paper on their board, draw a line down the middle, make a few measurements, and start blocking in the drawing without having given the subject to be drawn a thought, as if it were all there done before them, and only needed copying, as a clerk would copy a letter already drafted for him.

Now, nothing is being said against the practice of drawing guide lines and taking measurements and blocking in your work. This is very necessary in academic work, if rather fettering to expressive drawing; but even in the most academic drawing the artistic intelligence must be used, although that is not the kind of drawing this chapter is particularly referring to.

Look well at the model first; try and be moved by something in the form that you feel is fine or interesting, and try and see in your mind's eye what sort of drawing you mean to do before touching your paper. In school studies, be always unflinchingly honest to the impression the model gives you, but dismiss the camera idea of truth from your mind. Instead of converting yourself into a mechanical instrument for the copying of what is before you, let your drawing be an expression of truth perceived intelligently.

Be extremely careful about the first few strokes you put on your paper: the quality of your drawing is often decided in these early stages. If they are vital and expressive, you have started along lines you can develop, and have some hope of doing a good drawing. If they are feeble and poor, the chances are greatly against your getting anything good built upon them. If your start has been bad, pull yourself together, turn your paper over and start afresh, trying to seize upon the big, significant lines and swings in your subject at once. Remember it is much easier to put down a statement correctly than to correct a wrong one; so out with the whole part if you are convinced it is wrong. Train yourself to make direct, accurate statements in your drawings, and don't waste time trying to manœuvre a bad drawing into a good one. Stop as soon as you feel you have gone wrong and correct the work in its early stages, instead of rushing on upon a wrong foundation in the vague hope that it will all come right in the end. When out walking, if you find you have taken a wrong road you do not, if you are wise, go on in the hope that the wrong way will lead to the right one, but you turn round and go back to the point at which you left the right road. It is very much the same in drawing and painting. As soon as you become aware that you have got upon the wrong track, stop and rub out your work until an earlier stage that was right is reached, and start along again from this point. As your eye gets trained you will more quickly perceive when you have done a wrong stroke, and be able to correct it before having gone very far along the wrong road.

Do not work too long without giving your eye a little rest; a few moments will be quite sufficient. If things won't come, stop a minute; the eye often gets fatigued very quickly and refuses to see truly, but soon revives if rested a minute or two.

Do not go labouring at a drawing when your mind is not working; you are not doing any good, and probably are spoiling any good you have already done. Pull yourself together, and ask what it is you are trying to express, and having got this idea firmly fixed in your mind, go for your drawing with the determination that it shall express it.

All this will sound very trite to students of any mettle, but there are large numbers who waste no end of time working in a purely mechanical, lifeless way, and with their minds anywhere but concentrated upon the work before them. And if the mind is not working, the work of the hand will be of no account. My own experience is that one has constantly to be making fresh effort during the procedure of the work. The mind is apt to tire and needs rousing continually, otherwise the work will lack the impulse that shall make it vital. Particularly is this so in the final stages of a drawing or painting, when, in adding details and small refinements, it is doubly necessary for the mind to be on fire with the initial impulse, or the main qualities will be obscured and the result enfeebled by these smaller matters.

Do not rub out, if you can possibly help it, in drawings that aim at artistic expression. In academic work, where artistic feeling is less important than the discipline of your faculties, you may, of course, do so, but even here as little as possible. In beautiful drawing of any facility it has a weakening effect, somewhat similar to that produced by a person stopping in the middle of a witty or brilliant remark to correct a word. If a wrong line is made, it is left in by the side of the right one in the drawing of many of the masters. But the great aim of the draughtsman should be to train himself to draw cleanly and fearlessly, hand and eye going together. But this state of things cannot be expected for some time.

Let painstaking accuracy be your aim for a long time. When your eye and hand have acquired the power of seeing and expressing on paper with some degree of accuracy what you see, you will find facility and quickness of execution will come of their own accord. In drawing of any expressive power this quickness and facility of execution are absolutely essential. The waves of emotion, under the influence of which the eye really sees in any artistic sense, do not last long enough to allow of a slow, painstaking manner of execution. There must be no hitch in the machinery of expression when the consciousness is alive to the realisation of something fine. Fluency of hand and accuracy of eye are the things your academic studies should have taught you, and these powers will be needed if you are to catch the expression of any of the finer things in form that constitute good drawing.

Try and express yourself in as simple, not as complicated a manner as possible. Let every touch mean something, and if you don't see what to do next, don't fill in the time by meaningless shading and scribbling until you do. Wait awhile, rest your eye by looking away, and then see if you cannot find something right that needs doing.

Before beginning a drawing, it is not a bad idea to study carefully the work of some master draughtsman whom the subject to be drawn may suggest. If you do this carefully and thoughtfully, and take in a full enjoyment, your eye will unconsciously be led to see in nature some of the qualities of the master's work. And you will see the subject to be drawn as a much finer thing than would have been the case had you come to it with your eye unprepared in any way. Reproductions are now so good and cheap that the best drawings in the world can be had for a few pence, and every student should begin collecting reproductions of the things that interest him.

This is not the place to discuss questions of health, but perhaps it will not be thought grandmotherly to mention the extreme importance of nervous vitality in a fine draughtsman, and how his life should be ordered on such healthy lines that he has at his command the maximum instead of the

PROCEDURE

minimum of this faculty. After a certain point, it is a question of vitality how far an artist is likely to go in art. Given two men of equal ability, the one leading a careless life and the other a healthy one, as far as a healthy one is possible to such a supersensitive creature as an artist, there can be no doubt as to the result. It is because there is still a lingering idea in the minds of many that an artist must lead a dissipated life or he is not really an artist, that one feels it necessary to mention the subject. This idea has evidently arisen from the inability of the average person to associate an unconventional mode of life with anything but riotous dissipation. A conventional life is not the only wholesome form of existence, and is certainly a most unwholesome and deadening form to the artist; and neither is a dissipated life the only unconventional one open to him. It is as well that the young student should know this, and be led early to take great care of that most valuable of studio properties, vigorous health.

XX

MATERIALS

THE materials in which the artist works are of the greatest importance in determining what qualities in the infinite complexity of nature he selects for expression. And the good draughtsman will find out the particular ones that belong to whatever medium he selects for his drawing, and be careful never to attempt more than it is capable of doing. Every material he works with possesses certain vital qualities peculiar to itself, and it is his business to find out what these are and use them to the advantage of his drawing. When one is working with, say, pen and ink, the necessity for selecting only certain things is obvious enough. But when a medium with the vast capacity of oil paint is being used, the principle of its governing the nature of the work is more often lost sight of. So near can oil paint approach an actual illusion of natural appearances, that much misdirected effort has been wasted on this object, all enjoyment of the medium being subordinated to a meretricious attempt to deceive the eye. And I believe a popular idea of the art of painting is that it exists chiefly to produce this deception. No vital expression of nature can be achieved without the aid of the particular vitality possessed by the medium with which one is working. If this is lost sight of and the eye is

271

MATERIALS

tricked into thinking that it is looking at real
nature, it is not a fine picture. Art is not a substitute for nature, but an expression of feeling
produced in the consciousness of the artist, and
intimately associated with the material through
which it is expressed in his work. Inspired, it may
be, in the first instance, by something seen, and
expressed by him in painted symbols as true to
nature as he can make them while keeping in
tune to the emotional idea that prompted the work;
but never regarded by the fine artist as anything
but painted symbols nevertheless. Never for one
moment does he intend you to forget that it is a
painted picture you are looking at, however naturalistic the treatment his theme may demand.

In the earlier history of art it was not so necessary to insist on the limitations imposed by different
mediums. With their more limited knowledge of
the phenomena of vision, the early masters had
not the same opportunities of going astray in this
respect. But now that the whole field of vision
has been discovered, and that the subtlest effects
of light and atmosphere are capable of being
represented, it has become necessary to decide how
far complete accuracy of representation will help
the particular impression you may intend your
picture or drawing to create. The danger is that
in producing a complete illusion of representation,
the particular vitality of your medium, with all the
expressive power it is capable of yielding, may be
lost.

Perhaps the chief difference between the great
masters of the past and many modern painters is
the neglect of this principle. **They represented nature
in terms of whatever medium they worked in, and**

never overstepped this limitation. Modern artists, particularly in the nineteenth century, often attempted to copy nature, the medium being subordinated to the attempt to make it look like the real thing. In the same way, the drawings of the great masters were drawings. They did not attempt anything with a point that a point was not capable of expressing. The drawings of many modern artists are full of attempts to express tone and colour effects, things entirely outside the true province of drawing. The small but infinitely important part of nature that pure drawing is capable of conveying has been neglected, and line work, until recently, went out of fashion in our schools.

There is something that makes for power in the limitations your materials impose. Many artists whose work in some of the more limited mediums is fine, are utterly feeble when they attempt one with so few restrictions as oil paint. If students could only be induced to impose more restraint upon themselves when they attempt so difficult a medium as paint, it would be greatly to the advantage of their work. Beginning first with monochrome in three tones, as explained in a former chapter, they might then take for figure work ivory black and Venetian red. It is surprising what an amount of colour effect can be got with this simple means, and how much can be learned about the relative positions of the warm and cold colours. Do not attempt the full range of tone at first, but keep the darks rather lighter and the lights darker than nature. Attempt the full scale of tone only when you have acquired sufficient experience with the simpler range, and gradually add more colours as you learn to master a few. But restraints are not so fashionable just now as unbridled licence. Art students start in with a palette full of the most amazing colours, producing results that it were better not to discuss. It is a wise man who can discover his limitations and select a medium the capacities of which just tally with his own. To discover this, it is advisable to try many, and below is a short description of the chief ones used by the draughtsman. But very little can be said about them, and very little idea of their capacities given in a written description; they must be handled by the student, and are no doubt capable of many more qualities than have yet been got out of them.

This well-known medium is one of the most beautiful for pure line work, and its use is an excellent training to the eye and hand in **Lead Pencil.** precision of observation. Perhaps this is why it has not been so popular in our art schools recently, where the charms of severe discipline are not so much in favour as they should be. It is the first medium we are given to draw with, as the handiest and most convenient is unrivalled for sketch-book use.

It is made in a large variety of degrees, from the hardest and greyest to the softest and blackest, and is too well known to need much description. It does not need fixing.

For pure line drawing nothing equals it, except silver point, and great draughtsmen, like Ingres, have always loved it. It does not lend itself so readily to any form of mass drawing. Although it is sometimes used for this purpose, the offensive shine that occurs if dark masses are introduced is against its use in any but very lightly shaded work.

274

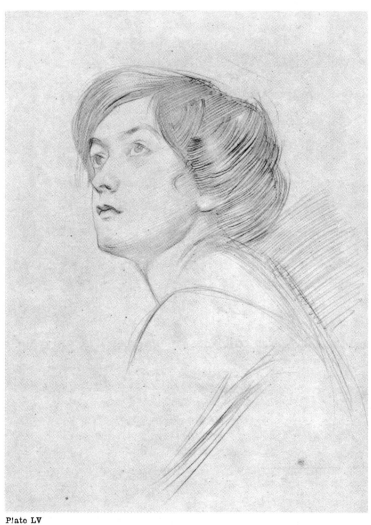

FROM A SILVER-POINT DRAWING

Its charm is the extreme delicacy of its grey-black lines.

Similar to lead pencil, and of even greater delicacy, is silver-point drawing. A more ancient method, it consists in drawing with a silver point on paper the surface of which has been treated with a faint wash of Chinese white. Without this wash the point will not make a mark. Silver and Gold Point.

For extreme delicacy and purity of line no medium can surpass this method. And for the expression of a beautiful line, such as a profile, nothing could be more suitable than a silver point. As a training to the eye and hand also, it is of great value, as no rubbing out of any sort is possible, and eye and hand must work together with great exactness. The discipline of silver-point drawing is to be recommended as a corrective to the picturesque vagaries of charcoal work.

A gold point, giving a warmer line, can also be used in the same way as a silver point, the paper first having been treated with Chinese white.

Two extreme points of view from which the rendering of form can be approached have been explained, and it has been suggested that students should study them both separately in the first instance, as they each have different things to teach. Of the mediums that are best suited to a drawing combining both points of view, the first and most popular is charcoal. Charcoal.

Charcoal is made in many different degrees of hardness and softness, the harder varieties being capable of quite a fine point. A chisel-shaped point is the most convenient, as it does not wear away so quickly. And if the broad side of the chisel point is used when a dark mass is wanted, the edge can constantly be kept sharp. With this edge a very fine line can be drawn.

Charcoal works with great freedom, and answers readily when forceful expression is wanted. It is much more like painting than any other form of drawing, a wide piece of charcoal making a wide mark similar to a brush. The delicacy and lightness with which it has to be handled is also much more like the handling of a brush than any other point drawing. When rubbed with the finger, it sheds a soft grey tone over the whole work. With a piece of bread pressed by thumb and finger into a pellet, high lights can be taken out with the precision of white chalk; or rubber can be used. Bread is, perhaps, the best, as it does not smudge the charcoal but lifts it readily off. When rubbed with the finger, the darks, of course, are lightened in tone. It is therefore useful to draw in the general proportions roughly and rub down in this way. You then have a middle tone over the work, with the rough drawing showing through. Now proceed carefully to draw your lights with bread or rubber, and your shadows with charcoal, in much the same manner as you did in the monochrome exercises already described.

All the preliminary setting out of work on canvas is usually done with charcoal, which must of course be fixed with a spray diffuser. For large work, such as a full-length portrait, sticks of charcoal nearly an inch in diameter are made, and a long swinging line can be done without their breaking.

For drawings that are intended as things of beauty in themselves, and are not merely done as a preparatory study for a painting, charcoal is perhaps not so refined a medium as a great many others. It is too much like painting to have the particular beauties of a drawing, and too much like drawing to have the qualities of a painting. However, some beautiful things have been done with it.

It is useful in doing studies where much finish is desired, to fix the work slightly when drawn in and carried some way on. You can work over this again without continually rubbing out with your hand what you have already drawn. If necessary you can rub out with a hard piece of rubber any parts that have already been fixed, or even scrape with a pen-knife. But this is not advisable for anything but an academic study, or working drawings, as it spoils the beauty and freshness of charcoal work. Studies done in this medium can also be finished with Conté chalk.

There is also an artificial charcoal put up in sticks, that is very good for refined work. It has some advantages over natural charcoal, in that there are no knots and it works much more evenly. The best natural charcoal I have used is the French make known as "Fusain Rouget." It is made in three degrees, No. 3 being the softest, and, of course, the blackest. But some of the ordinary Venetian and vine charcoals sold are good. But don't get the cheaper varieties: a bad piece of charcoal is worse than useless.

Charcoal is fixed by means of a solution of white shellac dissolved in spirits of wine, blown on with a spray diffuser. This is sold by the artists' colourmen, or can be easily made by the student. It lightly deposits a thin film of shellac over the work, acting as a varnish and preventing its rubbing off

MATERIALS

Charcoal is not on the whole the medium an artist with a pure love of form selects, but rather that of the painter, who uses it when his brushes and paints are not handy.

A delightful medium that can be used for either pure line work or a mixed method of drawing, is
Red Chalk   red chalk. This natural red earth is one
(San-   of the most ancient materials for drawing.
guine).   It is a lovely Venetian red in colour, and works well in the natural state, if you get a good piece. It is sold by the ounce, and it is advisable to try the pieces as they vary very much, some being hard and gritty and some more soft and smooth. It is also made by Messrs. Conté of Paris in sticks artificially prepared. These work well and are never gritty, but are not so hard as the natural chalk, and consequently wear away quickly and do not make fine lines as well.

Red chalk when rubbed with the finger or a rag spreads evenly on paper, and produces a middle tone on which lights can be drawn with rubber or bread. Sticks of hard, pointed rubber are everywhere sold, which, cut in a chisel shape, work beautifully on red chalk drawings. Bread is also excellent when a softer light is wanted. You can continually correct and redraw in this medium by rubbing it with the finger or a rag, thus destroying the lights and shadows to a large extent, and enabling you to draw them again more carefully. For this reason red chalk is greatly to be recommended for making drawings for a picture where much fumbling may be necessary before you find what you want. Unlike charcoal, it hardly needs fixing, and much more intimate study of the forms can be got into it.

MATERIALS

Most of the drawings by the author reproduced in this book are done in this medium. For drawings intended to have a separate existence it is one of the prettiest mediums. In fact, this is the danger to the student while studying : your drawing looks so much at its best that you are apt to be satisfied too soon. But for portrait drawings there is no medium to equal it.

Additional quality of dark is occasionally got by mixing a little of this red chalk in a powdered state with water and a very little gum-arabic. This can be applied with a sable brush as in water-colour painting, and makes a rich velvety dark.

It is necessary to select your paper with some care. The ordinary paper has too much size on it. This is picked up by the chalk, and will prevent its marking. A paper with little size is best, or old paper where the size has perished. I find an O.W. paper, made for printing etchings, as good as any for ordinary work. It is not perfect, but works very well. What one wants is the smoothest paper without a faced and hot-pressed surface, and it is difficult to find.

Occasionally black chalk is used with the red to add strength to it. And some draughtsmen use it with the red in such a manner as to produce almost a full colour effect.

Holbein, who used this medium largely, tinted the paper in most of his portrait drawings, varying the tint very much, and sometimes using zinc white as a wash, which enabled him to supplement his work with a silver-point line here and there, and also got over any difficulty the size in the paper might cause. His aim seems to have been to select the few essential things in a head and draw them with great finality and exactness. In many of the drawings the earlier work has been done with red or black chalk and then rubbed down and the drawing redone with either a brush and some of the chalk rubbed up with water and gum or a silver-point line of great purity, while in others he has tinted the paper with water-colour and rubbed this away to the white paper where he wanted a light, or Chinese white has been used for the same purpose.

Black Conté is a hard black chalk made in small sticks of different degrees. It is also put up in cedar pencils. Rather more gritty **Black Conté and** than red chalk or charcoal, it is a favourite **Carbon Pencil.** medium with some, and can be used with advantage to supplement charcoal when more precision and definition are wanted. It has very much the same quality of line and so does not show as a different medium. It can be rubbed like charcoal and red chalk and will spread a tone over the paper in very much the same way.

Carbon pencils are similar to Conté, but smoother in working and do not rub.

White chalk is sometimes used on toned paper to draw the lights, the paper serving as a half tone **White Chalk.** while the shadows and outlines are drawn in black or red. In this kind of drawing the chalk should never be allowed to come in contact with the black or red chalk of the shadows, the half tone of the paper should always be between them.

For rubbed work white pastel is better than the ordinary white chalk sold for drawing, as it is not so hard. A drawing done in this method with white pastel and red chalk is reproduced on

280

MATERIALS

page 43, and one with the hard white chalk, on page 260.

This is the method commonly used for making studies of drapery, the extreme rapidity with which the position of the lights and shadows can be expressed being of great importance when so unstable a subject as an arrangement of drapery is being drawn.

Lithography as a means of artistic reproduction has suffered much in public esteem by being put to all manner of inartistic trade uses. It is really one of the most wonderful means Litho-graphy. of reproducing an artist's actual work, the result being, in most cases, so identical with the original that, seen together, if the original drawing has been done on paper, it is almost impossible to distinguish any difference. And of course, as in etching, it is the prints that are really the originals. The initial work is only done as a means of producing these.

A drawing is made on a lithographic stone, that is, a piece of limestone that has been prepared with an almost perfectly smooth surface. The chalk used is a special kind of a greasy nature, and is made in several degrees of hardness and softness. No rubbing out is possible, but lines can be scratched out with a knife, or parts made lighter by white lines being drawn by a knife over them. A great range of freedom and variety is possible in these initial drawings on stone. The chalk can be rubbed up with a little water, like a cake of water-colour, and applied with a brush. And every variety of tone can be made with the side of the chalk.

Some care should be taken not to let the warm finger touch the stone, or it may make a greasy mark that will print.

281

MATERIALS

When this initial drawing is done to the artist's satisfaction, the most usual method is to treat the stone with a solution of gum-arabic and a little nitric acid. After this is dry, the gum is washed off as far as may be with water; some of the gum is left in the porous stone, but it is rejected where the greasy lines and tones of the drawing come. Prints may now be obtained by rolling up the stone with an inked roller. The ink is composed of a varnish of boiled linseed oil and any of the lithographic colours to be commercially obtained.

The ink does not take on the damp gummed stone, but only where the lithographic chalk has made a greasy mark, so that a perfect facsimile of the drawing on stone is obtained, when a sheet of paper is placed on the stone and the whole put through the press.

The medium deserves to be much more popular with draughtsmen than it is, as no more perfect means of reproduction could be devised.

The lithographic stone is rather a cumbersome thing to handle, but the initial drawing can be done on paper and afterwards transferred to the stone. In the case of line work the result is practically identical, but where much tone and playing about with the chalk is indulged in, the stone is much better. Lithographic papers of different textures are made for this purpose, but almost any paper will do, provided the drawing is done with the special lithographic chalk.

Pen and ink was a favourite means of making studies with many old masters, notably Rembrandt. Often heightening the effect with a wash, he conveyed marvellous suggestions with the simplest scribbles. But it is a difficult medium for the young

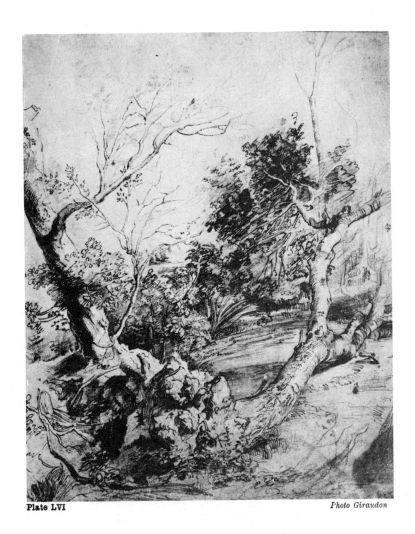

Study in Pen and Ink and Wash for Tree in "The Boar Hunt"
Rubens (Louvre)

student to hope to do much with in his studies, although for training the eye and hand to quick definite statement of impressions, there is much to be said for it. No hugging of half **Pen and Ink.** tones is possible, things must be reduced to a statement of clear darks—which would be a useful corrective to the tendency so many students have of seeing chiefly the half tones in their work.

The kind of pen used will depend on the kind of drawing you wish to make. In steel pens there are innumerable varieties, from the fine crow-quills to the thick "J" nibs. The natural crow-quill is a much more sympathetic tool than a steel pen, although not quite so certain in its line. But more play and variety is to be got out of it, and when a free pen drawing is wanted it is preferable.

Reed pens are also made, and are useful when thick lines are wanted. They sometimes have a steel spring underneath to hold the ink somewhat in the same manner as some fountain pens.

There is even a glass pen, consisting of a sharp-pointed cone of glass with grooves running down to the point. The ink is held in these grooves, and runs down and is deposited freely as the pen is used. A line of only one thickness can be drawn with it, but this can be drawn in any direction, an advantage over most other shapes.

Etching is a process of reproduction that consists in drawing with a steel point on a waxed plate of copper or zinc, and then putting it in a **Etching.** bath of diluted nitric acid to bite in the lines. The longer the plate remains in the bath the deeper and darker the lines become, so that variety in thickness is got by stopping out with a varnish the light lines when they are sufficiently strong, and letting the darker ones have a longer exposure to the acid.

Many wonderful and beautiful things have been done with this simple means. The printing consists in inking the plate all over and wiping off until only the lines retain any ink, when the plate is put in a press and an impression taken. Or some slight amount of ink may be left on the plate in certain places where a tint is wanted, and a little may be smudged out of the lines themselves to give them a softer quality. In fact there are no end of tricks a clever etching printer will adopt to give quality to his print.

The varieties of paper on the market at the service of the artist are innumerable, and nothing **Paper.** need be said here except that the texture of your paper will have a considerable influence on your drawing. But try every sort of paper so as to find what suits the particular things you want to express. I make a point of buying every new paper I see, and a new paper is often a stimulant to some new quality in drawing. Avoid the wood-pulp papers, as they turn dark after a time. Linen rag is the only safe substance for good papers, and artists now have in the O.W. papers a large series that they can rely on being made of linen only.

It is sometimes advisable, when you are not drawing a subject that demands a clear hard line, but where more sympathetic qualities are wanted, to have a wad of several sheets of paper under the one you are working on, pinned on the drawing-board. This gives you a more sympathetic surface to work upon and improves the quality of your work. In redrawing a study with which you are not quite satisfied, it is a good plan to use a thin paper, pinning it over the first study so that it can be seen through. One can by this means start as it were from the point where one left off. Good papers of this description are now on the market. I fancy they are called "bank-note" papers.

XXI

CONCLUSION

MECHANICAL invention, mechanical knowledge, and even a mechanical theory of the universe, have so influenced the average modern mind, that it has been thought necessary in the foregoing pages to speak out strongly against the idea of a mechanical standard of accuracy in artistic drawing. If there were such a standard, the photographic camera would serve our purpose well enough. And, considering how largely this idea is held, one need not be surprised that some painters use the camera; indeed, the wonder is that they do not use it more, as it gives in some perfection the mechanical accuracy which is all they seem to aim at in their work. There may be times when the camera can be of use to artists, but only to those who are thoroughly competent to do without it—to those who can look, as it were, through the photograph and draw from it with the same freedom and spontaneity with which they would draw from nature, thus avoiding its dead mechanical accuracy, which is a very difficult thing to do. But the camera is a convenience to be avoided by the student.

Now, although it has been necessary to insist strongly on the difference between phenomena mechanically recorded and the records of a living individual consciousness, I should be very sorry if

CONCLUSION

anything said should lead students to assume that a loose and careless manner of study was in any way advocated. The training of his eye and hand to the most painstaking accuracy of observation and record must be the student's aim for many years. The variations on mechanical accuracy in the work of a fine draughtsman need not be, and seldom are, conscious variations. Mechanical accuracy is a much easier thing to accomplish than accuracy to the subtle perceptions of the artist. And he who cannot draw with great precision the ordinary cold aspect of things cannot hope to catch the fleeting aspect of his finer vision.

Those artists who can only draw in some weird fashion remote from nature may produce work of some interest; but they are too much at the mercy of a natural trick of hand to hope to be more than interesting curiosities in art.

The object of your training in drawing should be to develop to the uttermost the observation of form and all that it signifies, and your powers of accurately portraying this on paper.

Unflinching honesty must be observed in all your studies. It is only then that the "you" in you will eventually find expression in your work. And it is this personal quality, this recording of the impressions of life as felt by a conscious individual that is the very essence of distinction in art.

The "seeking after originality" so much advocated would be better put "seeking for sincerity." Seeking for originality usually resolves itself into running after any peculiarity in manner that the changing fashions of a restless age may throw up. One of the most original men who ever lived did not trouble to invent the plots of more than three or four of his plays, but was content to take the hackneyed work of his time as the vehicle through which to pour the rich treasures of his vision of life. And wrote:

" What custom wills in all things do you do it."

Individual style will come to you naturally as you become more conscious of what it is you wish to express. There are two kinds of insincerity in style, the employment of a ready-made conventional manner that is not understood and that does not fit the matter; and the running after and laboriously seeking an original manner when no original matter exists. Good style depends on a clear idea of what it is you wish to do; it is the shortest means to the end aimed at, the most apt manner of conveying that personal "something" that is in all good work. "The style is the man," as Buffon says. The splendour and value of your style will depend on the splendour and value of the mental vision inspired in you, that you seek to convey; on the quality of the man, in other words. And this is not a matter where direct teaching can help you, but rests between your own consciousness and those higher powers that move it.

APPENDIX

IF you add a line of 5 inches to one of 8 inches you produce one 13 inches long, and if you proceed by always adding the last two you arrive at a series of lengths, 5, 8, 13, 21, 34, 55 inches, &c. Mr. William Schooling tells me that any two of these lines adjoining one another are practically in the same proportion to each other; that is to say, one 8 inches is 1·600 times the size of one 5 inches, and the 13-inch line is 1·625 the size of the 8-inch, and the 21-inch line being 1·615 times the 13-inch line, and so on. With the mathematician's love of accuracy, Mr. Schooling has worked out the exact proportion that should exist between a series of quantities for them to be in the same proportion to their neighbours, and in which any two added together would produce the next. There is only one proportion that will do this, and although very formidable, stated exactly, for practical purposes, it is that between 5 and a fraction over 8. Stated accurately to eleven places of decimals it is $(1 + \sqrt{5}) \div 2 = 1·61803398875$ (nearly).

We have evidently here a very unique proportion. Mr. Schooling has called this the Phi proportion, and it will be convenient to refer to it by this name.

THE PHI PROPORTION

BC is 1·618033, &c., times size of AB,
CD „ „ „ „ BC,
DE „ „ „ „ CD, &c.,
AC = CD
BD = DE, &c.

APPENDIX

Testing this proportion on the reproductions of pictures in this book in the order of their appearing, we find the following remarkable results :

"Los Meninas," Velazquez, page 60.—The right-hand side of light opening of door at the end of the room is exactly Phi proportion with the two sides of picture; and further, the bottom of this opening is exactly Phi proportion with the top and bottom of canvas.

It will be noticed that this is a very important point in the "placing" of the composition.

"Fête Champêtre," Giorgione, page 150.—Lower end of flute held by seated female figure exactly Phi proportion with sides of picture, and lower side of hand holding it (a point slightly above the end of flute) exactly Phi proportion with top and bottom of canvas. This is also an important centre in the construction of the composition.

"Bacchus and Ariadne," Titian, page 154.—The proportion in this picture both with top and bottom and sides of canvas comes in the shadow under chin of Bacchus; the most important point in the composition being the placing of this head.

"Love and Death," by Watts, page 158.—Point from which drapery radiates on figure of Death exactly Phi proportion with top and bottom of picture.

Point where right-hand side of right leg of Love cuts dark edge of steps exactly Phi proportion with sides of picture.

"Surrender of Breda," by Velazquez, page 160.— First spear in upright row on the right top of picture, exactly Phi proportion with sides of canvas. Height of gun carried horizontally by man in middle distance above central group, exactly Phi proportion with top and bottom of picture. This line gives height of group of figures on left, and is the most important horizontal line in the picture.

"Birth of Venus," Botticelli, page 166.—Height of horizon line Phi proportion with top and bottom of picture. Height of shell on which Venus stands Phi proportion with top and bottom of picture, the smaller quantity being below this time. Laterally the extreme edge of dark drapery held by figure on right that blows towards Venus is Phi proportion with sides of picture.

"The Rape of Europa," by Paolo Veronese, page 168.—Top of head of Europa exactly Phi proportion with top and bottom of picture. Right-hand side of same head slightly to left of Phi proportion with sides of picture (unless in the reproduction a part of the picture on the left has been trimmed away, as is likely, in which case it would be exactly Phi proportion).

I have taken the first seven pictures reproduced in this book that were not selected with any idea of illustrating this point, and I think you will admit that in each some very important quantity has been placed in this proportion. One could go on through all the illustrations were it not for the fear of becoming wearisome; and also, one could go on through some of the minor relationships, and point out how often this proportion turns up in compositions. But enough has been said to show that the eye evidently takes some especial pleasure in it, whatever may eventually be found to be the physiological reason underlying it.

INDEX

INDEX

China and Japan, the art of, 59
Colour, contrasts of, 208
Colours for figure work, 273
Colours, a useful chart of, 191
Classic architecture, 148
Claude Monet, 62, 190
Clothes, the treatment of, 253
Composition of a picture, the, 216
Constable, 149
Conté crayon, 192, 277
"Contrasts in Harmony," 136
Conventional art, 74
Conventional life, deadness of the, 270
Corners of the panel or canvas, the, 160
Corot, his masses of foliage, 197, 214
Correggio, 206
Crow-quill pen, the, 283
Curves, how to observe the shape of, 90, 162, 209
Curves and straight lines, 220

Darwin, anecdote of, 243
Deadness, to avoid, 132, 193
Decorative work, 183
Degas, 66
"Dither," 71
Diagonal lines, 160
Discord and harmony, 173
Discordant lines, 172
Draperies of Watteau, the, 211
Drapery studies in chalks, 125
Drapery in portrait-drawing, 253
Draughtsmanship and impressionism, 66
Drawing, academic, 35
Drawing, definition of, 31

East, arts of the, 57
Edges, variety of, 192
Edges, the importance of the subject of, 198
Egg and dart moulding, 138
Egyptian sculpture, 135
Egyptian wall paintings, 51
El Greco, 169
Elgin Marbles, the, 135
Ellipse, the, 138
"Embarquement pour l'Ile de Cythère," Watteau's, 211
Emerson on the beautiful, 214

Emotional power of the arts, 20
Emotional significance of objects, 31
Erechtheum, moulding from the, 138
Etching, 283
Exercises in mass drawing, 110
Exhibitions, 57
Expression in portrait-drawing, 242
Eye, anatomy of the, 105
Eye, the, in portrait-drawing, 242
Eyebrow, the, 105
Eyelashes, the, 108
Eyelids, the, 106

"Fête Champêtre," Giorgioni's, 151
Figure work, colours for, 273
"Finding of the Body of St. Mark," 123, 236
Fixing positions of salient points, 86
Flaubert, 68
Foliage, treatment of, 196
Foreshortenings, 93
Form and colour, 18
Form, the influence of, 32
Form, the study of, 81
Frans Hals, 246
French Revolution, Carlyle's, 64
French schools, 68
Fripp, Sir Alfred, 91
Fromentin's definition of art, 23
Fulness of form indicated by shading, 102, 124

Gainsborough, the charm of, 209, 223
Genius and talent, 17
Geology, the study of, 36
Giorgioni, 151, 196
"Giorgioni, The School of," Walter Pater's, 29
Giotto, 222
Glass pens, 283
Goethe, 64
Gold point, 275
Gold and silver paint for shading, 125
Gothic architecture, 148, 150
Gradation, variety of, 199
Greek architecture, 221
Greek art in the Middle Ages, 130
Greek art, variety in, 133
Greek vivacity of moulding, 134
Greek and Gothic sculpture, 147

INDEX

INDEX

INDEX

A CATALOG OF SELECTED DOVER
BOOKS IN ALL FIELDS OF INTEREST

100 BEST-LOVED POEMS, Edited by Philip Smith. "The Passionate Shepherd to His Love," "Shall I compare thee to a summer's day?" "Death, be not proud," "The Raven," "The Road Not Taken," plus works by Blake, Wordsworth, Byron, Shelley, Keats, many others. 96pp. 5³⁄₁₆ x 8¼. 0-486-28553-7

100 SMALL HOUSES OF THE THIRTIES, Brown-Blodgett Company. Exterior photographs and floor plans for 100 charming structures. Illustrations of models accompanied by descriptions of interiors, color schemes, closet space, and other amenities. 200 illustrations. 112pp. 8⅜ x 11. 0-486-44131-8

1000 TURN-OF-THE-CENTURY HOUSES: With Illustrations and Floor Plans, Herbert C. Chivers. Reproduced from a rare edition, this showcase of homes ranges from cottages and bungalows to sprawling mansions. Each house is meticulously illustrated and accompanied by complete floor plans. 256pp. 9⅜ x 12¼.
0-486-45596-3

101 GREAT AMERICAN POEMS, Edited by The American Poetry & Literacy Project. Rich treasury of verse from the 19th and 20th centuries includes works by Edgar Allan Poe, Robert Frost, Walt Whitman, Langston Hughes, Emily Dickinson, T. S. Eliot, other notables. 96pp. 5³⁄₁₆ x 8¼. 0-486-40158-8

101 GREAT SAMURAI PRINTS, Utagawa Kuniyoshi. Kuniyoshi was a master of the warrior woodblock print — and these 18th-century illustrations represent the pinnacle of his craft. Full-color portraits of renowned Japanese samurais pulse with movement, passion, and remarkably fine detail. 112pp. 8⅜ x 11. 0-486-46523-3

ABC OF BALLET, Janet Grosser. Clearly worded, abundantly illustrated little guide defines basic ballet-related terms: arabesque, battement, pas de chat, relevé, sissonne, many others. Pronunciation guide included. Excellent primer. 48pp. 4³⁄₁₆ x 5¾.
0-486-40871-X

ACCESSORIES OF DRESS: An Illustrated Encyclopedia, Katherine Lester and Bess Viola Oerke. Illustrations of hats, veils, wigs, cravats, shawls, shoes, gloves, and other accessories enhance an engaging commentary that reveals the humor and charm of the many-sided story of accessorized apparel. 644 figures and 59 plates. 608pp. 6 ⅛ x 9¼.
0-486-43378-1

ADVENTURES OF HUCKLEBERRY FINN, Mark Twain. Join Huck and Jim as their boyhood adventures along the Mississippi River lead them into a world of excitement, danger, and self-discovery. Humorous narrative, lyrical descriptions of the Mississippi valley, and memorable characters. 224pp. 5³⁄₁₆ x 8¼. 0-486-28061-6

ALICE STARMORE'S BOOK OF FAIR ISLE KNITTING, Alice Starmore. A noted designer from the region of Scotland's Fair Isle explores the history and techniques of this distinctive, stranded-color knitting style and provides copious illustrated instructions for 14 original knitwear designs. 208pp. 8⅜ x 10⅞. 0-486-47218-3

Browse over 9,000 books at www.doverpublications.com

CATALOG OF DOVER BOOKS

ALICE'S ADVENTURES IN WONDERLAND, Lewis Carroll. Beloved classic about a little girl lost in a topsy-turvy land and her encounters with the White Rabbit, March Hare, Mad Hatter, Cheshire Cat, and other delightfully improbable characters. 42 illustrations by Sir John Tenniel. 96pp. 5³⁄₁₆ x 8¼.   0-486-27543-4

AMERICA'S LIGHTHOUSES: An Illustrated History, Francis Ross Holland. Profusely illustrated fact-filled survey of American lighthouses since 1716. Over 200 stations — East, Gulf, and West coasts, Great Lakes, Hawaii, Alaska, Puerto Rico, the Virgin Islands, and the Mississippi and St. Lawrence Rivers. 240pp. 8 x 10¾.
0-486-25576-X

AN ENCYCLOPEDIA OF THE VIOLIN, Alberto Bachmann. Translated by Frederick H. Martens. Introduction by Eugene Ysaye. First published in 1925, this renowned reference remains unsurpassed as a source of essential information, from construction and evolution to repertoire and technique. Includes a glossary and 73 illustrations. 496pp. 6⅛ x 9¼.   0-486-46618-3

ANIMALS: 1,419 Copyright-Free Illustrations of Mammals, Birds, Fish, Insects, etc., Selected by Jim Harter. Selected for its visual impact and ease of use, this outstanding collection of wood engravings presents over 1,000 species of animals in extremely lifelike poses. Includes mammals, birds, reptiles, amphibians, fish, insects, and other invertebrates. 284pp. 9 x 12.   0-486-23766-4

THE ANNALS, Tacitus. Translated by Alfred John Church and William Jackson Brodribb. This vital chronicle of Imperial Rome, written by the era's great historian, spans A.D. 14-68 and paints incisive psychological portraits of major figures, from Tiberius to Nero. 416pp. 5³⁄₁₆ x 8¼.   0-486-45236-0

ANTIGONE, Sophocles. Filled with passionate speeches and sensitive probing of moral and philosophical issues, this powerful and often-performed Greek drama reveals the grim fate that befalls the children of Oedipus. Footnotes. 64pp. 5³⁄₁₆ x 8 ¼.   0-486-27804-2

ART DECO DECORATIVE PATTERNS IN FULL COLOR, Christian Stoll. Reprinted from a rare 1910 portfolio, 160 sensuous and exotic images depict a breathtaking array of florals, geometrics, and abstracts — all elegant in their stark simplicity. 64pp. 8⅜ x 11.   0-486-44862-2

THE ARTHUR RACKHAM TREASURY: 86 Full-Color Illustrations, Arthur Rackham. Selected and Edited by Jeff A. Menges. A stunning treasury of 86 full-page plates span the famed English artist's career, from *Rip Van Winkle* (1905) to masterworks such as *Undine, A Midsummer Night's Dream,* and *Wind in the Willows* (1939). 96pp. 8⅜ x 11.
0-486-44685-9

THE AUTHENTIC GILBERT & SULLIVAN SONGBOOK, W. S. Gilbert and A. S. Sullivan. The most comprehensive collection available, this songbook includes selections from every one of Gilbert and Sullivan's light operas. Ninety-two numbers are presented uncut and unedited, and in their original keys. 410pp. 9 x 12.
0-486-23482-7

THE AWAKENING, Kate Chopin. First published in 1899, this controversial novel of a New Orleans wife's search for love outside a stifling marriage shocked readers. Today, it remains a first-rate narrative with superb characterization. New introductory Note. 128pp. 5³⁄₁₆ x 8¼.   0-486-27786-0

BASIC DRAWING, Louis Priscilla. Beginning with perspective, this commonsense manual progresses to the figure in movement, light and shade, anatomy, drapery, composition, trees and landscape, and outdoor sketching. Black-and-white illustrations throughout. 128pp. 8⅜ x 11.   0-486-45815-6

Browse over 9,000 books at www.doverpublications.com

THE BATTLES THAT CHANGED HISTORY, Fletcher Pratt. Historian profiles 16 crucial conflicts, ancient to modern, that changed the course of Western civilization. Gripping accounts of battles led by Alexander the Great, Joan of Arc, Ulysses S. Grant, other commanders. 27 maps. 352pp. 5⅜ x 8½.   0-486-41129-X

BEETHOVEN'S LETTERS, Ludwig van Beethoven. Edited by Dr. A. C. Kalischer. Features 457 letters to fellow musicians, friends, greats, patrons, and literary men. Reveals musical thoughts, quirks of personality, insights, and daily events. Includes 15 plates. 410pp. 5⅜ x 8½.   0-486-22769-3

BERNICE BOBS HER HAIR AND OTHER STORIES, F. Scott Fitzgerald. This brilliant anthology includes 6 of Fitzgerald's most popular stories: "The Diamond as Big as the Ritz," the title tale, "The Offshore Pirate," "The Ice Palace," "The Jelly Bean," and "May Day." 176pp. 5⅜ x 8½.   0-486-47049-0

BESLER'S BOOK OF FLOWERS AND PLANTS: 73 Full-Color Plates from Hortus Eystettensis, 1613, Basilius Besler. Here is a selection of magnificent plates from the *Hortus Eystettensis,* which vividly illustrated and identified the plants, flowers, and trees that thrived in the legendary German garden at Eichstätt. 80pp. 8⅜ x 11.
0-486-46005-3

THE BOOK OF KELLS, Edited by Blanche Cirker. Painstakingly reproduced from a rare facsimile edition, this volume contains full-page decorations, portraits, illustrations, plus a sampling of textual leaves with exquisite calligraphy and ornamentation. 32 full-color illustrations. 32pp. 9⅜ x 12¼.   0-486-24345-1

THE BOOK OF THE CROSSBOW: With an Additional Section on Catapults and Other Siege Engines, Ralph Payne-Gallwey. Fascinating study traces history and use of crossbow as military and sporting weapon, from Middle Ages to modern times. Also covers related weapons: balistas, catapults, Turkish bows, more. Over 240 illustrations. 400pp. 7¼ x 10⅛.   0-486-28720-3

THE BUNGALOW BOOK: Floor Plans and Photos of 112 Houses, 1910, Henry L. Wilson. Here are 112 of the most popular and economic blueprints of the early 20th century — plus an illustration or photograph of each completed house. A wonderful time capsule that still offers a wealth of valuable insights. 160pp. 8⅜ x 11.
0-486-45104-6

THE CALL OF THE WILD, Jack London. A classic novel of adventure, drawn from London's own experiences as a Klondike adventurer, relating the story of a heroic dog caught in the brutal life of the Alaska Gold Rush. Note. 64pp. 5³⁄₁₆ x 8¼.
0-486-26472-6

CANDIDE, Voltaire. Edited by Francois-Marie Arouet. One of the world's great satires since its first publication in 1759. Witty, caustic skewering of romance, science, philosophy, religion, government — nearly all human ideals and institutions. 112pp. 5³⁄₁₆ x 8¼.   0-486-26689-3

CELEBRATED IN THEIR TIME: Photographic Portraits from the George Grantham Bain Collection, Edited by Amy Pastan. With an Introduction by Michael Carlebach. Remarkable portrait gallery features 112 rare images of Albert Einstein, Charlie Chaplin, the Wright Brothers, Henry Ford, and other luminaries from the worlds of politics, art, entertainment, and industry. 128pp. 8⅜ x 11.   0-486-46754-6

CHARIOTS FOR APOLLO: The NASA History of Manned Lunar Spacecraft to 1969, Courtney G. Brooks, James M. Grimwood, and Loyd S. Swenson, Jr. This illustrated history by a trio of experts is the definitive reference on the Apollo spacecraft and lunar modules. It traces the vehicles' design, development, and operation in space. More than 100 photographs and illustrations. 576pp. 6¾ x 9¼. 0-486-46756-2

Browse over 9,000 books at www.doverpublications.com

AN ENCYCLOPEDIA OF BATTLES: Accounts of Over 1,560 Battles from 1479 B.C. to the Present, David Eggenberger. Essential details of every major battle in recorded history from the first battle of Megiddo in 1479 B.C. to Grenada in 1984. List of battle maps. 99 illustrations. 544pp. 6½ x 9¼. 0-486-24913-1

ENCYCLOPEDIA OF EMBROIDERY STITCHES, INCLUDING CREWEL, Marion Nichols. Precise explanations and instructions, clearly illustrated, on how to work chain, back, cross, knotted, woven stitches, and many more — 178 in all, including Cable Outline, Whipped Satin, and Eyelet Buttonhole. Over 1400 illustrations. 219pp. 8⅜ x 11¼. 0-486-22929-7

ENTER JEEVES: 15 Early Stories, P. G. Wodehouse. Splendid collection contains first 8 stories featuring Bertie Wooster, the deliciously dim aristocrat and Jeeves, his brainy, imperturbable manservant. Also, the complete Reggie Pepper (Bertie's prototype) series. 288pp. 5⅜ x 8½. 0-486-29717-9

ERIC SLOANE'S AMERICA: Paintings in Oil, Michael Wigley. With a Foreword by Mimi Sloane. Eric Sloane's evocative oils of America's landscape and material culture shimmer with immense historical and nostalgic appeal. This original hardcover collection gathers nearly a hundred of his finest paintings, with subjects ranging from New England to the American Southwest. 128pp. 10⅝ x 9.
0-486-46525-X

ETHAN FROME, Edith Wharton. Classic story of wasted lives, set against a bleak New England background. Superbly delineated characters in a hauntingly grim tale of thwarted love. Considered by many to be Wharton's masterpiece. 96pp. 5 3/16 x 8 ¼.
0-486-26690-7

THE EVERLASTING MAN, G. K. Chesterton. Chesterton's view of Christianity — as a blend of philosophy and mythology, satisfying intellect and spirit — applies to his brilliant book, which appeals to readers' heads as well as their hearts. 288pp. 5⅜ x 8½.
0-486-46036-3

THE FIELD AND FOREST HANDY BOOK, Daniel Beard. Written by a co-founder of the Boy Scouts, this appealing guide offers illustrated instructions for building kites, birdhouses, boats, igloos, and other fun projects, plus numerous helpful tips for campers. 448pp. 5 3/16 x 8¼. 0-486-46191-2

FINDING YOUR WAY WITHOUT MAP OR COMPASS, Harold Gatty. Useful, instructive manual shows would-be explorers, hikers, bikers, scouts, sailors, and survivalists how to find their way outdoors by observing animals, weather patterns, shifting sands, and other elements of nature. 288pp. 5⅜ x 8½. 0-486-40613-X

FIRST FRENCH READER: A Beginner's Dual-Language Book, Edited and Translated by Stanley Appelbaum. This anthology introduces 50 legendary writers — Voltaire, Balzac, Baudelaire, Proust, more — through passages from *The Red and the Black, Les Misérables, Madame Bovary,* and other classics. Original French text plus English translation on facing pages. 240pp. 5⅜ x 8½. 0-486-46178-5

FIRST GERMAN READER: A Beginner's Dual-Language Book, Edited by Harry Steinhauer. Specially chosen for their power to evoke German life and culture, these short, simple readings include poems, stories, essays, and anecdotes by Goethe, Hesse, Heine, Schiller, and others. 224pp. 5⅜ x 8½. 0-486-46179-3

FIRST SPANISH READER: A Beginner's Dual-Language Book, Angel Flores. Delightful stories, other material based on works of Don Juan Manuel, Luis Taboada, Ricardo Palma, other noted writers. Complete faithful English translations on facing pages. Exercises. 176pp. 5⅜ x 8½. 0-486-25810-6

FIVE ACRES AND INDEPENDENCE, Maurice G. Kains. Great back-to-the-land classic explains basics of self-sufficient farming. The one book to get. 95 illustrations. 397pp. 5⅜ x 8½.   0-486-20974-1

FLAGG'S SMALL HOUSES: Their Economic Design and Construction, 1922, Ernest Flagg. Although most famous for his skyscrapers, Flagg was also a proponent of the well-designed single-family dwelling. His classic treatise features innovations that save space, materials, and cost. 526 illustrations. 160pp. 9⅜ x 12¼.

0-486-45197-6

FLATLAND: A Romance of Many Dimensions, Edwin A. Abbott. Classic of science (and mathematical) fiction — charmingly illustrated by the author — describes the adventures of A. Square, a resident of Flatland, in Spaceland (three dimensions), Lineland (one dimension), and Pointland (no dimensions). 96pp. 5³⁄₁₆ x 8¼.

0-486-27263-X

FRANKENSTEIN, Mary Shelley. The story of Victor Frankenstein's monstrous creation and the havoc it caused has enthralled generations of readers and inspired countless writers of horror and suspense. With the author's own 1831 introduction. 176pp. 5³⁄₁₆ x 8¼.   0-486-28211-2

THE GARGOYLE BOOK: 572 Examples from Gothic Architecture, Lester Burbank Bridaham. Dispelling the conventional wisdom that French Gothic architectural flourishes were born of despair or gloom, Bridaham reveals the whimsical nature of these creations and the ingenious artisans who made them. 572 illustrations. 224pp. 8⅜ x 11.   0-486-44754-5

THE GIFT OF THE MAGI AND OTHER SHORT STORIES, O. Henry. Sixteen captivating stories by one of America's most popular storytellers. Included are such classics as "The Gift of the Magi," "The Last Leaf," and "The Ransom of Red Chief." Publisher's Note. 96pp. 5³⁄₁₆ x 8¼.   0-486-27061-0

THE GOETHE TREASURY: Selected Prose and Poetry, Johann Wolfgang von Goethe. Edited, Selected, and with an Introduction by Thomas Mann. In addition to his lyric poetry, Goethe wrote travel sketches, autobiographical studies, essays, letters, and proverbs in rhyme and prose. This collection presents outstanding examples from each genre. 368pp. 5⅜ x 8½.   0-486-44780-4

GREAT EXPECTATIONS, Charles Dickens. Orphaned Pip is apprenticed to the dirty work of the forge but dreams of becoming a gentleman — and one day finds himself in possession of "great expectations." Dickens' finest novel. 400pp. 5³⁄₁₆ x 8¼.

0-486-41586-4

GREAT WRITERS ON THE ART OF FICTION: From Mark Twain to Joyce Carol Oates, Edited by James Daley. An indispensable source of advice and inspiration, this anthology features essays by Henry James, Kate Chopin, Willa Cather, Sinclair Lewis, Jack London, Raymond Chandler, Raymond Carver, Eudora Welty, and Kurt Vonnegut, Jr. 192pp. 5⅜ x 8½.   0-486-45128-3

HAMLET, William Shakespeare. The quintessential Shakespearean tragedy, whose highly charged confrontations and anguished soliloquies probe depths of human feeling rarely sounded in any art. Reprinted from an authoritative British edition complete with illuminating footnotes. 128pp. 5³⁄₁₆ x 8¼.   0-486-27278-8

THE HAUNTED HOUSE, Charles Dickens. A Yuletide gathering in an eerie country retreat provides the backdrop for Dickens and his friends — including Elizabeth Gaskell and Wilkie Collins — who take turns spinning supernatural yarns. 144pp. 5⅜ x 8½.   0-486-46309-5

Browse over 9,000 books at www.doverpublications.com

HEART OF DARKNESS, Joseph Conrad. Dark allegory of a journey up the Congo River and the narrator's encounter with the mysterious Mr. Kurtz. Masterly blend of adventure, character study, psychological penetration. For many, Conrad's finest, most enigmatic story. 80pp. 5³⁄₁₆ x 8¼. 0-486-26464-5

HENSON AT THE NORTH POLE, Matthew A. Henson. This thrilling memoir by the heroic African-American who was Peary's companion through two decades of Arctic exploration recounts a tale of danger, courage, and determination. "Fascinating and exciting." — *Commonweal.* 128pp. 5⅜ x 8½. 0-486-45472-X

HISTORIC COSTUMES AND HOW TO MAKE THEM, Mary Fernald and E. Shenton. Practical, informative guidebook shows how to create everything from short tunics worn by Saxon men in the fifth century to a lady's bustle dress of the late 1800s. 81 illustrations. 176pp. 5⅜ x 8½. 0-486-44906-8

THE HOUND OF THE BASKERVILLES, Arthur Conan Doyle. A deadly curse in the form of a legendary ferocious beast continues to claim its victims from the Baskerville family until Holmes and Watson intervene. Often called the best detective story ever written. 128pp. 5³⁄₁₆ x 8¼. 0-486-28214-7

THE HOUSE BEHIND THE CEDARS, Charles W. Chesnutt. Originally published in 1900, this groundbreaking novel by a distinguished African-American author recounts the drama of a brother and sister who "pass for white" during the dangerous days of Reconstruction. 208pp. 5⅜ x 8½. 0-486-46144-0

THE HUMAN FIGURE IN MOTION, Eadweard Muybridge. The 4,789 photographs in this definitive selection show the human figure — models almost all undraped — engaged in over 160 different types of action: running, climbing stairs, etc. 390pp. 7⅞ x 10⅝. 0-486-20204-6

THE IMPORTANCE OF BEING EARNEST, Oscar Wilde. Wilde's witty and buoyant comedy of manners, filled with some of literature's most famous epigrams, reprinted from an authoritative British edition. Considered Wilde's most perfect work. 64pp. 5³⁄₁₆ x 8¼. 0-486-26478-5

THE INFERNO, Dante Alighieri. Translated and with notes by Henry Wadsworth Longfellow. The first stop on Dante's famous journey from Hell to Purgatory to Paradise, this 14th-century allegorical poem blends vivid and shocking imagery with graceful lyricism. Translated by the beloved 19th-century poet, Henry Wadsworth Longfellow. 256pp. 5³⁄₁₆ x 8¼. 0-486-44288-8

JANE EYRE, Charlotte Brontë. Written in 1847, *Jane Eyre* tells the tale of an orphan girl's progress from the custody of cruel relatives to an oppressive boarding school and its culmination in a troubled career as a governess. 448pp. 5³⁄₁₆ x 8¼.
0-486-42449-9

JAPANESE WOODBLOCK FLOWER PRINTS, Tanigami Kônan. Extraordinary collection of Japanese woodblock prints by a well-known artist features 120 plates in brilliant color. Realistic images from a rare edition include daffodils, tulips, and other familiar and unusual flowers. 128pp. 11 x 8¼. 0-486-46442-3

JEWELRY MAKING AND DESIGN, Augustus F. Rose and Antonio Cirino. Professional secrets of jewelry making are revealed in a thorough, practical guide. Over 200 illustrations. 306pp. 5⅜ x 8½. 0-486-21750-7

JULIUS CAESAR, William Shakespeare. Great tragedy based on Plutarch's account of the lives of Brutus, Julius Caesar and Mark Antony. Evil plotting, ringing oratory, high tragedy with Shakespeare's incomparable insight, dramatic power. Explanatory footnotes. 96pp. 5³⁄₁₆ x 8¼. 0-486-26876-4

Browse over 9,000 books at www.doverpublications.com

THE JUNGLE, Upton Sinclair. 1906 bestseller shockingly reveals intolerable labor practices and working conditions in the Chicago stockyards as it tells the grim story of a Slavic family that emigrates to America full of optimism but soon faces despair. 320pp. 5³⁄₁₆ x 8¼. 0-486-41923-1

THE KINGDOM OF GOD IS WITHIN YOU, Leo Tolstoy. The soul-searching book that inspired Gandhi to embrace the concept of passive resistance, Tolstoy's 1894 polemic clearly outlines a radical, well-reasoned revision of traditional Christian thinking. 352pp. 5³⁄₁₆ x 8¼. 0-486-45138-0

THE LADY OR THE TIGER?: and Other Logic Puzzles, Raymond M. Smullyan. Created by a renowned puzzle master, these whimsically themed challenges involve paradoxes about probability, time, and change; metapuzzles; and self-referentiality. Nineteen chapters advance in difficulty from relatively simple to highly complex. 1982 edition. 240pp. 5⅜ x 8½. 0-486-47027-X

LEAVES OF GRASS: The Original 1855 Edition, Walt Whitman. Whitman's immortal collection includes some of the greatest poems of modern times, including his masterpiece, "Song of Myself." Shattering standard conventions, it stands as an unabashed celebration of body and nature. 128pp. 5³⁄₁₆ x 8¼. 0-486-45676-5

LES MISÉRABLES, Victor Hugo. Translated by Charles E. Wilbour. Abridged by James K. Robinson. A convict's heroic struggle for justice and redemption plays out against a fiery backdrop of the Napoleonic wars. This edition features the excellent original translation and a sensitive abridgment. 304pp. 6⅛ x 9¼. 0-486-45789-3

LILITH: A Romance, George MacDonald. In this novel by the father of fantasy literature, a man travels through time to meet Adam and Eve and to explore humanity's fall from grace and ultimate redemption. 240pp. 5⅜ x 8½. 0-486-46818-6

THE LOST LANGUAGE OF SYMBOLISM, Harold Bayley. This remarkable book reveals the hidden meaning behind familiar images and words, from the origins of Santa Claus to the fleur-de-lys, drawing from mythology, folklore, religious texts, and fairy tales. 1,418 illustrations. 784pp. 5⅜ x 8½. 0-486-44787-1

MACBETH, William Shakespeare. A Scottish nobleman murders the king in order to succeed to the throne. Tortured by his conscience and fearful of discovery, he becomes tangled in a web of treachery and deceit that ultimately spells his doom. 96pp. 5³⁄₁₆ x 8¼. 0-486-27802-6

MAKING AUTHENTIC CRAFTSMAN FURNITURE: Instructions and Plans for 62 Projects, Gustav Stickley. Make authentic reproductions of handsome, functional, durable furniture: tables, chairs, wall cabinets, desks, a hall tree, and more. Construction plans with drawings, schematics, dimensions, and lumber specs reprinted from 1900s The Craftsman magazine. 128pp. 8⅛ x 11. 0-486-25000-8

MATHEMATICS FOR THE NONMATHEMATICIAN, Morris Kline. Erudite and entertaining overview follows development of mathematics from ancient Greeks to present. Topics include logic and mathematics, the fundamental concept, differential calculus, probability theory, much more. Exercises and problems. 641pp. 5⅜ x 8½. 0-486-24823-2

MEMOIRS OF AN ARABIAN PRINCESS FROM ZANZIBAR, Emily Ruete. This 19th-century autobiography offers a rare inside look at the society surrounding a sultan's palace. A real-life princess in exile recalls her vanished world of harems, slave trading, and court intrigues. 288pp. 5⅜ x 8½. 0-486-47121-7

Browse over 9,000 books at www.doverpublications.com

THE METAMORPHOSIS AND OTHER STORIES, Franz Kafka. Excellent new English translations of title story (considered by many critics Kafka's most perfect work), plus "The Judgment," "In the Penal Colony," "A Country Doctor," and "A Report to an Academy." Note. 96pp. 5³⁄₁₆ x 8¼.　　　0-486-29030-1

MICROSCOPIC ART FORMS FROM THE PLANT WORLD, R. Anheisser. From undulating curves to complex geometrics, a world of fascinating images abound in this classic, illustrated survey of microscopic plants. Features 400 detailed illustrations of nature's minute but magnificent handiwork. The accompanying CD-ROM includes all of the images in the book. 128pp. 9 x 9.　　　0-486-46013-4

A MIDSUMMER NIGHT'S DREAM, William Shakespeare. Among the most popular of Shakespeare's comedies, this enchanting play humorously celebrates the vagaries of love as it focuses upon the intertwined romances of several pairs of lovers. Explanatory footnotes. 80pp. 5³⁄₁₆ x 8¼.　　　0-486-27067-X

THE MONEY CHANGERS, Upton Sinclair. Originally published in 1908, this cautionary novel from the author of *The Jungle* explores corruption within the American system as a group of power brokers joins forces for personal gain, triggering a crash on Wall Street. 192pp. 5⅜ x 8½.　　　0-486-46917-4

THE MOST POPULAR HOMES OF THE TWENTIES, William A. Radford. With a New Introduction by Daniel D. Reiff. Based on a rare 1925 catalog, this architectural showcase features floor plans, construction details, and photos of 26 homes, plus articles on entrances, porches, garages, and more. 250 illustrations, 21 color plates. 176pp. 8⅜ x 11.　　　0-486-47028-8

MY 66 YEARS IN THE BIG LEAGUES, Connie Mack. With a New Introduction by Rich Westcott. A Founding Father of modern baseball, Mack holds the record for most wins — and losses — by a major league manager. Enhanced by 70 photographs, his warmhearted autobiography is populated by many legends of the game. 288pp. 5⅜ x 8½.　　　0-486-47184-5

NARRATIVE OF THE LIFE OF FREDERICK DOUGLASS, Frederick Douglass. Douglass's graphic depictions of slavery, harrowing escape to freedom, and life as a newspaper editor, eloquent orator, and impassioned abolitionist. 96pp. 5³⁄₁₆ x 8¼.　　　0-486-28499-9

THE NIGHTLESS CITY: Geisha and Courtesan Life in Old Tokyo, J. E. de Becker. This unsurpassed study from 100 years ago ventured into Tokyo's red-light district to survey geisha and courtesan life and offer meticulous descriptions of training, dress, social hierarchy, and erotic practices. 49 black-and-white illustrations; 2 maps. 496pp. 5⅜ x 8½.　　　0-486-45563-7

THE ODYSSEY, Homer. Excellent prose translation of ancient epic recounts adventures of the homeward-bound Odysseus. Fantastic cast of gods, giants, cannibals, sirens, other supernatural creatures — true classic of Western literature. 256pp. 5³⁄₁₆ x 8¼.　　　0-486-40654-7

OEDIPUS REX, Sophocles. Landmark of Western drama concerns the catastrophe that ensues when King Oedipus discovers he has inadvertently killed his father and married his mother. Masterly construction, dramatic irony. Explanatory footnotes. 64pp. 5³⁄₁₆ x 8¼.　　　0-486-26877-2

ONCE UPON A TIME: The Way America Was, Eric Sloane. Nostalgic text and drawings brim with gentle philosophies and descriptions of how we used to live — self-sufficiently — on the land, in homes, and among the things built by hand. 44 line illustrations. 64pp. 8⅜ x 11.　　　0-486-44411-2

CATALOG OF DOVER BOOKS

ONE OF OURS, Willa Cather. The Pulitzer Prize–winning novel about a young Nebraskan looking for something to believe in. Alienated from his parents, rejected by his wife, he finds his destiny on the bloody battlefields of World War I. 352pp. 5³⁄₁₆ x 8¼. 0-486-45599-8

ORIGAMI YOU CAN USE: 27 Practical Projects, Rick Beech. Origami models can be more than decorative, and this unique volume shows how! The 27 practical projects include a CD case, frame, napkin ring, and dish. Easy instructions feature 400 two-color illustrations. 96pp. 8¼ x 11. 0-486-47057-1

OTHELLO, William Shakespeare. Towering tragedy tells the story of a Moorish general who earns the enmity of his ensign Iago when he passes him over for a promotion. Masterly portrait of an archvillain. Explanatory footnotes. 112pp. 5³⁄₁₆ x 8¼. 0-486-29097-2

PARADISE LOST, John Milton. Notes by John A. Himes. First published in 1667, *Paradise Lost* ranks among the greatest of English literature's epic poems. It's a sublime retelling of Adam and Eve's fall from grace and expulsion from Eden. Notes by John A. Himes. 480pp. 5³⁄₁₆ x 8¼. 0-486-44287-X

PASSING, Nella Larsen. Married to a successful physician and prominently ensconced in society, Irene Redfield leads a charmed existence — until a chance encounter with a childhood friend who has been "passing for white." 112pp. 5⅜ x 8½. 0-486-43713-2

PERSPECTIVE DRAWING FOR BEGINNERS, Len A. Doust. Doust carefully explains the roles of lines, boxes, and circles, and shows how visualizing shapes and forms can be used in accurate depictions of perspective. One of the most concise introductions available. 33 illustrations. 64pp. 5⅜ x 8½. 0-486-45149-6

PERSPECTIVE MADE EASY, Ernest R. Norling. Perspective is easy; yet, surprisingly few artists know the simple rules that make it so. Remedy that situation with this simple, step-by-step book, the first devoted entirely to the topic. 256 illustrations. 224pp. 5⅜ x 8½. 0-486-40473-0

THE PICTURE OF DORIAN GRAY, Oscar Wilde. Celebrated novel involves a handsome young Londoner who sinks into a life of depravity. His body retains perfect youth and vigor while his recent portrait reflects the ravages of his crime and sensuality. 176pp. 5³⁄₁₆ x 8¼. 0-486-27807-7

PRIDE AND PREJUDICE, Jane Austen. One of the most universally loved and admired English novels, an effervescent tale of rural romance transformed by Jane Austen's art into a witty, shrewdly observed satire of English country life. 272pp. 5³⁄₁₆ x 8¼. 0-486-28473-5

THE PRINCE, Niccolò Machiavelli. Classic, Renaissance-era guide to acquiring and maintaining political power. Today, nearly 500 years after it was written, this calculating prescription for autocratic rule continues to be much read and studied. 80pp. 5³⁄₁₆ x 8¼. 0-486-27274-5

QUICK SKETCHING, Carl Cheek. A perfect introduction to the technique of "quick sketching." Drawing upon an artist's immediate emotional responses, this is an extremely effective means of capturing the essential form and features of a subject. More than 100 black-and-white illustrations throughout. 48pp. 11 x 8¼. 0-486-46608-6

RANCH LIFE AND THE HUNTING TRAIL, Theodore Roosevelt. Illustrated by Frederic Remington. Beautifully illustrated by Remington, Roosevelt's celebration of the Old West recounts his adventures in the Dakota Badlands of the 1880s, from round-ups to Indian encounters to hunting bighorn sheep. 208pp. 6¼ x 9¼. 0-486-47340-6

Browse over 9,000 books at www.doverpublications.com

THE RED BADGE OF COURAGE, Stephen Crane. Amid the nightmarish chaos of a Civil War battle, a young soldier discovers courage, humility, and, perhaps, wisdom. Uncanny re-creation of actual combat. Enduring landmark of American fiction. 112pp. 5³⁄₁₆ x 8¼. 0-486-26465-3

RELATIVITY SIMPLY EXPLAINED, Martin Gardner. One of the subject's clearest, most entertaining introductions offers lucid explanations of special and general theories of relativity, gravity, and spacetime, models of the universe, and more. 100 illustrations. 224pp. 5⅜ x 8½. 0-486-29315-7

REMBRANDT DRAWINGS: 116 Masterpieces in Original Color, Rembrandt van Rijn. This deluxe hardcover edition features drawings from throughout the Dutch master's prolific career. Informative captions accompany these beautifully reproduced landscapes, biblical vignettes, figure studies, animal sketches, and portraits. 128pp. 8⅜ x 11. 0-486-46149-1

THE ROAD NOT TAKEN AND OTHER POEMS, Robert Frost. A treasury of Frost's most expressive verse. In addition to the title poem: "An Old Man's Winter Night," "In the Home Stretch," "Meeting and Passing," "Putting in the Seed," many more. All complete and unabridged. 64pp. 5³⁄₁₆ x 8¼. 0-486-27550-7

ROMEO AND JULIET, William Shakespeare. Tragic tale of star-crossed lovers, feuding families and timeless passion contains some of Shakespeare's most beautiful and lyrical love poetry. Complete, unabridged text with explanatory footnotes. 96pp. 5³⁄₁₆ x 8¼. 0-486-27557-4

SANDITON AND THE WATSONS: Austen's Unfinished Novels, Jane Austen. Two tantalizing incomplete stories revisit Austen's customary milieu of courtship and venture into new territory, amid guests at a seaside resort. Both are worth reading for pleasure and study. 112pp. 5⅜ x 8½. 0-486-45793-1

THE SCARLET LETTER, Nathaniel Hawthorne. With stark power and emotional depth, Hawthorne's masterpiece explores sin, guilt, and redemption in a story of adultery in the early days of the Massachusetts Colony. 192pp. 5³⁄₁₆ x 8¼. 0-486-28048-9

THE SEASONS OF AMERICA PAST, Eric Sloane. Seventy-five illustrations depict cider mills and presses, sleds, pumps, stump-pulling equipment, plows, and other elements of America's rural heritage. A section of old recipes and household hints adds additional color. 160pp. 8⅜ x 11. 0-486-44220-9

SELECTED CANTERBURY TALES, Geoffrey Chaucer. Delightful collection includes the General Prologue plus three of the most popular tales: "The Knight's Tale," "The Miller's Prologue and Tale," and "The Wife of Bath's Prologue and Tale." In modern English. 144pp. 5³⁄₁₆ x 8¼. 0-486-28241-4

SELECTED POEMS, Emily Dickinson. Over 100 best-known, best-loved poems by one of America's foremost poets, reprinted from authoritative early editions. No comparable edition at this price. Index of first lines. 64pp. 5³⁄₁₆ x 8¼. 0-486-26466-1

SIDDHARTHA, Hermann Hesse. Classic novel that has inspired generations of seekers. Blending Eastern mysticism and psychoanalysis, Hesse presents a strikingly original view of man and culture and the arduous process of self-discovery, reconciliation, harmony, and peace. 112pp. 5³⁄₁₆ x 8¼. 0-486-40653-9

SKETCHING OUTDOORS, Leonard Richmond. This guide offers beginners step-by-step demonstrations of how to depict clouds, trees, buildings, and other outdoor sights. Explanations of a variety of techniques include shading and constructional drawing. 48pp. 11 x 8¼. 0-486-46922-0

SMALL HOUSES OF THE FORTIES: With Illustrations and Floor Plans, Harold E. Group. 56 floor plans and elevations of houses that originally cost less than $15,000 to build. Recommended by financial institutions of the era, they range from Colonials to Cape Cods. 144pp. 8⅜ x 11. 0-486-45598-X

SOME CHINESE GHOSTS, Lafcadio Hearn. Rooted in ancient Chinese legends, these richly atmospheric supernatural tales are recounted by an expert in Oriental lore. Their originality, power, and literary charm will captivate readers of all ages. 96pp. 5⅜ x 8½. 0-486-46306-0

SONGS FOR THE OPEN ROAD: Poems of Travel and Adventure, Edited by The American Poetry & Literacy Project. More than 80 poems by 50 American and British masters celebrate real and metaphorical journeys. Poems by Whitman, Byron, Millay, Sandburg, Langston Hughes, Emily Dickinson, Robert Frost, Shelley, Tennyson, Yeats, many others. Note. 80pp. 5³⁄₁₆ x 8¼. 0-486-40646-6

SPOON RIVER ANTHOLOGY, Edgar Lee Masters. An American poetry classic, in which former citizens of a mythical midwestern town speak touchingly from the grave of the thwarted hopes and dreams of their lives. 144pp. 5³⁄₁₆ x 8¼. 0-486-27275-3

STAR LORE: Myths, Legends, and Facts, William Tyler Olcott. Captivating retellings of the origins and histories of ancient star groups include Pegasus, Ursa Major, Pleiades, signs of the zodiac, and other constellations. "Classic." — *Sky & Telescope.* 58 illustrations. 544pp. 5⅜ x 8½. 0-486-43581-4

THE STRANGE CASE OF DR. JEKYLL AND MR. HYDE, Robert Louis Stevenson. This intriguing novel, both fantasy thriller and moral allegory, depicts the struggle of two opposing personalities — one essentially good, the other evil — for the soul of one man. 64pp. 5³⁄₁₆ x 8¼. 0-486-26688-5

SURVIVAL HANDBOOK: The Official U.S. Army Guide, Department of the Army. This special edition of the Army field manual is geared toward civilians. An essential companion for campers and all lovers of the outdoors, it constitutes the most authoritative wilderness guide. 288pp. 5³⁄₁₆ x 8¼. 0-486-46184-X

A TALE OF TWO CITIES, Charles Dickens. Against the backdrop of the French Revolution, Dickens unfolds his masterpiece of drama, adventure, and romance about a man falsely accused of treason. Excitement and derring-do in the shadow of the guillotine. 304pp. 5³⁄₁₆ x 8¼. 0-486-40651-2

TEN PLAYS, Anton Chekhov. *The Sea Gull, Uncle Vanya, The Three Sisters, The Cherry Orchard,* and *Ivanov,* plus 5 one-act comedies: *The Anniversary, An Unwilling Martyr, The Wedding, The Bear,* and *The Proposal.* 336pp. 5³⁄₁₆ x 8¼. 0-486-46560-8

THE FLYING INN, G. K. Chesterton. Hilarious romp in which pub owner Humphrey Hump and friend take to the road in a donkey cart filled with rum and cheese, inveighing against Prohibition and other "oppressive forms of modernity." 320pp. 5⅜ x 8½. 0-486-41910-X

THIRTY YEARS THAT SHOOK PHYSICS: The Story of Quantum Theory, George Gamow. Lucid, accessible introduction to the influential theory of energy and matter features careful explanations of Dirac's anti-particles, Bohr's model of the atom, and much more. Numerous drawings. 1966 edition. 240pp. 5⅜ x 8½. 0-486-24895-X

TREASURE ISLAND, Robert Louis Stevenson. Classic adventure story of a perilous sea journey, a mutiny led by the infamous Long John Silver, and a lethal scramble for buried treasure — seen through the eyes of cabin boy Jim Hawkins. 160pp. 5³⁄₁₆ x 8¼. 0-486-27559-0

Browse over 9,000 books at www.doverpublications.com

CATALOG OF DOVER BOOKS

THE TRIAL, Franz Kafka. Translated by David Wyllie. From its gripping first sentence onward, this novel exemplifies the term "Kafkaesque." Its darkly humorous narrative recounts a bank clerk's entrapment in a bureaucratic maze, based on an undisclosed charge. 176pp. 5³⁄₁₆ x 8¼. 0-486-47061-X

THE TURN OF THE SCREW, Henry James. Gripping ghost story by great novelist depicts the sinister transformation of 2 innocent children into flagrant liars and hypocrites. An elegantly told tale of unspoken horror and psychological terror. 96pp. 5³⁄₁₆ x 8¼. 0-486-26684-2

UP FROM SLAVERY, Booker T. Washington. Washington (1856-1915) rose to become the most influential spokesman for African-Americans of his day. In this eloquently written book, he describes events in a remarkable life that began in bondage and culminated in worldwide recognition. 160pp. 5³⁄₁₆ x 8¼. 0-486-28738-6

VICTORIAN HOUSE DESIGNS IN AUTHENTIC FULL COLOR: 75 Plates from the "Scientific American – Architects and Builders Edition," 1885-1894, Edited by Blanche Cirker. Exquisitely detailed, exceptionally handsome designs for an enormous variety of attractive city dwellings, spacious suburban and country homes, charming "cottages" and other structures — all accompanied by perspective views and floor plans. 80pp. 9¼ x 12¼. 0-486-29438-2

VILLETTE, Charlotte Brontë. Acclaimed by Virginia Woolf as "Brontë's finest novel," this moving psychological study features a remarkably modern heroine who abandons her native England for a new life as a schoolteacher in Belgium. 480pp. 5³⁄₁₆ x 8¼. 0-486-45557-2

THE VOYAGE OUT, Virginia Woolf. A moving depiction of the thrills and confusion of youth, Woolf's acclaimed first novel traces a shipboard journey to South America for a captivating exploration of a woman's growing self-awareness. 288pp. 5³⁄₁₆ x 8¼. 0-486-45005-8

WALDEN; OR, LIFE IN THE WOODS, Henry David Thoreau. Accounts of Thoreau's daily life on the shores of Walden Pond outside Concord, Massachusetts, are interwoven with musings on the virtues of self-reliance and individual freedom, on society, government, and other topics. 224pp. 5³⁄₁₆ x 8¼. 0-486-28495-6

WILD PILGRIMAGE: A Novel in Woodcuts, Lynd Ward. Through startling engravings shaded in black and red, Ward wordlessly tells the story of a man trapped in an industrial world, struggling between the grim reality around him and the fantasies his imagination creates. 112pp. 6⅛ x 9¼. 0-486-46583-7

WILLY POGÁNY REDISCOVERED, Willy Pogány. Selected and Edited by Jeff A. Menges. More than 100 color and black-and-white Art Nouveau–style illustrations from fairy tales and adventure stories include scenes from Wagner's "Ring" cycle, *The Rime of the Ancient Mariner, Gulliver's Travels,* and *Faust.* 144pp. 8⅜ x 11. 0-486-47046-6

WOOLLY THOUGHTS: Unlock Your Creative Genius with Modular Knitting, Pat Ashforth and Steve Plummer. Here's the revolutionary way to knit — easy, fun, and foolproof! Beginners and experienced knitters need only master a single stitch to create their own designs with patchwork squares. More than 100 illustrations. 128pp. 6½ x 9¼. 0-486-46084-3

WUTHERING HEIGHTS, Emily Brontë. Somber tale of consuming passions and vengeance — played out amid the lonely English moors — recounts the turbulent and tempestuous love story of Cathy and Heathcliff. Poignant and compelling. 256pp. 5³⁄₁₆ x 8¼. 0-486-29256-8

Browse over 9,000 books at www.doverpublications.com